WOMEN OF PRIVILEGE

Women of Privilege

100 Years of Love and Loss in a Family of the Hudson River Valley

Susan Gillotti

ACADEMY CHICAGO PUBLISHERS

Published in 2013 by
Academy Chicago Publishers
363 West Erie Street
Chicago, Illinois 60654

First edition.

Printed and bound in the U.S.A.

Cover: Fanny Schieffelin Crosby (standing), Maunsell Schieffelin Crosby,
Minnie Schieffelin (seated left to right), circa 1894.

All photographs courtesy of the author's collection.

Grateful acknowledgment is made to Yale University Press for permission
to excerpt from Beulah Parker: *The Evolution of a Psychiatrist*.
© 1987 by Yale University.

For Sheila and Judy

Ex Libris
HELEN E. CROSBY

PREFACE

THE HUDSON RIVER VALLEY EXTENDS along the east and west banks of the river from Manhattan to Albany. For many, its core is the section of river that runs for approximately fifteen miles north and south of Rhinebeck. Settled in the 1700s by Beekmans and Livingstons, it is a place where many descendents of the early settlers still live. It is their love of the land and the life style—quiet, nature-loving, unostentatious—that keeps them there.

The Beekman Arms, in the center of Rhinebeck, claims to be the oldest continuously operated inn in the country. As one enters its dark, low-ceilinged tavern, it transports one to an earlier time. North and south of Rhinebeck are houses representing every style of American architecture from Colonial, Georgian, and Federal to Greek Revival, Italianate, and Late Victorian.

Grasmere, on Mill Road a mile south of the Beekman Arms, was not a grand house, but it was grand enough. Its history began with Janet Livingston, a granddaughter of Col. Henry Beekman, when she inherited 618 acres of land. She married General Richard Montgomery in 1773 and together they planned a house. Construction began, but the Revolutionary War intervened. Richard was killed in the Battle of Quebec in 1775 and after a few years, Janet wanted to leave. As a memorial to her husband, she planted a long driveway with locust seeds.

Many of these seeds grew into beautiful trees. She moved north to Red Hook, to a house she named Montgomery Place, and Grasmere fell into the ownership of Peter Livingston.

The original house burned down in the 1820s. It was rebuilt as a red-brick mansion with white marble trim. In 1850, Lewis Livingston, Peter's nephew, became the owner. He made further enlargements from 1861 to 1862, at the same time acquiring an additional 280 acres of farmland.

Sarah Minerva Schieffelin, my great-great grandmother, bought the 898-acre estate in the 1890s, when Lewis died. She was living in Manhattan at the time, expecting to stay in her Fifth Avenue house with her daughters nearby. But one thing led to another, and her son-in-law, Ernest Crosby, crossed the line with his political beliefs. Sarah felt certain that she could save her family embarrassment if she bought a country estate and offered it to Ernest as a home where he could write poetry and entertain his country neighbors rather than the socialists he preferred.

It didn't turn out as Sarah had hoped. For the next forty years, Grasmere experienced a number of family upheavals. The house was beautiful, and the farm prospered. Guests came and enjoyed the gardens and distant views. But money started to run out, and my grandfather, Maunsell Schieffelin Crosby, didn't invest in improvements as he should have. Eventually, after my mother inherited the house and land, it had to be sold. I didn't know about the upheavals. As a child, I was entranced by the stories my mother told about her childhood there, and I conjured up a world in which I, too, could have been a part.

It was only after my mother died in Florida, in 1995, that I learned the true story of what happened. The women who lived at Grasmere kept diaries, the earliest of which dates back to 1876. My grandmother, Elizabeth Coolidge, wrote letters daily. My mother, Helen Crosby, kept a diary, wrote letters, and kept a journal. She also wrote short autobiographical stories for the Famous Writers School, hiding her family's identity by calling herself Ann Pell. I discovered all of these documents in a closet. Attached to them was a note: "For my daughters to read after I am gone. In these papers you will find answers to questions I know you have had."

I shipped the papers from Florida to Martha's Vineyard, where I lived at the time. Three years later, when I'd finished reading everything, I realized I'd been given a rare glimpse into the lives of privileged women who were searching for an identity and power in a cultural system dominated by patriarchy.

The writing of the book took several years, and three drafts. As I wrote, the characters began to speak. I was faced with the problem of how to use dialogue in scenes where I hadn't been present.

I didn't want to write strictly as a historian. I wanted to develop character. I wanted the facts of the family history to be told, but I also wanted the characters to interact with each other. The result is what some might call "literary history" or "creative non-fiction." For me, it is the true story of my family. Every imagined conversation in the book is linked to diaries, journals, letters or other documentation in my archive.

The worlds of my forebears have gone forever. But I am their legacy, a woman who more than once has wondered how I acquired the sense of entitlement that sometimes gets in my way. By having written this book, I understand those influences better. Whoever we are, wherever we come from, we carry within us parts of those who came before.

CHAPTER 1

I HAVE IN FRONT OF ME a photograph of my great-great-grandmother's drawing room on Fifth Avenue in New York. I don't know its date, except that it is more than a hundred years old. I do know that at that time, 665 Fifth Avenue was a five-story row house with twelve steps rising to its front door. Many of the houses on Fifth Avenue once had front stoops. I found a picture of the house in Burton Welles's *Fifth Avenue from Start to Finish 1911*, a photographic record of every building on Fifth Avenue from Washington Square to East 93rd Street. My great-great-grandmother, Sarah Minerva Schieffelin (Mrs. Henry Maunsell Schieffelin), is listed as the owner of the house that stood between East 53rd and East 54th Street. She lived there for many years.

My photograph of the drawing room shows that Sarah Minerva and her family lived a comfortable life. There is a cream and gold Steinway piano with a collection of scores on it. A large gilded mirror hangs opposite. The chairs and sofa are upholstered in silk and a white polar bear skin rug lies on the parquet floor. Sitting on a marble-topped table is a Meissen porcelain cockatoo, its head tilted downwards as if it wanted to eavesdrop. Happily, the cockatoo is now in my house in Vermont. It sits on a bookshelf next to an Abenaki carved bear. The cockatoo and the bear come from different worlds, just as I live in a world that is different from my maternal ancestor's world.

The story of my family begins with Sarah Minerva Schieffelin, whose values left an imprint on those of us who followed. I came to know her through reading a diary she began on June 28, 1876. She was the devoted wife of Henry Maunsell Schieffelin, a scion of a successful importing firm. The diary begins as she and Henry, and their two daughters, Minnie and Fanny, are preparing to leave for an extended trip to Europe.

The purpose of the trip was to introduce Minnie and Fanny to the cultural treasures of Great Britain. They planned to visit important sites in Ireland, Scotland, Wales, and England. They'd booked passage on the Cunard Line which, beginning in 1840, offered private staterooms on scheduled passenger service across the Atlantic. Mrs. Schieffelin had written letters to friends living abroad announcing their dates of arrival in Dublin, Edinburgh, and London. Because Henry had earlier served as Consul General in Liberia, they knew many people in diplomatic circles.

On June 28, 1876, Sarah Schieffelin stood in the doorway of her drawing room surveying its contents. She was intent on assuring that everything was in place for their departure. She'd instructed the servants to remove breakable objects and store them elsewhere. Once the tabletops were cleared, the servants covered the settees and chairs with white sheets. Two sheets covered the Steinway grand piano. The white bear-skin rug—one of six in the house—had been pulled to a corner of the room to protect it from the sun. Two small palm trees had been taken to the downstairs kitchen where the servants could water them during the family's absence.

She paused at one of the front windows and looked across Fifth Avenue at St. Thomas's Church. Horse-drawn carriages passed by, taking their passengers north to the houses overlooking Central Park. Other carriages traveled south to the haber-dashers, florists, banks, and booksellers that served New York's growing population. She folded the wooden shutters across the windows and turned towards the hallway. They would be leaving within the hour. She descended to the butler's pantry to look once again at her china. Her dining room seated twenty and broken pieces needed to be replaced. They would be buying soup bowls and fruit dishes, oyster plates, and finger bowls.

She went to her bedroom on the third floor and attended to the final packing of her personal traveling case. Into it she put a silver comb, hairbrush, hand mirror, tortoiseshell pill box, ivory glove stretcher and tortoiseshell letter opener. Each was initialed with her monogram, SMS. She added a lace fan for when the weather would be hot. She also made certain to pack laudanum, a form of opium, which she always carried with her to give to Fanny when the child had headaches.

On the fourth floor, Minnie and Fanny, now thirteen and fifteen, were putting the last of their summer frocks into valises. Their steamer trunks had already been sent to the pier. They contained not only practical cotton dresses for daytime travel but also fancier lace and silk ones, along with ribbons for their hair and kidskin gloves.

Henry Schieffelin, looking forward to a long holiday, had packed his steamer trunk with the help of a manservant. Henry was a cultivated man who enjoyed reading and music, but who also spent time in men's clubs. As his wife had sent letters ahead to families they would meet, so Henry had obtained letters of introduction to clubs in Britain. He was taking informal clothes for the country and suits and dinner attire for town. His trunk had also been sent ahead.

Henry and the manservant collected the valises from the ladies' rooms and took them downstairs to the front door. Minnie and Fanny descended, stopping at a hallway mirror to tie the bows of their new straw hats. Sarah Schieffelin emerged from her bedroom carrying her personal traveling case. A carriage with two horses was waiting and the manservant helped each of them step up into it. Within a short period of time (they had only to cross Manhattan to the west side), they would board the Cunard Line's *RMS Bothnia*, destined for Ireland.

* * *

As the ship left the harbor, most passengers remained on deck to watch the slowly receding skyline of New York, an experience few wanted to miss. As Mr. and Mrs. Schieffelin stood at the railing, John Schuyler Crosby, an acquaintance, approached. A lawyer in his thirties, and a bachelor, he was just the sort of young man Fanny and Minnie should meet. The Schieffelins invited him to join their table at dinner and for the remainder of the voyage the family saw him often.

During the early part of the voyage it was only Minnie, the younger daughter, who managed to eat meals. Fanny was not a good sailor and when the *Bothnia* hit rough sea just outside the harbor, she became seasick. She lay in her berth for three days, and opening the porthole provided no relief. Minnie and Mrs. Schieffelin stayed on deck while Mr. Schieffelin went down from time to time to look after Fanny. "I despair so for the child, she is so prostrated," Mrs. Schieffelin confided to her diary. Wanting to be helpful, she gave Fanny laudanum.

The seas subsided and Fanny returned to the upper deck. "Bring your shawl," said Mrs. Schieffelin, "and we'll enjoy ourselves on a deck chair." They passed their days reading books from the ship's library, the first of its kind on a passenger ship, and in the ladies' saloon, the first such room offered exclusively for the use of women on a transatlantic crossing. They read about the abbeys, churches, and castles they would visit. Mrs. Schieffelin had made clear to her daughters the importance of being well-educated. "If you want to marry well, which I know you do, you'll need to be able to talk about art and music and architecture at home." 'At home' meant the stretch of Fifth Avenue lined with New York's best houses.

The family disembarked at Cork and spent several weeks in Ireland. Mrs. Schieffelin recorded their activities in her diary every day. In Belfast, "Minnie celebrated her fourteenth birthday with a tea party with cakes." They took a steamer across the Irish Sea to Scotland and traveled three hours by train to the Kings Arms Hotel in Dumfries. The hotel proved a disappointment. "It was a dirty little house we reached at last," Mrs. Schieffelin wrote. Her diary noted both pleasure about the places they saw and exasperation with how long it took to reach them. The roads were often rough. They all felt stiffness after traveling by omnibus, a four-wheeled conveyance with covered seating inside and open seats on the roof. It frequently rained and they were often soaked. They were not traveling with a personal servant and depended on the hotels where they stayed to have their laundry done. There are many references in Mrs. Schieffelin's diary to the need to repack their valises or send their trunks ahead, and to the need for clothes to be mended. Mending took place at least one day a week. On these occasions Mr. Schieffelin took himself off to gentlemen's clubs.

A frequent notation in Mrs. Schieffelin's diary is of Fanny's headaches and the need to give her opium. Fanny, we will discover later, found opium useful during much of her life—she became addicted.

When the family reached Aberdeen, there's the first mention of lighthearted fun. Near a bridge in the center of the town, villagers were competing in a swimming match. The Schieffelins stopped and joined the crowd of spectators. Mr. Schieffelin spied a market where a florist was selling roses at a penny apiece. He bought a bouquet. Near the florist was a fruit stand. It was the height of the strawberry season. In the rear garden of their hotel the girls noticed a large strawberry patch.

"Oh, Mama, look at the strawberries. Can we pick them?" they asked. Their mother approved, and Fanny and Minnie ran freely with baskets given to them by the owner of the hotel. Mrs. Schieffelin recorded in her diary that it was one of the loveliest days yet.

Mrs. Schieffelin looked forward to reaching Leamington Spa in Warwickshire. This was where aristocratic Englishmen and women rejuvenated themselves in heated waters and gathered for entertainment at night. The girls' prettiest dresses were pressed to be ready for what Mrs. Schieffelin was certain would be a lively time. To her dismay, they arrived too late. The season had just ended and 'no one' was there.

"I am so disappointed," she said. "I had my heart set on being here so Minnie and Fanny could see such a beautiful place and enjoy the dancing." She told the girls about grand country houses and how lucky one would be if invited to stay.

London was their last stop. They took rooms at 13 Albemarle Street in the heart of Mayfair; for a time the Duke of Roxburghe was in adjacent rooms. They were close to Bond Street and Piccadilly and many of London's best shops. Green Park, with its expanse of lawns, was only a minute or two away. Mr. Schieffelin encouraged his wife and daughters to enjoy themselves.

"Buy three-buttoned gloves, be sure to get a hat, and remember umbrellas. They are well-made here," he said, before leaving with a friend to order suits for himself. The girls and their mother took him at his word. They went to a shop that sold kid gloves and tried on many pairs, pulling the soft leather over their elbows, and testing the ease of buttoning and unbuttoning the gloves at the wrist. The girls found sealskin purses for a shilling. They bought hats at Brown's on New Bond Street and umbrellas at W.W. Martin's in the Burlington Arcade. Mrs. Schieffelin took them to a custom fitter on Curzon Street for riding habits and to a bookseller for prayer books. They bought three Bibles, bound in blue velvet with their names engraved on gold clasps.

Mrs. Schieffelin didn't forget the china she wanted for her dining room in New York and they went to A.B. Daniell & Son, 46 Wigmore Street, purveyors of "the choicest productions from Messrs. Mintons the Coalbrookdale & the Worcester manufactories." In addition to replacing broken pieces in the patterns she owned, she bought a soup tureen.

When they weren't shopping, they went sightseeing. They saw Big Ben and toured the Houses of Parliament. They crossed Westminster Bridge by foot and viewed the Palace of Westminister from the embankment on the other side of the Thames. They visited Eton College and Windsor Castle. Fanny missed some of these excursions. "She has another headache," Mrs. Schieffelin wrote in her diary early in October. "She remained in her room not just for an hour or two, but the entire day. I gave her laudanum."

"I need a nice carriage *à deux chevaux* for calling on our new friends," Mrs. Schieffelin said to her husband one morning, and Mr. Schieffelin agreed. Their final week was spent traveling about in a private carriage to the rhythm of the horses' feet.

* * *

When the Schieffelins returned to New York, the winter social season had begun. Fanny, turning sixteen, was old enough to receive invitations to parties in her own name. She'd taken piano lessons from the age of eight, as had many of the children of their neighbors, and musical evenings were popular. Minnie had a good voice and she and Fanny often performed together.

On one of these occasions, Fanny was introduced to Ernest Crosby, a law student at Columbia.

"I recognize your name," he said. "You met my cousin, John Crosby, on your voyage to Europe last year. He told me how much he enjoyed sitting with your family at dinner." They sat down together on a settee and he asked her about her travels abroad.

Ernest was a good-looking young man, with brown hair, a carefully trimmed beard and intense brown eyes. He and Fanny talked easily about the places they'd been; Ernest's father was a Greek scholar and had taken him to the Holy Land several years earlier.

Fanny and Ernest saw each other again at subsequent parties, and it was not long before they fell in love. He went to her parents and asked for her hand. Her parents liked Ernest but said no; Fanny was only seventeen and Ernest was twenty-one. "Wait," they told him. "Wait until you've finished law school and begun to work. If you're still in love when Fanny is twenty-one, we will give the marriage our blessing."

* * *

Sarah and Henry Schieffelin were quietly pleased by Fanny's choice of suitor. Ernest was descended from a long line of distinguished forebears. His earliest American ancestor was Simon Crosby, who emigrated from England to Massachusetts in 1636. Crosby had acquired two acres of land on Brattle Street in Cambridge and farmed it profitably. The next several generations of Crosbys settled in Braintree. Ebenezer Crosby, Ernest's great-grandfather, graduated from Harvard in 1777 with a specialty in medicine. The Revolutionary War was in progress and he was chosen to join George Washington's Corps of Guards as a surgeon. When the war ended, he took further degrees in medicine and settled in New York. He married Catharine Bedlow, daughter of William Bedlow and a niece of Col. Henry Rutgers, thus aligning himself with two of New York's oldest families.

Ebenezer and Catharine had two sons: John Player Crosby and William Bedlow Crosby. When the boys were four and three, Ebenezer died. Catharine survived her husband by seven months. The two children were legally adopted by her uncle, Col. Rutgers, a bachelor who had made a fortune by investing in land along the East River. John Player Crosby died in his twenties, leaving William Bedlow Crosby the sole beneficiary of Col. Rutgers' estate, which in 1830 was valued at a million dollars. William was Ernest's grandfather.

William married Harriet Clarkson, a granddaughter of General William Floyd, a signer of the Declaration of Independence. They had twelve children. With his inheritance, they built, in Lower Manhattan, one of New York's largest private houses, modeled on a Regency house in London. The estate occupied two blocks of Monroe Street, now renamed Rutgers Place, with lawns, a garden, and stables. The house stood until 1865 when it was torn down in a rising real estate market, and the land divided into city lots and sold.

Ernest's father, Howard Crosby, was one of the twelve children. He grew up in the house on Rutgers Place with private tutors and very little chance to leave the grounds. He married Margaret Evertson, descended from a family of Scottish intellectuals, in 1847. "He had always had every luxury," Margaret wrote in a memoir for her children, "but he was most simple in his tastes."

Howard and Margaret traveled in Egypt, Turkey, Palestine, and Northern Europe for two years after they married. Howard's knowledge of Greek was so advanced that when given in English lines from the *Iliad* or the *Odyssey*, he could instantly translate them back to the original. When they returned from their travels, Howard accepted a position as Professor of Greek at City University, his alma mater. "We lived much at Rutgers Place when we came home," Margaret wrote. "It was rather doleful to me; when the great gates would clang shut after our daily drive, I had a prison-like sensation! But Howard's parents were very good to me."

Before marrying, Howard had promised Margaret that he would never speak to her of religion, and never be a clergyman. When poor health led to his physician's suggesting he move to the country, he accepted a professorship at Rutgers in New Brunswick, New Jersey (formerly Queens College, but renamed in 1825 in recognition of money given to the college by Col. Rutgers). Howard recovered, but Margaret fell ill. Her illness was so serious that Howard prayed for her survival. When she returned to health, he told her of his newfound faith and asked that she let him become a minister.

Howard spent two years studying for the ministry and in 1861 was invited to become pastor of the Fourth Avenue Presbyterian Church in New York. He and Margaret moved back to the city, together with their children, and bought a house on East 19th Street. They filled it with books and often invited scholars and clergy to dine with them. Howard was named Chancellor of the University of the City of New York in 1870 and was minister of the church for thirty years, until his death in 1891.

Ernest, Fanny's suitor, grew up meeting scholars and participating in his parents' social gatherings. He and his father often took walks together, exploring the streets of New York and talking about what they saw. They both noticed the plight of recently arrived immigrants on the Lower East Side, many of whom drowned their sorrows in alcohol. Howard was happy to have an occasional drink, and wine with a meal, but believed drunkenness to be "a crime against God and Man." He campaigned against 'dram shops' and 'drinking saloons' where drinking was the purpose, not eating. In 1877 he founded the Society for the Prevention of Crime, to punish those who sold alcohol illegally. He made enemies, but, because of the evenness of his manners and his ability to speak equally with all classes of persons, never lost their respect.

During the four years that Fanny and Ernest waited to be married, Ernest thought about the proper ways to treat mankind. He shared his father's concerns about the hard life so many in New York endured. He graduated from Columbia Law School with honors and went to work as a lawyer. Fanny went with him to parties and envisioned an exciting future in New York as the wife of a rising legal scholar. She looked forward to having children and entertaining in a house of her own.

They were married on October 12, 1881. Mr. and Mrs. Schieffelin welcomed them to 665 Fifth Avenue and gave them rooms at the back of the house. When the *Social Register* was first published in 1887, the two families were listed at the Schieffelins' address. Ernest's parents, Howard and Margaret Crosby, were listed as well, at their town house on East 19th Street.

The 1887 *Social Register* appeared on the scene as an aid to prominent families. It offered the following statement of its purpose:

> [The publication is to be] a record of society, comprising an accurate and careful list of its members, with their addresses, many of the maiden names of the married women, the club addresses of the men, officers of the leading clubs and social organizations, opera box holders, and other useful social information.

The inside front cover lists its contents in more detail. The book is:

A Systematic Index to Married & Maiden Names, Home & Club Addresses, Removals and Departures, Summer and Foreign Residences, Club Elections, Marriages, and Social Events, Revised and Noted Monthly. $3.25 Per Annum.

Only the club addresses of men were included. Women did not yet have their own prestigious clubs. The Colony Club and Cosmopolitan Club were founded much later. Woman's place was in the home. Women who wanted an independent life didn't receive encouragement. Fanny Crosby was content with her role, just as her mother, Sarah Schieffelin, had been. Fanny's daughter-in-law, my grandmother, rebelled. She would have a terrible life. My mother rebelled too, but she had a somewhat easier time.

CHAPTER 2

ERNEST'S CONCERNS ABOUT NEW YORK weren't so much
about the presence of illegal alcohol. He was concerned about
immigrant labor and poverty. He saw men in the streets trying to find work. He met Italians digging the subway and listened to their requests for better working conditions. He began
to question why he had so much, while others had so little. He
joined the newly formed Society for the Protection of Italian
Immigrants and went to their meetings.

Fanny wasn't initially concerned about Ernest's progressive
views. She was concentrating on learning how to run a house.
Their first child, Margaret Eleanor, was born in 1884. Eleanor,
as the baby was called, began her life learning languages. She
said her morning and evening prayers in three languages, and
quickly learned foreign words. Pointing to an owl in a storybook
one evening, she looked up at her mother and said "*hibou.*"

"I think," Fanny said to her mother one morning, "that
when Eleanor is older, she will want to live in Europe. She
should marry a duke."

"She might," said Eleanor's grandmother, and wrote this
pleasant thought in her diary.

Three years later, a son, Maunsell Schieffelin Crosby,
was born. Both children showed an early interest in music. The

family sang hymns together on Sunday evenings. Fanny's sister, Minnie, accompanied them on the piano, and Maunsell often sat beside her watching her fingers move up and down the keys. Little Eleanor learned the melodies and was soon experimenting with them on her Schieffelin grandfather's flute and accordion.

Ernest was a doting father during these early years. He marked Eleanor's growing height on a door jamb. He listened to her when she learned new words. He enjoyed taking her out in a landau. The top of the horse-drawn carriage came in two parts so that it could be closed. Ernest liked it open and held Eleanor on his lap. Fanny took her out as well. One morning she dressed Eleanor in a white plush coat and bonnet and took her shopping. The sales clerks clustered around. "They called her a little snowflake," she said to Ernest on their return.

During the first several years of their marriage, Fanny and Ernest remained close to both their families. They spent Monday evenings at the Crosbys' house on East 19th Street. They joined Fanny's parents in Rhode Island in the summer. But things began to change when Ernest, whose law practice was well regarded, was invited to stand for election to the New York State Assembly. He liked the idea.

"I'd like to do something useful," he said to Fanny, "and maybe I can do that by creating laws rather than interpreting them." He began to dislike many aspects of the practice of law, especially its use against poor people. "I don't like seeing children work," he said, "so I'm pleased to have this opportunity to work against it." He ran on the Republican ticket and won, succeeding Theodore Roosevelt. His election meant spending time in Albany instead of New York.

In Albany he introduced bills to outlaw the hiring of child workers. His fellow legislators laughed, arguing that restricting the working rights of children was tantamount to taking their rights away.

Ernest wasn't deterred. He continued to notice inequities and work against them. For the next several years he commuted from New York to Albany by train, a trip that took several hours. The railroad was on the east bank of the Hudson River and factories were rising on both sides. Their ugliness so close to the river jarred him. Above Poughkeepsie, he saw the Catskill Mountains to the west and recalled childhood summers there with his parents. As a youngster he joined his father on long 'tramps' through the woods. Now, as a young legislator, he pondered these things. He used his time on the train to draft legislation and write speeches; but he also wrote poetry. His poem, "Civilization," condemning the desecration of the landscape, remains as relevant in the twenty-first century as it was in the late nineteenth.

Fanny's parents became concerned about Ernest's growing progressive ideas. They weren't political activists. They weren't used to speaking in public about issues. They pondered how to silence their son-in-law without embarrassing their daughter. Henry Schieffelin decided to draw on his friendships in Washington. He and Sarah knew President Benjamin Harrison. They wrote to him about Ernest's altruism and legal talent. Was there a foreign country, they wondered, where Ernest might serve?

Thus it happened that when Eleanor was five and Maunsell two, Ernest and Fanny left America. In 1889 President Harrison nominated Ernest to be a judge on the Mixed Tribunals in Alexandria, Egypt—a lifelong appointment. The court adjudicated grievances between foreigners living in Egypt, and grievances between foreigners and Egyptians. To the Schieffelins' delight, Ernest and Fanny didn't hesitate to accept the appointment. They believed the presence of so many nationalities in Alexandria would foster in Eleanor and Maunsell a good ear for foreign languages.

Ernest left first, sailing to France and transferring to a second ship that took him to Cairo. Fanny, Mrs. Schieffelin, and the two children followed a month later. Mrs. Schieffelin stayed in Alexandria for several weeks, helping the family settle into the large, well-staffed house that came with Ernest's position. She then went back to New York, related to her husband Henry how interesting Alexandria was, and persuaded him to return with her for a holiday.

Disaster struck. Two weeks after their arrival, without any warning that he was ill, Henry Schieffelin collapsed and died. Mrs. Schieffelin returned to New York where her other daughter, Minnie, had remained. Minnie died a few years later, unmarried, leaving Mrs. Schieffelin alone in her Fifth Avenue house.

In Alexandria, Ernest spent his days sitting in court or working in his chambers. He attended many dinners, only a few of which included Fanny. Sometimes the invitations were to Ernest only, and other times to them both. Fanny usually offered a mild ailment as a reason for declining to go.

As had been the case in New York, Ernest noticed the social and economic conditions around him. He visited many parts of the city and once again felt distressed by the poverty. It wasn't long before Ernest the judge became Ernest the activist. In this he was much like his father, Howard Crosby, the minister. He couldn't rid himself of the thought that he enjoyed unearned privileges. He discovered that he didn't care for his responsibilities as a judge in Alexandria any more than he'd cared for his duties as a lawyer in New York. The injustices in Egypt were in his eyes even greater than those on the Lower East Side.

Sitting in his library one night, he explained it to Fanny. "I don't like that I authorized the burning of a farmer's house. I don't like sending men to prison. I especially did not like authorizing an execution. I don't, in fact, like being in the position of having to make these decisions about my fellow human beings."

By chance, Ernest came upon a copy of Tolstoy's *My Life*. Reading it affected him deeply. He discovered in Tolstoy a writer whose feelings for the underclass resonated with his own. He wrote to Tolstoy and a correspondence began that would span thirteen years (the letters are now in the Rare Books Collection at Vassar College). Ernest decided he had to meet Tolstoy. He resigned from the international court in 1894 and made plans to visit Russia. "You go to New York," he said to Fanny, "and take the children with you. I will join you when I can." Fanny returned to 665 Fifth Avenue, and Ernest went alone to Warsaw and Moscow.

"My compartment companions were reading *War and Peace* in Russian," he wrote Fanny. "I have arrived in Moscow and am awaiting the arrival of the Tolstoys from the country. I have been to a public bath where twenty-five men bathed naked, and to an orphanage with 1,100 babies and peasant wet nurses. I have not dined in the same restaurant twice, and the food and wine are splendid."

The Tolstoys invited Ernest to their house in the country. He spent several days there, and had conversations with both the Countess and the Count. "We talked of many matters that required delicacy—the Emperor, his poor advisors, the difficulties the family has had with their children, and friends who do not share their views."

When Ernest returned to New York, he announced to all his friends that he was opposed to imperialism and military power. "It should be the power of ideas that changes peoples' minds," he said, "not the power of force." He wanted international peace, and for it to be achieved by non-violent resistance to oppression. He planned to spend the rest of his life writing books and articles. He said he would no longer attend frivolous parties.

As could have been expected, Ernest's friends and former associates formed new opinions of him. The Rev. Leighton

Williams, who when younger had felt unable to attain intimacy with Ernest, found now that "the aristocrat had become a democrat. He became joyful. He cared for the wage earners."

Ernest's first book was a novel, *Captain Jinx, Hero,* in which he satirized the Spanish-American War. He based his hero on Cervantes' *Don Quixote,* but added more violence. The novel brought a rebuke from President Harrison. Ernest wasn't troubled. He joined the Manhattan Single Tax Club and founded the Social Welfare Club of New York. There was almost no subject about which he didn't now have an opinion. He advocated vegetarianism and supported the building of playgrounds for children. He forbade Fanny to buy new gowns when the poor were starving.

Fanny and her mother were stunned. Ernest told them he didn't care. He felt so indebted to Tolstoy that he wrote a tribute to him, *Tolstoy and his Message,* published in London in 1903 with a second edition the following year. The opening page tells us much about Tolstoy's early epiphany and reveals by association the values Ernest was choosing for himself:

> They tell a story of Leo Tolstoy which may or may not be true, but which at any rate is characteristic of the man, and brings into relief the peculiar dramatic quality of his mind. He was a student at the University of Kazan, and had only spent a few months at that great Russian seat of learning, when he was invited to attend a ball at the house of a nobleman, who lived upon his estate near the city. It was a bitter cold winter night, and the snow lay heavy upon the ground, and young Tolstoy went out from town in a sleigh driven by a peasant-coachman, for there was then no separate liveried class in Russia, and the farm-hand in summer might become a driver in winter. Tolstoy passed the night in feasting and dancing, enjoying himself as a youth of eighteen would be likely to under the circumstances, and when he came out

at an early hour of the morning wrapped in his furs, he was horrified to find his coachman half-frozen to death. It was with the greatest difficulty, and only after hours of chafing and rubbing, that the man was brought back to consciousness and his life finally saved.

This scene remained graven upon the heart of the young student, and he could not dismiss it from his thoughts. Why, thought he, should I, a young nobleman of eighteen, who has never been of any use to any one and perhaps never shall be—why should I be permitted to pass the night in this great house, elegantly furnished and comfortably warmed, and to consume in wine and delicacies the value of many days' labour, while this poor peasant, the representative of the class that builds and heats the houses and provides the food and drink, is shut out in the cold? He saw, with the true instinct of a seer, that it was no accidental event, but the picture in miniature of the civilization of the day, in which one class sowed and reaped, and another enjoyed the harvest. Tolstoy took this lesson so to heart that he abandoned his university career as a selfish luxury, and went down to his country estate, which the early death of his parents had already placed in his hands, with the determination of devoting his life to the serfs whose interests he found entrusted to him. It was thus a dramatic incident which formed the first turning-point in Tolstoy's life, and we shall see that again and again he has been influenced by such sights when book or argument could never have moved him.

Ernest finally went too far for the Schieffelins when he brought unpredictable acquaintances home for dinner. The most notable was Maxim Gorky, the Russian novelist and playwright. Gorky had been welcomed in New York until it was discovered he was traveling with his mistress. While others, including Mark Twain and William Dean Howells, turned their backs on him, Ernest welcomed him.

Fanny couldn't understand how the charming man she'd married, with a brilliant lawyer's future, had become an embarrassment. She was made noticeably nervous by the strain of entertaining Marxists instead of patricians. Mrs. Schieffelin thought the best solution would be for Fanny and Ernest to leave New York City permanently.

"If he were safely ensconced in the country," she suggested, "he wouldn't be able to bring such politically volatile acquaintances home for dinner. A country village would hardly provide him a forum for his public utterances." Thus, Grasmere, a nine-hundred-acre property in Rhinebeck, ninety miles north of Manhattan, became my great-grandparents' house. Ernest and Fanny agreed to live there most of the year, while Mrs. Schieffelin kept the house on Fifth Avenue for herself.

The Grasmere estate was primarily farm land and woods, dominated by a Georgian brick house with more than thirty rooms. The fields and woods surrounding the house had names: Long Meadow, Fifty Acre Lot, Oak Field, Square Meadow, East Woods, Brick Lot, Mill Lot, Camp Meeting Woods, and South Pines. The main driveway, called North, was lined with the now fully grown locust trees planted by seed after the Revolutionary War. The other drives were named West, East, and South (also called "The Ladies' Mile").

Ernest and Fanny made improvements to the house and land. They added another story, under a mansard roof. They built a stone barn, believed by many to be at the time the largest stone barn in America. They built two gatehouses to a design characterized as "Lake District Revival" in style. They planted beautiful lawns and laid out carefully spaced beds of rhododendrons and flowering shrubs. They created a walk leading from the formal garden to provide views of the mountains to the west.

Mrs. Schieffelin listed 665 Fifth Avenue in the *Social Register* as her winter residence, and Grasmere as her summer residence.

As Grasmere became more beautiful, she spent more time there. 'Summer residence' didn't mean precisely what it might seem to mean, as 'summer' for the owners of big houses on the Hudson River lasted well beyond the hot summer months. Henry Noble MacCracken, Dutchess County historian, described the life style well in his book, *Blithe Dutchess*. According to him, it was the skippers of the Hudson River boats who knew when summer ended. Unlike rich landowners in Newport or on Long Island, the Hudson River people could commute by boat from New York. As long as the river was free from ice, they could travel. And when the river froze over, they had the New York Central Railroad. It was said that if they owned shares, they could stop the southbound train by waving a hand. When they traveled north from Manhattan, they told the conductor to instruct the engineer where to stop.

There were life style differences between these Hudson River millionaires and their counterparts in Newport and elsewhere. The river families, including the Delanos, Roosevelts, Livingstons, and Chanlers, sought privacy above all else. They built libraries instead of ballrooms. They would see other families at church or at the boat landing, but otherwise live quietly on their estates. The children were taught by tutors, and those who had horses had riding instructors. It was in this world that Eleanor and Maunsell, Fanny and Ernest's two children, now lived.

The farm, according to notes made by my mother, was devoted to raising livestock—Jerseys, Holsteins, and Brown Swiss cattle, hogs, a few colts for farm work, chickens, turkeys, and ducks—and to agriculture, including apples, pears, hay and grain, potatoes, and beans. There were beehives for honey and a dairy route to manage; Grasmere supplied most of the milk in Rhinebeck. The farm also produced lumber, stone, and sand. The superintendent, Jacob V. Beach, lived in a separate house.

Two farmers lived in tenant cottages with their families and fifteen male summer laborers had beds in the large stone barn.

For playmates, Maunsell and Eleanor could count on the farmers' children. The outdoor entertainments were plentiful. There were several ponds, numerous trails, the animals themselves, and Mr. Beach, who enjoyed answering the children's questions. Maunsell felt immediately at home. He was healthy, strong, and an athlete in the making. He loved running and tore off down one of the drives when his tutorials were done. Fanny encouraged this: she wanted him to know every foot of the estate, because she expected him to run it eventually. She was certain his explorations would lead to good stewardship on his part.

In the summer of 1900, when Maunsell was thirteen, his parents hired an amateur ornithologist as his tutor. Clinton Abbott saw in Maunsell the makings of an excellent birder. Maunsell could hear a bird sing once and remember its call. He soon mastered all the different calls of warblers. He and Abbott took long walks early every morning, with binoculars around their necks and field guides and notebooks in their pockets. The neighbors gave them free access to their fields and woods. "Don't ask in advance," they said. "Just come when you wish." One friend further south, in Hyde Park, was Franklin Roosevelt, who, when Maunsell was older, would invite him to join him on vacations in the south (a climate Maunsell came to love).

Clinton Abbott returned the following summer and Maunsell's interest in birds grew. He decided the village of Rhinebeck needed an official bird count. By himself, at age fourteen, he did the preparatory work and, that winter, organized an annual bird count that continues to this day.

Abbott returned to Rhinebeck on his own for several more years. He and Maunsell always found time to go out together. When Maunsell was seventeen, Ernest considered him old enough to meet Abbott at the railroad station by himself. Abbott recorded how they started their search for birds from the station:

> I saw practically nothing from the train but crows, with one kingfisher to vary the monotony. . . As we drove up we spied an evidently new vireo's nest at the end of one of the limbs directly over the road. . . Veeries were singing beautifully in the woods all about. Maunsell showed me where a pair of red-shouldered hawks nested.

Their field notes reveal rich bird life everywhere, so different from today, a hundred years later. Here is what they saw on June 24, 1905:

> We walked down the Lady's Mile (where chickadees were seen feeding full-grown young), and out through the South Gate to a scrubby field with a brook running through it, where we knew we should find many birds. Here we soon had yellowthroats, chats, chestnut-sided warblers, golden-winged warblers, towhees and catbirds all scolding us at once. Apparently all were solicitous over full-grown young, however, which in most cases we found. I might state that, as usual, golden-winged warblers are the most abundant warblers here. It is very interesting what a local species this is and how it is always to be found here. They all seem to be entirely full grown young birds. . . .
>
> When we left the scrubby field our list of species for the day stood at 59, and with a desire to raise it to 60 we returned to the Mill Pond in the hope of seeing a night heron, but we were not to be rewarded.

Maunsell and Clinton Abbott remained good friends for life. Abbott's dream was eventually to become a farmer, and when he married years later and was at last able to buy land,

Maunsell gave him a handsome wedding present: one of his most valuable prize cows.

* * *

Those experiences run a little ahead of the story, and we need to return to Ernest Crosby. Ernest had no interest in actually running Grasmere, nor any interest in the needs of his farmers, despite the example of Tolstoy he'd said he admired. He also now had little interest in his children. Grasmere interested him solely as a place to write. "My father spent his life teaching and writing," he said, "and therefore so shall I." He built himself an outdoor place to be alone, and called it Cedar Hut. In addition to *Captain Jinx Hero,* and *Tolstoy and his Message*, he published a volume of poetry, *Swords and Ploughshares,* in 1902. He wrote *Tolstoy as a Schoolmaster* in 1904 and *Garrison, The Non-Resistant and Abolitionist* in 1905. It was not until 1973, however, more than sixty years after his death, that he gained broad recognition as an early pacifist. In *Peace Movements in America*, edited by Charles Chatfield at Wittenberg University in Ohio, a chapter is devoted to him.

Grasmere was dependent on Mrs. Schieffelin's money. She found discussions with Ernest useless and turned to her daughter, Fanny, for decisions about how the estate would be run. While Grasmere gave the appearance of being a farm that made a profit, it was not a real farm. The pastures with their barns and dairy cows functioned more as a background for the 'big house' with its lawns, Italianate gardens, and driveways. The social life revolved around guests who came from nearby estates where life was lived the same way, though some had more efficient methods of running things.

Ernest, despite his writings in support of the less privileged, managed to protect his son Maunsell from any acute knowledge of the 'lower classes.' He seemed blindly unaware that although he'd become a vegetarian and lived simply, his simplicity was supported at great cost and was, in reality, maintained in the manner of a Roman patrician. Maunsell learned only a little about how the estate was really run.

Ernest Crosby was a man of his time and class. I have a hard time thinking of him as selfish, because I'm attracted to his intellectualism, but Fanny certainly found him difficult. Maunsell, my grandfather, grew up between his ever more possessive and nervous mother, Fanny, and the stern political rhetoric of his father. When it came time for him to make decisions about the estate after Ernest's death, he deferred to Fanny, because his father didn't take him under his wing. Maunsell became oblivious to the social and economic problems of others. He did not inherit the intellectual concerns of his father. He waited on the friends of his mother and sister with gallant gracefulness, albeit shyly. Children who came to visit called Eleanor and Maunsell "goodie goodies." Only when Maunsell was able to get away and go to boarding school did he begin to make good friends. Of women, he knew only that they seemed to be the ones who made decisions.

* * *

After five years of tutoring at Grasmere, Maunsell went to boarding school in northern New Jersey. He was eighteen, older than his classmates. Because he was outgoing and charming and good at music, he made many friends. One was John Hall Wheelock, who would go on to publish fourteen volumes of poetry and win the Bollingen Prize in 1962. Maunsell and Wheelock decided to apply to Harvard together, and easily won acceptance with the class of 1908. There they met Maxwell Perkins, class of 1907, later to be Scribner's editor of Ernest Hemingway, Thomas Wolfe, and F. Scott Fitzgerald. Two other new friends were Edward Sheldon, a future playwright, and Van Wyck Brooks, who became a historian of American literature. They were a close-knit group. Wheelock, Perkins, Sheldon, and Brooks visited Grasmere, where they enjoyed long walks in the woods, and in turn introduced Maunsell to the literary life of Boston and New York. If one did not know Maunsell well, and met him then, one would assume that he, too, was destined for literary success.

Maunsell qualified for Harvard's intercollegiate track team and was one of its fastest runners. By the time he graduated, he'd won more than twenty races and almost as many glass-bottomed pewter mugs, each engraved with the dates of his victories. His name began to appear in New York and Boston society columns, where he was described as a young man of promise. He was invited to skating parties and dances.

Young women in Boston and Cambridge enjoyed going to Harvard's athletic competitions. In the early 1900s, wearing long skirts and fitted blouses with puffy sleeves, they sat on the sidelines and cheered. On April 13, 1906, a pretty sixteen-year-old was at the track. Maunsell was competing in a two-mile run. It was cold and the wind blew hard on the runners' faces. Maunsell fell behind during the first seven laps. On the final go around of the quarter-mile path, he burst ahead and won. His two-mile running time was ten minutes and eight seconds.

The pretty sixteen-year-old had met Maunsell six months earlier. They'd seen each other at skating parties and she'd talked with him at supper parties. They'd enjoyed arguing points with each other, as if neither had had the opportunity to converse in this spirited way before. She liked his literary friends. She'd come specifically to watch him run. When the race was over, she left the bench on which she'd been sitting and congratulated him. Her name was Elizabeth Coolidge.

CHAPTER 3

HOW I WISH I COULD HAVE KNOWN Elizabeth as she was then. She seems so vivacious and outgoing. For the first twenty years of my life, I barely knew she existed. I was a senior at college in 1960 when my mother took me to meet her. Elizabeth was then seventy-one and had spent half of her life as a psychiatric inpatient in a state hospital. My mother's papers at last gave me a chance to get to know her. Helen, I think correctly, had shielded my sisters and me from learning about her earlier.

Aside from finding a few Coolidge photographs among Helen's papers, my first awareness of her family came from a newspaper clipping. Her father, Albert Leighton Coolidge, had died. There were cover-ups in the press, because suicide wasn't something one talked about. But there is no doubt that Albert killed himself. Shortly after lunch, on June 29, 1891, at the age of fifty-nine, he opened the window of a tall office building on the outskirts of Boston and stepped onto the ledge. An active partner of Houghton, Coolidge & Co., boot and shoe manufacturers, he was also a director of the Central National Bank, the American Loan & Trust Company, and the Home Savings Bank. He lived on Commonwealth Avenue in Boston with his second wife, Evelyn Wiggin, originally from Saco, Maine. They had a daughter, Bertha, now twelve, and Elizabeth, not yet two.

Albert Coolidge was a good-looking man, with dark, penetrating eyes and a graying beard. He was a member of the Commercial, Algonquin, and Eastern Yacht Clubs, and he kept a boat. He was also an enlightened progressive, supporting what were then called colored institutions of higher learning in the south. Later that week he was to open his home on Commonwealth Avenue for a concert in support of unmarried pregnant women. There were no indications that he was about to take his life. But that is what he did, while Evelyn was at home arranging flowers and consulting with the cook.

I learned how Albert died from reading my mother's letters and diaries. She wondered, in her journal, whether Elizabeth's growing up with a depressed mother and a sister ten years older could have contributed to Elizabeth's willfulness later. The *Boston Post* reported that Albert Coolidge "died of a cerebral hemorrhage at Dr. Channing's home at Brookline." The *Boston Journal* said he "died at his home." Elizabeth herself left no clues.

I haven't been able to locate any financial records for the family. But my guess is that they were financially secure while Albert was alive because of his earnings, rather than an inheritance. My earliest photographs of Elizabeth, Bertha, and their mother show them wearing handsome clothes. In one, Elizabeth wears a shaggy wool cape and white bonnet. In another, Evelyn is wearing a satin and velvet evening suit with a bustle and train.

There are suggestions, however, that after Albert died, Evelyn had trouble making ends meet. She and her daughters stayed in the house on Commonwealth Avenue for less than a year. The summer after Albert died, Evelyn took Bertha and Elizabeth to Manchester-by-the-Sea, where they stayed with a cousin. They returned to Commonwealth Avenue for several months, then stayed with relations for varying periods of time in Lexington, Massachusetts, Richmond, Virginia, and

Fryeburg, Maine. Gossips said the Coolidge girls were poor and that any semblances of prosperity were the result of the kindness of relatives.

Six years after Albert died, Evelyn moved to 396 Harvard Street in Cambridge. Elizabeth entered the Cambridge School on Concord Avenue. The prospectus promised "admirable buildings: well equipped, hot-water heated, sunny in every room, with unexcelled ventilation." The girls wore blue uniforms and aviator hats, and were assured of "special attention to posture and carriage." Tennis and softball games were closely supervised by the teachers. Alone with tutors until she was seven, Elizabeth was now under scrutiny every minute. There was no opportunity for the girls to enjoy unstructured play.

Elizabeth's teachers thought she was mature for her age, but it may be that she had simply never had friends her own age. On Christmas Day 1897, she felt compelled to write a will:

Miss E. Coolidge

My Will

1. All my jewelry to Bertha my sister
2. All my dolls are to be given to all the poor children in the hospitels
3. All my dresses to the poor women
4. All my mony to Mamma
5. All the rest of the things to the poor
6. Give my house to Bertha if she has none. If she has give it to my children an husband.

I am 8 years old.

The ten-year difference in age between Bertha and Elizabeth was always to provoke discord between them. Elizabeth found her older sister overbearing and bossy. Bertha thought Elizabeth reckless. They had lots of time to observe each other, because Evelyn, their mother, took herself elsewhere, leaving Bertha in charge. Elizabeth wrote in her diary: "Bertha is keeping house. Bertha knows very little about it, and we get rather queer meals. And there are mishaps. The maid has broken the water pitcher and the fernery and the Japanese pot it was in, and I don't know what mamma will say!"

Evelyn Coolidge, their often-absent mother, was born in 1851, the product of an age when most women didn't have opportunities to express themselves freely. Women of her class were expected to welcome the protection of men. They looked to their husbands, uncles, and brothers for economic support. Their own realm of influence was at home, where they often set a severe moral tone. If they were sufficiently compliant, they had a place in society. If they questioned their gender role, they were ostracized. Evelyn expected her daughters to want what she had achieved for herself: a husband whose name she could take as her own.

But there was now acrimony at 396 Harvard Street. Bertha, entering her twenties, wanted independence. She noted the opening of colleges for women: Wellesley, Mt. Holyoke, Radcliffe, Vassar, Barnard, Bryn Mawr, and Smith. Women could now obtain an education comparable to the educations men received at Yale, Harvard, and Princeton. Bertha fretted about not having enough money to enter one of these women's colleges, and sought the company of other young women who felt as she did. She joined the Sewing Circle, a forerunner of the Junior League, where, while sewing for the poor, she enjoyed intellectual conversation away from the ears of men. In World War I, she became a driver for the Red Cross in France. In her thirties, she made a name for herself, and a little money, as a miniaturist, painting small portraits of people in her social class.

She told her mother she didn't want to marry. "All the young men I've met are not to my requirements."

Evelyn eventually gave up on Bertha and focused her attention on her much younger daughter, Elizabeth. She asked her siblings to help with Elizabeth's upbringing. One of her sisters was married to the portrait painter Frederic Porter Vinton, who took Elizabeth to art exhibits in Boston. In 1904, when Elizabeth was fifteen, Evelyn moved back to Boston. She rented an apartment in the Back Bay on Marlborough Street. Bertha stayed in the house in Cambridge, sharing its cost with friends and effectively leaving Elizabeth without an intermediary.

A neighbor on Marlborough Street, Miss Mary Haskell, headmistress of a fashionable Boston school, became a new friend of Evelyn and Elizabeth. Elizabeth was now a trim and pretty teenager, her long, brown hair tied in a ribbon. Evelyn explained to Miss Haskell that Elizabeth would soon be "entering society" and needed to learn the basics of social letter writing. Miss Haskell offered to help and suggested that Elizabeth compose letters on a variety of subjects.

"Think of a delicate situation," she said, "and let's decide how to handle it."

"I've just planted spring bulbs in the communal grass beside our house," Elizabeth replied.

"And?" Miss Haskell asked.

"Mrs. Brown seems not to have noticed. She lets her children walk on the bulbs."

"Ah," said Miss Haskell, "put that into a letter you can give her." Elizabeth picked up her pen and wrote in the third person manner customary for formal notes:

Miss Elizabeth Coolidge
begs that Mrs. Brown will do her the kindness
to ask her children not to walk on the grass plot
adjoining the houses of Mrs. Brown and Miss Coolidge,

as it has lately been planted with crocuses.
224 Marlborough Street

Miss Haskell then asked Elizabeth to compose the reply. She took a second piece of paper and wrote:

Mrs. Brown will be
very happy to grant Miss Coolidge's request
that her children shall not walk upon the grass plot
adjacent to Miss Coolidge's and Mrs. Brown's houses.
226 Marlborough Street

"That was good," said Miss Haskell. "Now let's suppose you're planning a picnic and would like to invite me." Elizabeth wrote:

Miss Elizabeth Coolidge
requests the pleasure of
Miss Mary Haskell's
company on Saturday, May the third,
at a picnic, starting at half after eleven o'clock
224 Marlborough Street
Boston

Miss Haskell frowned slightly and drew a line through the word "Mary" in the third line. "We don't use the overly familiar first name in a formal invitation," she said.

* * *

Elizabeth was glad she'd moved back to Boston. Her mother let her roam freely. She explored the city on foot, going to art exhibitions almost daily. She told Miss Haskell she'd enjoyed seeing Monet's work.

"Why?" Miss Haskell asked.

"I liked his method and the pigments," Elizabeth replied. "I sat down before his picture of the Thames with the ships moving back and forth. My uncle was with me. I called those pale foggy ones 'muslin' pictures and told him I liked them best, and he made great fun of me, but he decided he liked them too, after a while."

Boston at this time was known for the number of its theaters. Famous actors came to the city on a regular basis and Elizabeth's uncle Vinton and his wife often took Elizabeth to performances. Not all Bostonians approved of these productions; they thought them too bold, and censors were introduced. This had an opposite effect from what the protestors had hoped. While "Banned in Boston" made some citizens feel virtuous, others found the labeling enticing. Elizabeth's uncle took her to a musical. She was shocked by the short dresses on the chorus girls, but also fascinated. "I'd like to be an actress," she said.

In 1906, Sarah Bernhardt, the legendary French actress, came to Boston. Afterwards, she was initiated into the *Cercle Français* at Harvard. Elizabeth was invited to the event by a friend. A number of Harvard faculty and students went onstage for a group photograph and Elizabeth joined them. The next day the photograph appeared in the *Boston American*. Elizabeth clipped it for her scrapbook and wrote in the margin, "Can you find me? I was there!" Two months later, she joined the Vincent Club, an upper class women's social club known for its theatrical productions, and attended dress rehearsals.

While Elizabeth loved visiting art galleries and going to the theater, she also excelled at hand-eye sports, enjoying softball, ping pong, and tennis, even in a long skirt. She was a graceful ice skater. One cold February day she traveled from North Station to Kendal Green with a friend, and found the skating pond hadn't been cleaned.

"We took a long, long walk into the country," she told her sister, Bertha. "It was quite wonderful. Everything is so white and snowy away from Boston."

* * *

Before a young woman was formally presented to society, she received invitations to afternoon teas and dinners. She met the other socially prominent young women who would be part of her group presentation, so that they could become friends. There was an understanding that each of the young women would give a party of her own; in return for the parties Elizabeth attended, she was expected to give one herself. As each girl grew a little older, the afternoon teas and dinners turned into evening dances and country weekends. The purpose was to introduce young men and women to one another in a wide variety of situations, including cotillions for which there was a subscription price. Elizabeth filled a scrapbook with mementoes of the parties she'd attended: engraved invitations to dances, handwritten invitations to house parties, dance cards, and dinner menus. Most invitations came by post, usually weeks in advance (*"You are invited to subscribe to five small dances to be given in Copley Hall December 1st and 15th, January 5th and 19th and February 16th"*); but some arrived just days, or even the day, before. One, from 417 Beacon Street, began, "I am writing to enquire whether you could join me for dinner tomorrow evening at a quarter to seven at the University Club and accompany me afterwards to Mrs. Kingsland's concert?" The postal service could be relied upon to deliver the answer in time. (Mrs. Coolidge installed a telephone in February 1906, but it wasn't yet considered a completely polite way of communicating socially.)

It's not clear how much time Elizabeth spent by herself in the apartment on Marlborough Street. No papers survive that indicate whether there was a live-in housekeeper. Elizabeth bought herself a five-year diary that she kept beginning in 1906. The diary offered printed advice on the inside front cover:

You have neither the time nor the inclination, possibly, to keep a full diary. Suppose, however, out of the multitude of matters that crowd each day, you jot down in a line or two those most worthy of remembrance. Such a book will be of the greatest value in after years. What a record of events, incidents, joys, sorrows, successes, failures, things accomplished, things attempted. This book is designed for just such a record. It can be commenced at any day of the year, and is so printed that it is good for any five years.

I was stunned when I found this diary, tucked deep in a box under my mother's diaries. In it I discovered a young woman who gave no clue that incarceration in a mental hospital would be her fate. Her words expressed the concerns and desires of a normal young woman of her age and background. In the five years that it spans, she chronicles her life in Boston and meeting my grandfather, Maunsell Crosby. She writes about their wedding, honeymoon and early married life. It concludes with her recognition that her marriage is failing, for which she blames Maunsell and his mother. Her handwriting is cramped, seven lines squeezed into space meant for four. She frequently uses abbreviations. On a blank page at the back, she lists more than 150 names under the heading, *Boys I Know*, following each name with initials. Maunsell Schieffelin Crosby is "MSC."

Early in 1906 she refers to MSC and a "long talk about drinking." There were whisky and sherry decanters on side tables in many houses in the early 1900s (as there were in my mother's in the 1960s, and my own in the 1990s; a silver tray that held them was passed along to younger generations). Elizabeth writes that she'd gone to a New Year's party where someone drank too much. When she saw Maunsell that week, she wanted to know if he drank. He said he didn't. She said she did, though not daily. She said she liked it.

By the end of April, despite knowing that she was expected to have a coming-out party in a year or two, she decided to see Maunsell exclusively. She refused invitations from all other suitors, though she did dance with other young men at parties. In June, Maunsell asked his mother to invite Elizabeth to Grasmere. Evelyn Coolidge was ambivalent about the invitation; Elizabeth was too young to be seeing just one person. Nonetheless, she said she could go, and allowed her to travel unchaperoned. "I will come to get you at the end of your visit, and meet Mrs. Crosby then," Evelyn had said. This decision strikes me today as very odd, since young women were usually watched over carefully. Elizabeth traveled on her own when other young women did not.

* * *

Elizabeth arrived at Grasmere on June 21st and stayed four days. The locust and maple trees were in full leaf. The couple walked over the estate, peering into the stone barn, stopping beside ponds, and following paths into the woods. Maunsell identified bird calls. Occasionally they heard the sound of a train traveling in the distance. Elizabeth noticed how easy it was to get to New York.

"You can get to the city by train almost anytime you want," she said.

"Yes, if being in the city is what you want," Maunsell replied.

"It is," Elizabeth said.

Evelyn Coolidge came to collect Elizabeth at the end of the visit, and wasn't happy about the deepening relationship. She told Elizabeth that New Yorkers were "undercivilized." She considered Maunsell's philosophy of life "rural."

"The Crosbys aren't like us," she said on the train back to Boston. "Maunsell's a nice young man, but he's only a temporary Bostonian. He's a student at Harvard but he's not going to stay in New England. Your roots are in New England. Boston–New York marriages don't work."

"But, Mama," Elizabeth pleaded, "there's so much beauty here."

"There's beauty in New England too," her mother replied. "The Crosbys are farmers. Their lives are isolated. There will be nothing for you to do. You mustn't let this relationship develop any further. I intend to see that you don't. We're going to Squam Lake for the remainder of the summer. New Hampshire will get your mind off this.

"And after that," she added, "you're going to Germany. Uncle Vinton has agreed to pay the tuition at a finishing school in Munich. You'll learn lots of things you need to know when you're married to a more suitable husband. Uncle Vinton is paying for your coming-out party too, at his house on Newbury Street. You'll meet some very nice Bostonians I'm sure you'll like."

Unable to fight back (she was too young and she had nowhere else to go), Elizabeth stayed with her mother the rest of the summer in a rented gray-shingle cottage near Center Sandwich, New Hampshire. They rowed, sailed, picked blueberries along country lanes, and sketched. In the evenings, Mrs. Coolidge sewed while Elizabeth learned to play the mandolin. On Sundays Elizabeth played the organ at church. She wrote Maunsell often, and he wrote back. On August 25th they returned to Boston and spent a week cleaning and mending clothes in preparation for their trip to Europe. The plan was to stay in Europe for a year, Elizabeth in a finishing school in Munich, while Bertha and her mother traveled elsewhere.

Evelyn, Bertha, and Elizabeth sailed to Genoa in early September. Elizabeth's only recorded pleasure on board was watching the moon rise over the ocean. She would have liked to have spent her nights in a deck chair, tucked under a blanket, but had to make do with gazing through a porthole in their stateroom while her mother and Bertha slept. They traveled by train from Milan to Innsbruck and from there by bus to Munich. Elizabeth was left at Miss Wilson's School and began a long, wet, lonely year.

Miss Wilson's School prepared girls for a life of privilege. It was understood that if they wished to marry someone who owned a big house and held an important job, they would have to be his equal on the domestic side. There might be foreign visitors or foreign travel, requiring that they be able to speak a second language, or even a third one. They needed to master the art of conversation. They were taught to paint and draw, play musical instruments, arrange flowers, and cook. "By mastering these things," the girls were told, "you will be able to teach your staff what they need to know, and entertain those who come to visit you."

Elizabeth's diary for the last three months of 1906 makes for melancholy reading. She mentions few new friends by name. There are no references to boys at all, except for the initials of boys who wrote her letters. She read classics like *Silas Marner* and *The Scarlet Letter* and translated French and German short stories. She complained about the weather: "The skies are thick with rain, rain, rain." Yet she ended her diary for 1906 with the note, "Despite the separation, this is the happiest year I've ever had, I think."

But there was a turn of events in January 1907 that would affect Maunsell in unalterable ways. He had lost any chance of having a paternal role model, and became dominated by his mother. During Maunsell's junior year at Harvard, Fanny developed a kidney ailment and traveled to Johns Hopkins in Baltimore for surgery. Ernest went with her. After the operation, Fanny was sedated with opium. Ernest, staying in an adjacent room, contracted influenza and died of its complications three days later. Fanny called on Maunsell at once to come from Cambridge to Baltimore to help her. With painkillers, and Maunsell beside her, she made the trip back to Rhinebeck with Ernest's body. She purchased a large plot in the Rhinebeck cemetery, and buried him there under tall trees near the main gate of Grasmere.

The opium Fanny took in Baltimore was not her first experience with the drug. We learned of her early use of laudanum from Sarah Schieffelin's 1876 record of their trip to Europe. Fanny continued to have headaches after her marriage, and continued to take opium. She turned to it sometimes when she was feeling the stress of Ernest's political activism. On her return to Rhinebeck, she depended on a local doctor willing to supply her on a regular basis. The neighbors and servants noticed her volatility; but since Grasmere was a big house, and the family was locally revered, no one spoke to her about it directly. The servants did as they were told.

As soon as she had sufficiently recovered from her surgery, Fanny went through all the rooms at Grasmere and cleaned the drawers and closets of any reminder of Ernest. He'd bought many artifacts in Egypt, which she took to the attic. She put the books he'd written in a trunk and locked it. She put his portrait in an upstairs closet. They were not looked at again during Maunsell's lifetime. He never learned they were there.

"We will not mention Judge Crosby's name again," Fanny announced to her son and daughter, her staff, and her neighbors. "That is a closed chapter. I shall manage by myself now." She was confident she would succeed: Maunsell had only another eighteen months before his graduation from Harvard, when she knew he'd come back to her.

Fanny vaguely thought Maunsell might want a wife, but she didn't ponder the question unduly. She was not thinking his wife would be the very young Boston débutante who'd visited Grasmere the summer before.

* * *

Maunsell, however, very much had Elizabeth on his mind. He went to a jeweler in Harvard Square and bought her a bracelet for Valentine's Day. February 14th coincided with his nineteenth birthday. He sent the bracelet to Elizabeth in Germany. She wrote back, thanking him, and said she was tired of Germany and wanted to come home. With the coming of winter, the gray skies and constant rain had turned into snow, thunder, and hail. She was tired of her advanced German and French lessons. She was tired of making marmalade. There was so little to do in the midst of winter that she'd begun to note in her diary, as activities of great moment, the times she had a bath or washed her hair.

The part of her stay in Germany that Elizabeth enjoyed was going to concerts at the Hof Theater. She practiced the piano. She learned Schumann's compositions and played in recitals. "I want to become good," she wrote. "I like being on the stage." But she missed the art shows in Boston and her long walks in Cambridge with friends.

Something else she liked about being in Germany was that her mother and Bertha weren't there. This was the longest she'd been free from their presence. She wrote Maunsell about their influence:

> Mama and Bertha criticize me. They tell me they're doing it for my good, but they're severe. Mama says I can't think for myself. I want to be free. Do you think marriage can make us free?

At last, Evelyn and Bertha came to collect Elizabeth. They went directly from Munich to Paris. Elizabeth was to have new afternoon dresses, long dinner dresses (simple ones, to be adorned only by a brooch or necklace), a ball gown, new hats, corsets, shoes, and gloves. Her coming-out party in Boston had been arranged: an afternoon tea at her aunt and uncle's house. Elizabeth remonstrated. "I'll go to Paris," she said, "but not to buy frou-frou dresses. If I'm going to Paris, I want clothes for my trousseau."

Mrs. Coolidge said no. "Why do you think the family arranged for you to spend a year in Germany? Why do you think Bertha and I spent this long winter in Europe? Don't you see this year abroad has been good for you?"

"It's been good for me," Elizabeth agreed. "But I don't want to go to all those Boston parties. I don't want different escorts. I want to go out with Maunsell."

"You'll do as I say. You're going to marry someone from Boston and we'll discuss it no further."

Mrs. Coolidge was countering her daughter in the only way she knew. Her responsibility was to prepare her daughter to accept familial authority and marry within the conventions of her upbringing. Independent thinking on the part of a daughter was out of the question. But she did relent in Paris, and Elizabeth came home with three dresses with short hems.

The determined mother, detached older sister, and rebellious younger daughter returned to New York on the *SS Ryndam*, "an unpleasant journey in a curly sea with everyone ill," and were met at the dock by Maunsell. He was now a senior at Harvard. He sent his mother a letter immediately afterwards, intent on announcing their engagement if he could:

> I got permission—as you know—to go down to N.Y. on Sunday, & while there saw Max Perkins and two plays. Tuesday A.M. at eight, the 'Ryndam' docked at Hoboken, & I met it. Elizabeth looks simply wonderful in her new Paris outfit and has improved tremendously in every way. We both

care for each other a great deal more than we ever did before. In fact, we are going to have an awful time keeping it from leaking out, as most people have suspicions from two years ago. Do you think it will be all right to announce it at Lent? We will have to lie up & down till then anyway, because we have to keep the bluff up on account of Elizabeth's coming-out. I predict that she will be the Belle of Boston. I didn't know I ever could be so happy.

Elizabeth consented to the coming-out party and to maintaining the appearance of being unattached, but extracted from her mother a promise that Maunsell could be her frequent escort. When the social season began that fall in Boston, she paid attention to what she wore. She smiled her way through the afternoon tea given jointly by her mother and uncle at the Vinton residence on Newbury Street. She was, as Maunsell was certain she would be, the belle of the Copley Ball. She wore a white-satin ball gown from Paris.

Maunsell gave Elizabeth a ring on Christmas Day 1907. She named her diary for 1908 "The Year of the Engaged Débutante." Her engagement was no longer secret. In "The Dowager's Views," a society column in *The Boston Sunday Post*, the following gossip appeared:

Dearest of Girls,

Today I have such an interesting engagement to tell you about, which came out on Monday, that of Miss Elizabeth Coolidge and Mr. Maunsell S. Crosby of New York. Miss Coolidge is the first of this winter's crop of buds to become engaged and her debut only dates back a few weeks. I am not in the least surprised to find that she has been appropriated this early in the season, for she is the most delightful girl imaginable, and ever since she has worn short frocks (which is not so very long ago) has been a great favorite with the sterner sex.

Several years ago, while Miss Coolidge was at an extremely tender age, a young man was calling at her home, and when Mrs. Coolidge reprimanded her daughter for some trifling misdemeanor she had made, the youth remarked, "You know, Mrs. Coolidge, I am quite willing to take Elizabeth off your hands at any time." I fancy he was only one of many who would have been extremely glad of the chance of securing Miss Coolidge as his fiancée.

One glimpse at the radiant Elizabeth is quite sufficient to prove that the charm of which her girlhood days gave evidence has been increased. She is strikingly handsome, knows exactly how to wear her clothes, and better than all the rest, possesses wonderful mentality, and fairly scintillates in conversation. She "came, saw and conquered," and of all the youths who looked longingly upon her, selected young Crosby. His upbringing has been in the rarified atmosphere of Fifth Avenue, and he is pronounced by the authorities to be a youth of much ability and promise. I believe the wedding date has not yet been discussed, but fortunately the principals can well afford to wait, since they are both young.

Social columns speak to the values women attach to surface and display, but sometimes, beneath their maunderings, truth lies in seemingly negligible comments. Maunsell was indeed a product of a "rarified atmosphere" and neither one had been permitted to be other than very young. Evelyn Coolidge and Fanny Crosby had both concentrated on the appealing charms of their younger children and had sheltered them from any possible emotional conflicts. As a couple now, Elizabeth and Maunsell went to parties in a round of happiness. Elizabeth learned that everything she wanted could be accomplished by talking. The girl who could talk most pleasingly won. Her courtship became a rapid succession of events and conversations about the couple—the Harvard-Yale game, the Pops, last night's dance, tomorrow's dinner. Therefore, in the midst of the flurry of their meetings for races and social gatherings in Cambridge, Elizabeth did not realize Maunsell's true reticence and retiring nature. Nor were there very many moments for Maunsell to discover that Elizabeth would want to be surrounded by admiration and excitement, not only while a débutante, but for many years. She looked forward to the stimulation of New York, whereas Maunsell was in search of a mother for his children and a fairly quiet life at Grasmere, where his own mother could grow old with them under the same roof. He was hopelessly in love with Elizabeth, but he was too country-quiet and lazy ever to control her.

Sarah Schieffelin, Maunsell's grandmother, now seventy-three, was fond of Maunsell. She still owned the house at 665 Fifth Avenue and invited the couple to visit. Elizabeth excitedly agreed.

"We'll have a wonderful time," she said to Maunsell. "It's so nice of your grandmother to invite us. We'll walk on Fifth Avenue and see the piano stores. We'll see plays." They did have a good time, attending a dance at the Waldorf and ice skating in the country at Tuxedo Park.

Maunsell wrote his Harvard friend, Maxwell Perkins, now working at the *New York Times,* about their plans. Perkins replied:

> I do hope that you won't put off getting married till you go through the law school, or the forestry school, or any other damn school; I hope you will get married as soon as you are graduated—next summer. These fellows who are all ready to marry and don't get around to it for several years make me tired.

In March, they set a wedding date and Mrs. Coolidge sent out invitations to fifty people. They spent many evenings at this time going out to dinner, paid for by Maunsell's monthly allowance. Their favorite restaurant in Boston was Touraine. In April Elizabeth's diary is decorated with little drawings of stars and exclamation points. She refers to "Heavenly 36 hours" and "Dearest for weekend, as usual."

Then, something happened. On May 16th Elizabeth and Maunsell abruptly changed their plans. Elizabeth instructed the stationer to print a notice canceling the formal wedding. Bertha was summoned. She helped them find a church and plan a smaller ceremony. She drafted the text of a wedding announcement and sent it to the newspapers. On June 11th they were married at Trinity Episcopal Church in Stockbridge, Massachusetts, halfway between Boston and Rhinebeck. *The New York Times* reported the event the following day:

> The wedding of Miss Elizabeth Coolidge, daughter of Mrs. Albert Leighton Coolidge of 224 Marlborough Street, Boston, to Maunsell Schieffelin Crosby, Harvard '08, son of Mrs. Ernest H. Crosby of Rhinebeck, N.Y., was celebrated in Trinity Episcopal Church at noon.
>
> It was an exceedingly simple wedding. Only a few very intimate friends were present. About fifty invitations had been recalled because of the serious illness of the bride's mother in Boston, who was unable to be present. Decorations in the church were of palms and potted plants in the chancel and bunches of white spiraea on the altar. There was a short recital before the service by the church organist.
>
> The only attendants were Miss Bertha Coolidge, the bride's sister, as maid of honor, and John Hall Wheelock of Morristown, N.J., as best man. The bride wore a simple gown of ivory white satin crepe de chine with lace guimpe and sleeves and a tulle veil. She carried a shower bouquet of

lilies of the valley. After the ceremony a wedding breakfast was served in the Curtis Hotel.

Mr. and Mrs. Crosby will go to Grasmere, the Crosby country place at Rhinebeck, N.Y., for a few days. Mr. Crosby will visit Cambridge on June 19 for class-day exercises and on the following day he and his bride will sail for Europe for an extended wedding journey.

After the wedding breakfast at the Curtis Hotel, the couple went to New York. They had dinner at the Knickerbocker Café, met with Maunsell's mother's bankers the following morning, had dinner that night at the Plaza Hotel, and then went by train to Grasmere. Fanny gave them a room a few doors down the hall from hers. They spent several days at Grasmere "doing nothing in particular," returned to Cambridge for Harvard's Class Day festivities on June 19th, and sailed for Liverpool the following afternoon.

No one knew at the time—except Elizabeth, Maunsell, and Bertha, and Elizabeth's mother, who it turns out was feigning an illness—that Elizabeth was pregnant.

CHAPTER 4

MAUNSELL AND ELIZABETH did on their honeymoon what many of my forebears did: they went to Europe. In 1908, it had become pleasurable (unlike traveling in open carriages as the Schieffelins did in 1876). There was now a well-developed system of train travel in Europe, there were comfortable hotels at the stations and luxury hotels in the city centers. Fanny gave Maunsell and Elizabeth a letter of credit against which they could draw foreign currencies. The young couple was confident they had enough money to enjoy any travel or entertainment they wished.

Their first stop was Oxford, where they stayed at The Mitre Inn, the four-hundred-year-old hostelry at which Henry and Sarah Schieffelin had stayed with their daughters thirty years before. Harvard friends were competing in the crew races at nearby Henley and they wanted to be there for the festivities.

Elizabeth immediately had difficulty with her clothes. English women dressed differently. "I don't understand the inconvenience of the style," she said to Maunsell. "The women wear long dresses during the *day,* and they keep having to lift their skirts out of the *mud.*" She had equal difficulty understanding cricket. "It is *the* most futile game I *ever* saw," she commented.

London gave greater pleasure. They took rooms at the Prince of Wales Hotel and spent two weeks sightseeing and going to restaurants. Van Wyck Brooks, Maunsell's Harvard friend, joined them at the Ritz and Savoy. They went to Winchester and Canterbury cathedrals. Maunsell visited a tailor on Bond Street for suits; Elizabeth shopped at Harrods. They sat in the sixth row at Covent Garden to watch a performance of *La Traviata*. Elizabeth wanted to go to the opera again. Maunsell said the tickets were too expensive. Elizabeth recorded in her diary their first concern about money. They then crossed the Channel by ferry and went by train to Frankfurt, Heidelberg, and Munich. Elizabeth showed Maunsell Miss Wilson's School. They took tea at *konditoreis* and conversed in German with everyone they met.

In August they went to Vienna and Salzburg. The charm of the trip was wearing off. Elizabeth wrote in her diary not that *they* didn't have enough money, but that *she* didn't. She didn't mention her pregnancy in her diary, but may have been feeling its effects. She began complaining. "We ate an awful lunch in Stephanplatz," she wrote. "It was hot and uncomfortable. I wanted to go to the opera again, but M. no."

They took the Orient Express to Paris and toured the chateaux in the Loire Valley: Blois, Chambord, Chantilly ("a *stupid* town"), Azay-le-Rideau, and Chinon. Maunsell now also complained about the food. They worried more about money; the letter of credit was being drawn down too quickly.

On August 23rd they went to the northern coast of France. "Carnac *plage* is awful," Elizabeth wrote on a postcard to Maunsell's mother, "and we left quickly." Quimper was no better: "A horrible night, we had to sleep in the dining room because they had no rooms." It rained every day, pelting water under gray skies. Their clothes got wet. They returned to Paris for the *Folies Bergères* and then scurried to the port of Cherbourg. Seven days later, they landed in New York. Edward Sheldon, Maunsell's playwright friend, met them at the dock at 8 a.m.

"Welcome home," he said. "I'm writing plays. I love New York. Come to the theater with me."

"We can't," Maunsell said. "Mama expects us at home."

Much as the honeymooning couple would have liked to stay in New York, it wasn't possible. It had been agreed before they left that immediately on their return, the couple would go to Rhinebeck. Fanny Crosby had made it clear to Elizabeth that she would have household duties to assume. Maunsell and Elizabeth spent their morning in New York hiring a laundress and personal maid from an agency in Manhattan. They took the train to Rhinebeck that afternoon. At the age of eighteen, and six months pregnant, Elizabeth became the ostensible head of the house. Fanny, however, retained control. She didn't settle any funds on Elizabeth. Maunsell was told that he would be given a little money for their personal expenses.

* * *

If Elizabeth thought that at last she might be welcomed by her mother-in-law, she was wrong. Two days after their return Fanny gave herself a forty-seventh birthday party. The cook baked a large cake. Elizabeth wondered why there was no party for herself, as a new bride at Grasmere, or a party for the two of them, to welcome them as a couple.

Two days after the party, four servants gave notice. They'd been awaiting Maunsell's return. Elizabeth Burroughs, the farm superintendent's daughter, had been Fanny's companion for much of the time that Maunsell was at Harvard. In a letter she wrote many years later to my mother, Elizabeth Burroughs said she'd found Mrs. Crosby difficult after Ernest died, as had all the servants.

> Mrs. Crosby did not appear to grieve as a widow for long. I do not believe she hated her husband, but she was a domineering person. She ruled everyone else and I do not recall

ever hearing her talked about admiringly by the other wealthy matrons. I read to Mrs. Crosby after school. She liked the 'Scarlet Pimpernel' books and other detective stories. She had real hero worship for Marie Antoinette. In the white and gold parlor there was a bust of Marie Antoinette. No servant was allowed to dust this. During the years I read to her I had to take it to the butler's pantry, wash it and carry it back. At this time she was a semi-invalid but never wore pretty negligees.

* * *

By October 4th, the house was fully staffed again, but on October 19th there was another crisis and the newly hired cook departed. Elizabeth was unnerved. She reacted by taking walks by herself to the Cedar Hut, a secluded cabin built years earlier by Ernest.

One Rhinebeck woman befriended Elizabeth. Daisy Suckley, from an old Hudson River family, lived two miles from Grasmere at "Wilderstein." She was close to Elizabeth in age and unmarried. Later in life, she would become a confidante of Franklin Roosevelt and give him his dog, Fala. She called on Elizabeth often and introduced her to Rhinebeck and the surrounding area. One morning they went to Poughkeepsie where Daisy pointed out, high on a hill, the red-brick insane asylum. Elizabeth noted that it was very large and very dark. "I don't like it," she said. "People are put there and they can't get out."

Dinners with Fanny were oppressive. The table in the formal dining room at Grasmere was set each night for three. Fanny sat at the head. She used these occasions to remonstrate over Elizabeth's failings.

"Did you not notice the roses in the front hall drooping?"

"I'm sorry, no, I didn't."

"Well, they were, and I had the parlor maid take them away. This is an important room in the house and you mustn't overlook this again. You *were* trained in flower arranging, weren't you?"

Elizabeth's latent impatience and her loneliness forced her into increasing dislike of her environment. She expressed her unhappiness to Maunsell, asking him to stand up for her. Maunsell felt helpless. No money had been settled on him. "What can I do?" he asked. "Where can I turn?" He had never challenged his mother and was afraid to do it.

Early in December a physician began coming to the house once a week. On January 13, 1909, Elizabeth gave birth. In her minuscule handwriting she wrote in her diary, "Maunsellina began to arrive at 12:30. Lunch with M. Bed at 2. Maunsellina all over 4.25. Tea 5. Turned out to be M. Jr." The hoped-for girl was a full-term baby boy.

Maunsell wrote the good news at once to Van Wyck Brooks, inviting him to be godfather. Brooks replied:

Dear Maunsell,

I am so happy about it, and you are just the man to make a perfect father, especially for a boy. I never dreamed that I could really love the whole idea of a youngster until I knew of this one.

And as for being Godfather—dear Maunsell, nothing in my whole life ever touched and blessed me so much. Why, it suddenly made me take a new and graver view of life! Indeed it will be one of the truest happinesses to feel a special right to watch him grow into just the kind of man he is going to make. Give Elizabeth my best and warmest regards. What a delight it will be for all of us to celebrate the double event of birth and christening next month! On that occasion, I think we can all manage to be non-abstainers in all respects.

Ever your devoted friend,
Van Wyck

Elizabeth rested. A nurse came to bathe, dress and feed the baby, which slept at night in the nurse's room. Elizabeth declined an invitation to play the organ on Sundays at church. She stopped going to church completely.

Maunsell developed a routine of rising before dawn. He went bird-watching and then joined the farm superintendent on his rounds. Elizabeth busied herself with painting watercolors and playing the piano. The baby was brought to Maunsell and Elizabeth before their supper each evening. On April 10th the child was christened Howard.

In May, John Butler Yeats, an Irish portraitist (and father of the poet, William Butler Yeats), came to visit. Maunsell and Elizabeth had met him at a party in New York. Yeats wrote his daughter, Lollie, in Dublin:

> I have just had five days, the best I ever had since I came to New York. Mr. and Mrs. Crosby, he 21 and she 19 with a baby 4 months old, and a big house with many servants and a large place and lots of birds in high trees—all strange to me and all singing. Crosby has counted 134 different species, and he says he has not counted them all—humming-birds, various wrens, various thrushes, orioles, two varieties of birds with scarlet and pink plumage, various woodpeck-ers. . . . The country is beautiful. I went on a long automo-bile drive—17 miles to Poughkeepsie. . . along a road which took us below tall trees, in deep shadow flecked by sunlight.

He returned a month later and wrote to his daughter again:

> I never saw a country so beautiful as Rhinebeck, with that kind of beauty Meredith praises when describing English landscape—so rich in hills and dales of fertile woods and crops, with fine houses dotted about everywhere. . . and the neighbours all so neighbourly. It was intoxicating. I felt as if I was walking on air. In England everywhere you feel yourself

in an atmosphere of critics. Here it is an atmosphere of good will. The people want to like you, and do not want to keep you off as is the way in England. . . .

As Elizabeth regained her strength, she and Maunsell invited more friends to visit. They enjoyed outdoor lunches and tennis matches. Sometimes they went riding. By late August the couple had become popular with many of their neighbors. Vincent Astor entertained them on his boat on September 20th.

Edward Sheldon, Maunsell's friend who'd met them on the dock on their return from their honeymoon, now had a producer for one of his plays. It opened in New York that fall. The following week he came to Grasmere to celebrate. Van Wyck Brooks arrived a week later with Maxwell Perkins. Each brought news of lively events in the city and Elizabeth became moody.

"I'd like some fresh air," she said one afternoon. "I'd like to take a walk." She went once again to the Cedar Hut.

After a shopping trip in New York, Elizabeth confided to her diary that she hadn't enjoyed it. "Endless calling on people, and tea." "Went to a dance: Bavarian costume. Stupid." In early December she went to the theater with Van Wyck Brooks. She had dinner with him alone afterwards. On December 9th she noted "M. didn't come home." On December 10th: "No sleep. M. to Rhinebeck 9.40."

They spent much of this winter at Maunsell's grandmother's house on Fifth Avenue. They went to dances and plays. In April, back in Rhinebeck with the arrival of warmer weather, Elizabeth said she was tired. Maunsell began to go to New York on his own, now sometimes staying at the Harvard Club.

In May, Elizabeth's diary records recurring arguments. "M. bed early. Horrid remark."

Summer arrived and there were more horrid days. John Butler Yeats came for a third visit and wrote his daughter on June 5, 1910:

Do you remember the Crosbys, those two young people with whom I stayed at Rhinebeck last year? She is 19, he 22, with a baby a year old. They are now arranging amicably for a divorce. She has determined it. They are still together in their beautiful home. . . It is a terrible trouble to him. He is the. . . most amiable and domestic of men and very handsome, really without a desire except to keep her in good humour and of course very well off, and will be better off, his mother being very rich. I don't in the least know what her game can be. I fancy she is quite without heart, absolutely without affection, yet with many valuable qualities. I suppose she wants to be a personage and thinks she can get a man who will give her a career, instead of poor Crosby whose only thought was to live quietly and love his neighbours, particularly his bird neighbours. He and I used to go walking together. He was completely under her thumb. He was clever with languages. Her mother would not come to the wedding, she hated her daughter so much. . . .

Yeats wrote his daughter again the following month:

Young Mrs. Crosby now says she is not going to have a divorce. . . She is only 19 and the husband 22—got married too young. But she is very fond of her husband. . . She is particularly alert and resolute in her housekeeping because her mother-in-law is pleasure-loving and lax, amusing but selfish, but adored by the son, which is another thorn to the young wife. You can see the situation is trying for a fiery young dame of 19.

Elizabeth couldn't think clearly about what her life should be. Maunsell's family money was committed to Grasmere. To leave Rhinebeck with Maunsell, which was what she wanted, would mean being without money. Maunsell would have to get a job and he couldn't conceive of getting one in New York. To leave Rhinebeck without Maunsell would mean having to depend on the support of friends and whatever money she could earn herself. She had a little capital, but it wouldn't go far.

Visitors to Grasmere noticed the changes in her. She now nagged Maunsell in front of his friends, rudely and cruelly, instead of waiting until they were alone. She got away with it because he was sensitive and abhorred scenes. She distanced herself from her young son. She seemed to think it out of fashion to be motherly, and the child now cried when he saw her coming.

* * *

After a year of these ups and downs, they agreed to separate. They would test what would make them happy. Elizabeth left her son in the care of Maunsell and his mother and sailed for England. She enrolled in an acting school and told Maunsell she'd return to New York when her acting teacher felt she was ready. Maunsell was dismayed by the choice of career and didn't tell his mother. He said only that Elizabeth wanted independence, and he hoped that by living apart for a time, they could resolve the situation.

It might have remained a separation indefinitely, so calm did the atmosphere at Grasmere suddenly become. But Maunsell had an aunt Grace, a missionary, who knew that Mrs. Crosby had been a trouble-maker. She thought Maunsell should try, after a year's separation, to continue with Elizabeth, if only for the sake of the child. She didn't approve of divorce and she had a forthrightness that made her the most respected person in her family. She didn't know whether Elizabeth was as difficult to live with as she seemed and she thought the intolerable situations had been mainly Mrs. Crosby's fault. So she urged both of them to meet again.

It was the fall of 1910 when Elizabeth returned from England. Maunsell took a suite at a hotel in New York and Elizabeth joined him. Since she was again in the city she most enjoyed, and he was away from his mother, dancing, gay, and vivacious, he was able to swing her into unexpected happiness. They gave parties, entertained merrily, and were the outstanding couple in any gathering. This came to an abrupt end when, in early 1911, she was once again with child and the only home he could bring her to was Grasmere.

They were trapped once more. Hoping against hope, they returned to the country. "This isn't going to work," Elizabeth said to Maunsell. "I am *furious* at the prospect of another infant. I don't want to bear this child at Grasmere. I don't want to see your mother and have her tell me what I must do."

Her revolt this time came from not only abhorrence of her situation but a growing physical hatred for the Crosbys. Day after day of the advancing pregnancy, she felt anger. She left Maunsell when it was time to give birth, and went to her mother's house in the coastal town of Marblehead, Massachusetts. The baby, my mother, was born on September 6, 1911. Elizabeth lay in bed for six weeks suffering from the carelessness of the doctor. She called my mother "the kid."

Elizabeth returned to Grasmere after six weeks because she wasn't strong enough to leave the marriage at once, as she wished to, and she filled the house once again with friends in an endeavor to shut out gloom. As a pastime for a late autumn Sunday afternoon, she suggested to her guests that "the kid" be christened that day. One of the guests was Helen Huntington, from nearby Staatsburg, who was being courted by Vincent Astor, who lived in Rhinebeck. A little riotously, the party filed into church, and Helen Elizabeth was duly christened. She was named Helen for her godmother, Helen Huntington, who married Vincent Astor two years later, and Elizabeth for her mother. Maunsell was mortified.

"That was an outrageous suggestion," he remonstrated when the guests had departed. "That was an embarrassment. You should have written to everyone first, to see if they would like to be godparents."

"It was not outrageous," Elizabeth replied. "It was an afternoon we'll remember and the kid will have good godparents. Why are you so unimaginative?"

"I'm not," Maunsell said. "But I do know what's appropriate and what's not. Why couldn't you have thought about it ahead of time and written a proper letter first?"

Elizabeth had no answer. There was a brief silence. "I think this really is the end," Maunsell said.

Elizabeth was insensitive to his anguish. She left Grasmere, taking little Helen with her. Maunsell gave her legal custody of the child, since he had the paternal viewpoint that a daughter needed its mother more than its father. Howard, now three, stayed with his father and grandmother at Grasmere.

* * *

Citing her acting lessons in London, Elizabeth immediately auditioned for a small part in Edward Sheldon's New York production, *Egypt*. She won the part and took the stage name Elizabeth Lane, a surname of one of her forebears. All of this was a crowning insult to the Crosbys, who thought her behavior scandalous.

Despite what she'd done, Elizabeth had friends who initially stood by her. These early days in New York were pleasurable for her. She employed a nurse to take care of Helen. When the play ended its New York run, she decided not to go with it to Chicago. She found a job translating German. Most evenings she went out, always with a man, to dinner and the theater.

Howard remained at Grasmere, adored by his father and grandmother. Mrs. Crosby gave reports of him to Elizabeth by telephone. She was peremptory and always quick to say that Howard was in perfect health. Elizabeth was never greatly concerned if the report was short and once a month.

But one day, after one of these reports of perfect health, the nurse at Grasmere called to say that Howard was terribly ill and dying. Apparently, Mrs. Crosby was unable to bear the thought of Elizabeth's presence, either in her house or at the side of the child she had never seemed to really love, and refused to make the call.

Elizabeth got to Grasmere in time to see Howard die. Mrs. Crosby shut herself in her room and told Maunsell she wouldn't come out until Elizabeth left the house. Elizabeth refused and ordered an autopsy. Since Mrs. Crosby had lied to her, she said, she suspected her of doing anything, including poisoning. To make matters even harder for Maunsell to bear, she sat through the procedure. The news hurtled through the house, upsetting the servants. There was no poison. The servants were told Howard had eaten green apples, causing a furry tongue, and had died from suffocation. To others it was explained that he'd had a ruptured appendix.

The day after the autopsy Maunsell asked Elizabeth to go once again, and this time to stay gone. He called a taxi, she stepped into it, and the taxi drove away. Neither waved.

Howard was buried in the Rhinebeck Crosby plot near his grandfather, Ernest Howard Crosby. His headstone, carved several months later, gives only the years of his birth and death. Without the months, no one in the village could pass by and count on their fingers how exactly soon after his parents' marriage he'd been born.

* * *

The moment Elizabeth left, Mrs. Crosby sat down with her son. "We'll have to do something about this. We can't have that wild woman going around New York spreading rumors that I poisoned her son."

"What do you propose?" said Maunsell.

"I think we need her watched," said his mother. "And we need to ask your grandmother to pay for it."

Sarah Schieffelin, Maunsell's grandmother, was unwell and had come from Fifth Avenue to Grasmere to rest. She lived in a bedroom at the rear of the house. Confined mostly to bed, she had no idea the autopsy had taken place. She had no concept of the family discord. Elizabeth had been gracious in all her dealings with her. And so it was with some difficulty that Maunsell and his mother relayed to Mrs. Schieffelin their concerns about Elizabeth and her free ways, and the fact of Helen, whom Maunsell wasn't at all sure he'd fathered.

"There's no chance of her coming back," said Fanny to her mother. "I won't have her, and Maunsell sees now that she's not the right wife for him. The problem is the baby. Elizabeth will want Maunsell's money for the child. It's problematic, of course," she said, smiling at Maunsell, "but if we can be discreet, and not have anyone know, I think there's a way we can cut her off. We will need private detectives," she said, turning now to her mother. "We need to prove she is seeing other men."

Mrs. Schieffelin held the ultimate purse strings. Every out-of-the-ordinary expenditure had to go through her. She recognized the threat to Maunsell's inheritance and listened solemnly while Fanny explained New York's adultery laws. A woman was divorceable if discovered to be an adulteress. All of Maunsell's college friends were suspect: Edward Sheldon, in whose play Elizabeth had appeared; John Hall Wheelock, writing poetry, and Van Wyck Brooks, beginning his career as a literary historian. They had all visited Grasmere. They had all gone on walks with Elizabeth. They had all entertained her at dinner in New York.

A Rhinebeck correspondent for "Town Topics" caught the distress in the family and wrote the following account:

Contrary to the usual rule in such cases, sympathy seems to be felt by friends of the Maunsell Crosbys with the husband rather than the wife in their strained relations. Mrs. Crosby left her home immediately after the funeral of their little boy, giving, it is understood, no reason whatever for a step that her husband's friends believe had no justification. Those who know Mrs. Crosby best say that she has always had more or less pronounced eccentricities that made the step not unexpected. It is now rumored that she is going to indulge in her craze for the stage, for which life her beauty and vivacity might, in a way, seem to promise success.

Maunsell contacted the family lawyer in New York, who counseled hiring Pinkertons' detective agency. Pinkertons were instructed to watch Elizabeth for a week to establish generally how she was spending her time. The family would then determine what further course to pursue. This first week of surveillance revealed that Elizabeth had dinner with five men and lunch with two. The detectives were instructed to watch her daily, until a compromising liaison could be proved.

* * *

Elizabeth lived in three rooms in a large apartment house on West 72nd Street. Her windows faced the back. She hired a live-in Irish nurse and left Helen, my mother, in her care. The nurse took my mother to Central Park each morning. They came back for lunch, then returned to the park for the afternoon. In more than two years of surveillance, Elizabeth was not once observed going into the park with Helen, who could easily have thought the nurse was her mother.

After a brief job translating German, Elizabeth found higher-paying work with the Edison Electric Light Company on East 42nd Street. She knew how to type and was hired to supervise the typists and telephone operators. She moved to an apartment on West 57th Street to shorten her walk to work. She excelled as a supervisor and was asked to take on additional responsibilities arranging exhibitions. She often worked late at night.

The Pinkertons reports were typewritten, double-spaced, and described in detail everything that could be observed without the use of electronics. Private detectives a hundred years ago worked on foot, or in taxicabs, or by hiding behind trees. The reports tell us what Elizabeth wore and where she went, and sometimes how much she smoked and drank; but nothing about liaisons. Yet one has to ask, why did so many men take her out, unless it was worth their while? Slipped between two of the Pinkertons reports I found a single sheet of paper in my mother's handwriting. It said: "My mother was a nymphomaniac. She slept with every member of the Harvard Club." Was this conjecture? Or did Elizabeth tell her this? Or was it a sudden insight that came to my mother years later? I read the reports more than once looking for clues. Who was the Edison employee who took her to dinner at the St. Regis, then back to her apartment where they were joined by another man at 10:00 p.m.? Who were the three men with whom she spent the day in New Jersey? Why did a man arrive at her apartment in a Daimler at 8:05 p.m, drive with her down 7th Avenue, then return at 11 p.m. and shake her hand at the door? The following evening he arrived in a Lancia. Why did she have dinner with a man in a hotel restaurant, easily observed through a window, then disappear with him through an inner door and emerge alone an hour and a half later? "Apartment hotels" were popular at this time. Did the men she was seeing live in apartment hotels, allowing a quick liaison without being seen?

It was not only the detectives who were aware of the situation. At one point during the almost two-year-long surveillance, Fanny Crosby traveled to London. She gleaned what she considered incontrovertible evidence of wrong-doing when she met a friend, Mrs. Wilkinson. She wrote to Maunsell from the Hotel Jules in Jermyn Street where she was staying:

Dearest M.,

I think you should know that a Mrs. Lucy Wilkinson, an American, told Sybil Kane that she had lent her handsomely furnished 57th Street flat to E.C.C. and a maid of hers was taken with the flat. This maid visited Mrs. Wilkinson and told her that she did not care very much for her new tenant. Mrs. E.C.C. had told her that "she believes in the sporting life" and sat in the parlour and drank gin an entire afternoon. Ask your lawyer if any judge would allow a woman of such habits to be the guardian of a little girl. It is horrible to think.

F.C.

P.S. Mrs. Wilkinson's name is in the Social Register.

Maunsell was considerably relieved that none of his friends' names appeared in the Pinkertons reports. There was just one puzzling instance. A misdirected Tiffany's bill came to him at Grasmere. Elizabeth had ordered a silver monogrammed cigarette case for John Hall Wheelock. Maunsell didn't know whether to confront her about it, or pay the bill without comment. Wheelock had been best man at their wedding. Perhaps the cigarette case was no more than an innocent expression of gratitude, though sent rather late in the day. He kept the bill to himself.

Becoming concerned about the expense of the surveillance, the family asked Pinkertons to move in more closely. The detectives took rooms in a building on West 56th Street whose rear windows looked out towards Elizabeth's. They observed Helen and the nurse night after night, and occasionally saw Elizabeth standing by a window smoking a cigarette, but they had no direct view of her hallway or sitting room. No implicating evidence was found. Fanny Crosby finally said it was time to force a dissolution of the marriage. Money would speak.

Lawyers drew up financial proposals and sent them to Elizabeth. Elizabeth bargained for more, insisting she'd done nothing wrong. Eventually, in return for a settlement of $30,000 and child support, she agreed to establish residency in Virginia, where divorce laws didn't require proof of adultery. Maunsell agreed to support Helen until she was eight, at which time he would agree to meet her.

Elizabeth resigned from the Edison Light Company in August of 1915. Her final day, she wrote a letter to the Clerk of the Company asking that he grant "the girls in the Contract & Inspection Department raises of $1.50 per week." She took a train to Richmond, Virginia with Helen and the Irish nurse. One of the typists in the secretarial pool wrote Elizabeth thanking her "for all the good things you did for us."

Old Mrs. Coolidge, Elizabeth's mother, wrote her in Richmond expressing sadness that the marriage hadn't succeeded, and hoping she would find happiness soon. To her mother's astonishment, Elizabeth did. In Virginia, she met Albert Cooley, a wine merchant originally from Manhattan. They took to each other at once, two escapees. When Elizabeth's divorce was granted in December of 1916, she took off with Albert. She discharged the nurse and told her mother she planned to work in England. Albert booked adjacent cabins on a ship, including a berth for Helen.

It was Mrs. Coolidge who was now scandalized. Newspapers published the names of transatlantic passengers. Gossip columnists mined them for stories. Mrs. Coolidge read in a newspaper that "a divorced New Yorker was fascinated by Elizabeth Crosby, who in turn was attracted by his worldliness, and they were traveling on the same boat." There was mention of a child. Genuinely fearful for her daughter, whom Mrs. Coolidge now considered errant, she cabled the U.S. Consul in Liverpool demanding that Elizabeth, who was now twenty-seven years old, not be allowed to disembark.

As the ship was docking in Liverpool, the Superintending Aliens Officer came on board and handed Elizabeth an official letter. It allowed her, with Mr. Cooley if she wished, "to go ashore for a few hours in order to do necessary shopping." She was otherwise refused permission to enter England.

Elizabeth, Albert, and Helen sailed back to New York on the ship's return voyage. Helen, my mother, recorded her memory of the trip in one of her early journals. She'd never been alone with her mother before. She recollected the happiness she'd felt when her mother gently brushed her hair each morning in their cabin.

The Liverpool incident caused small headlines in the social columns again. Elizabeth, furiously upset, and true to her training, which was to solve one problem at a time, took the obvious solution and married Albert. She didn't love him. She admitted to herself that she was more fascinated than in love. She did it as blithely as if she'd never suffered from the maladjustment of a premature marriage. She further satisfied her indignation by refusing to communicate with her mother for eleven years.

Looking around for the next step, anxious to establish herself and to succeed in her own name, Elizabeth took Maunsell's divorce settlement and bought a ranch, sight unseen, in eastern Montana. It had no buildings of any kind. Persuading the doubting second husband that there they would make more money than in any East Coast endeavor, they set out for Miles City, Montana in the spring of 1917.

CHAPTER 5

EASTERN MONTANA IS A TREELESS PLACE with endless open skies and a harsh climate. The winters are cold. Arctic winds blow. In the summer there is often drought. Yet for many, it's the most beautiful place in the world. The wide skies offer freedom. For a New Yorker bound to convention, being in Montana in 1917 brought the possibility of not only escape, but also renewal.

After the bison herds were killed and the Native Americans removed to reservations, ranchers bought up the grasslands for cattle. It didn't matter that the distances between ranches were great and that one's nearest neighbors might live hours away. The land promised riches. But, because neighbors were the only source of help, the land also required that people get along. An attitude of personal superiority would not serve one well; the ranchers knew how to read each other and with whom to do business.

Elizabeth and Albert brought with them a maid and cook, but hadn't explained that everyone would live in tents until the ranch house was built. The servants balked and returned to New York. Helen became acutely aware of how alone she was. Ever since the trip to Liverpool, she'd been without her nurse; now, she had no one. Albert was the first adult man with whom she lived. She took it for granted that her father was non-existent, assuming that he'd been killed in the war. She knew nothing of her mother's affairs, and still not even that her name was Helen. She was called "Baby" or "Kid."

The ranch was twenty-five miles by dirt roads from Miles City. Elizabeth and Albert bought a Ford Model T that functioned well enough when the roads were dry, but oftentimes they had to rely on a team of horses pulling a wagon. Elizabeth liked the idea of horses; she brought expensive riding britches with her, expecting to be in the saddle more than on the seat of a wagon. She wore the britches most days, contributing to a commanding masculine persona. She spoke peremptorily with people and early on they said of her that she didn't have the necessary sense of humor to make it as a rancher. Their nearest neighbors, the Shermans, didn't like Elizabeth, and worried about Helen, who had played with other children only occasionally in Central Park, and during a short time in kindergarten. She'd trusted the people she was with at these times. She developed strong attachments to anyone who showed affection. But she was almost never touched affectionately by Elizabeth.

Helen never told me, or my sisters, that she once lived in Montana. We learned it after she died, and found her papers. It appears that at some point in her life, she tried to write about her family. I found four drafts of short stories in her papers, written in the third person, in some of which the main character was named Ann Pell. Helen submitted at least two of them for criticism to the Famous Writers School in Westport, Connecticut. She may have shown them to her analyst, Hanna Colm. There are no surviving diaries that correspond to the years about which she wrote. Some of the events may be fictionalized, but I believe their essence to be true. Here is the first, in which Helen tells us what happened when she was seven.

The morning after the staff left, Elizabeth had heard Helen trying to memorize the Q, R, S, T, U, V, W part of the alphabet and had spanked her for being obstinate and slow. Helen was afraid to say she hadn't meant to be stupid. Elizabeth had said, "Wipe that expression off your face," and walked off furiously.

Helen thought Elizabeth looked beautiful in her riding britches, cool even in the hot sun, and wanted to tell her so. But it was so difficult to say anything. She'd never seen very much of her mother, perhaps that was why. This was too bad, because there were a lot of things she knew that were quite important that she would have liked to tell Elizabeth, if only her mother would be interested.

For instance, Helen recalled to herself, there was everything she knew about Ireland that she'd learned from her nurse. Whenever they'd gone to Central Park, they'd played "Going to Ireland." There was the secret in her mind about finding her fairy godmother's home. They hadn't gone in, it was just that they'd gone down the road to it, a road so highly and widely shaded by enormous trees that it undoubtedly belonged to an Important Person.

Then, she thought, she'd never been able to tell Elizabeth how much she'd liked the automobile trip from Richmond, because one afternoon she'd seen green clouds instead of white ones. Helen had never told Elizabeth about the night she dreamed dragons were chasing her and she'd woken up screaming under the bed.

These events had happened especially to her and they made her a person separate from other people. She thought Elizabeth might like her better if she knew about these things, but Elizabeth never seemed to have time to listen. Elizabeth didn't know that Helen could whistle on a blade of grass, or that she'd built clay cities and made paper garlands when she went to kindergarten in New York.

Helen remembered her trip to England on the boat. Elizabeth had been nice to her when the ship was pitching in the terrible storm and they thought it would go down either from the force of the wind or from an attack by Germans. That night Elizabeth read to her by candlelight, and in the morning combed her hair. It was the first time Helen remembered seeing Elizabeth undressed.

There was another time when Elizabeth had been nice. She'd sat beside Helen once before, when Helen had the croup, and in return for sniffing hot fumes of camphor, Elizabeth had read her a story she'd written. Helen didn't know that her mother wrote. Elizabeth had been grand those two times, but mostly she was scary. She'd sent away Helen's favorite New York City nurse when Helen had sneaked permission to play with the little boys across the street, a request expressly forbidden by Elizabeth. Helen missed her nurse for months afterwards, remembering how she'd brushed quickly by her on the stairway in her best blue suit. The nurse kissed her and Helen saw the suitcase in her other hand. Then she was gone. Elizabeth told Helen to go to her room until she could stop crying, then spanked her for being such a stupid little girl.

Helen decided Elizabeth knew very little about her except when she needed a spanking. One morning she wheeled her doll-carriage along the narrow dirt road until she found a big rock. She sat on the rock and annotated her existence by punishments. Then she annotated the activities of the last week. They had finished piping water from the spring in the red rocks of the hill. Elizabeth boasted that theirs would be the only bathroom for miles around. This was the first week that Helen had been able to wash without walking into the woods to the source of the water. It would be nice when the bathroom was finished and she didn't have to use a privy in the woods, where the pines next to it smelt burnt and the flies settled on the roll of paper.

They were going to raise cattle and sell them and then perhaps they would have a cook again. Helen wished this would be soon. Elizabeth was doing the cooking. Helen felt sick trying to get down the salty lima beans and canned codfish. Elizabeth had never cooked full meals before. Now, the biscuits were thick and heavy. Helen began to hide most of her luncheon in her room and bury it outside after her nap. If Albert saw, he wouldn't tell on her—he was nice to her—and he called her Helen instead of "Baby."

"Are you sure you won't tell?" she asked him once, when he saw her making another hole in the dirt.

"I won't," he said, giving her a smile and a wink. Helen liked his warmth and the way he smelled of sage brush.

Helen counted the number of prairie dogs sitting up in their holes on the other side of the road. The road was mostly just two ruts in the dust that came from the west past the pines and went through the cornfield to an unexplored east. She watched a jack-rabbit cross it with two bobbing crouches. Then she wiggled down the rock and carefully wheeled her doll-carriage along the narrow cow paths back to the house.

A month later, the house was finished. Helen was installed in a separate bedroom. Albert and Elizabeth had a big bedroom and a bureau with a triple mirror. Helen's room was small. There was a guest room and a living room with a long table, a red rug, a couch, fireplace, and desk. Helen spent her mornings doing lessons in her room, given to her by Elizabeth and corrected afterwards. She had to wear glasses to do her sums. She went into the living room only when summoned to present her work to Elizabeth.

The rest of the time she was supposed to be outdoors or in her room, even for meals. That was a good thing, because Elizabeth brought her meals in on a tray and then left. When Helen couldn't finish the big helpings, she could hide the food in her clothes. The khaki middies and bloomers from Sears, Roebuck and woolen union suits were piled on shelves behind a curtain. Elizabeth would come in and shout at her, "Baby, put it in your mouth, and swallow it." She wasn't allowed any water with her meals. Helen would chew and chew and it still wouldn't feel right for swallowing. Then she'd gag. If she'd swallowed after that, it choked her. She'd try to pretend it was down until Elizabeth left the room, then she'd spit the beans, potato and biscuit onto the napkin and tuck it under her clothes or hide it in her toy chest. She meant to clean out the little petrified bundles and hide them in the gully outside. The gully was the only good final hiding place for refuse. She kept putting it off because she was afraid of rattlesnakes ever since Elizabeth had nearly stepped on one curled up asleep on the back stoop.

Mostly Helen was happy when she was outdoors. The summer crops were in, the corral was finished and they worked endlessly in the garden. Each morning after breakfast, Helen fed the chickens, collected eggs and, when she was sure Elizabeth wasn't looking, held the newborn chicks in her hand. Then she picked up twigs for kindling and went as slowly as she dared. When her chores were finished, she had to do addition and subtraction.

Helen hoped Elizabeth would go out riding before it was time for doing homework. She never could get the answers anywhere near right and she was afraid to leave them on Elizabeth's desk while she was still in the house, because then she was sent back to her room to correct them. When Elizabeth went out first, she laid her answers on the desk and rushed outdoors. That way, she didn't have to tackle them again until the next morning. The reading was easy, it had come suddenly, and already she was doing the *Book of Knowledge*. She was fascinated by the picture of the ship cut in half to show its insides, and the pictures of Marie Antoinette and the bloody revolution. She had trouble reading the dialect of Br'er Rabbit and understanding how to read the stars. But the rest was easy: read a page or two or three at a time. Then Elizabeth would send her out to pick the nasturtiums, and train them up against the shingled walls of the house, or to train the sweet peas that ran up the wire around the vegetable garden, or to weed the potatoes and beans. Two hired men, one of them married with a family, lived in separate houses down the road. She often saw them working in the distance and sometimes they waved.

Afterwards, she played by herself behind the big odd rock that had fallen from the hill into the backyard. She baked mud-pies and rolls, and built houses with pebbles and stones and whispered endlessly in behalf of the occupants. She liked the ranch in the daytime, it was hot and friendly; the cows moved in the distance to the watering trough and salt lick, and Albert had fixed her a swing, though she was afraid to climb up to it on account of the snakes.

But, at night, when Elizabeth closed her door, after the sun had gone down, the North Wind came whistling through the screen and frightened Helen with every stir of the curtain. She felt the wind under her bed waiting to seize her if she moved a muscle. It was worse than thunder or lightning because it always came, each twilight. On the distant prairie ridge the coyotes howled, not the timid hunters of the day, but the dangerous lonely yelpers of the night, the only sound besides the shrill whistling of the wind. She plucked the blanket nervously and loosened fluff from the weave. She lay very flat, since she was not allowed a pillow, and, not daring to raise her head, peered into the ridges and valleys of the blanket. The fluff stood up like people, like naked men and women moving to protect her. There were thousands of people living in the blanket who crept out of the grey woolen hills and into the fluffy houses she arranged. They were a guard against the vengeance of the Wind.

One night Helen was able to hide a book in her night-clothes and lie in the twilight reading. The book helped her forget the terror. But Elizabeth came in, not knocking on the door, and caught her.

"This will teach you to disobey me," she said, fastening Helen's wrists together with a little chain. Naturally Helen did not tell her that she could still hold a book with her hands free above the wrists—although it was heavy and uncomfortable.

Helen was afraid of so many things. She didn't dare go all the way to the top of the one nearby hill, a hill not soft

and wild with pine needles and underbrush but barren of
all save glittering piles of deep red rock: rocks hunched and
piled against each other with dark holes for rattlesnakes. She
climbed up beyond the cow paths once, and a little higher,
but not to the very top. It was so big and lonely and creep-
ingly alive—and when a jackrabbit rustled in the sage brush,
she was sick with fear and ran quickly down. She was afraid
of her pony too, ever since he had bucked her neatly under
a barbed wire fence. She hated to be left sitting alone in a
car with its engine running because she was sure it would
start off by itself and run down the road and crash. She never
told anyone how afraid she was. She didn't want to lose the
opportunity of going to Miles City. That at least was like
going into safety.

"Hurry up, Baby," Elizabeth said one morning. "We're
going for the mail and Albert and I need supplies. Feed the
chickens and make sure you close the gate and put on your
leather shoes and find your coat and come to the car."

Helen did as she was told and climbed into the back seat.
They went south past the Venables and five miles more until
they got to their mailbox on the wide dirt road, then they
drove west past flat cultivated ranchland until they came to
the unpainted schoolhouse. After that they had to go uphill,
through sheep country, and along a two-mile chasm. The
road was narrow but not single-track. Travelers in a caravan
approached from the opposite direction.

"Back up," said the leader to Elizabeth, after her car and
his wagon had stopped hood to horse. "There are wagons
behind me and you are just one Ford."

"I won't," said Elizabeth, indignantly. "This is a road for
the people who live here, not travelers looking for a place to
camp. There's a pullover you just passed, I know this road
well. Turn round your horses and go back to the pullover and
let us pass by."

Helen couldn't imagine how the travelers could do this
and lowered her head and peered between her mother's

and Albert's shoulders. She hoped they couldn't see her. The leader turned to the driver behind him and told him to maneuver his horses as close to the hill as he could. He walked further back and told two other drivers to do the same. It took several minutes for this to be accomplished. Elizabeth put her car into first gear and went forward. Helen was certain there were only inches between the car wheels and the edge of the chasm.

They drove through more miles of scrubby pines until, twenty-five miles in all, they came to the mud banks of the Yellowstone River, and trees with leaves on them, the soft green of the cottonwood.

They parked on the dusty square of Miles City and Albert and Elizabeth filled up the car with canned goods and supplies. They went to the man who sold forty crates of liquor a week and bought a crate of bourbon. Helen looked into the wide windowpanes of the harness store, where gleaming saddles rode wooden saw horses and bridles hung on pegs.

One winter day Elizabeth decided to go to town alone. Albert stayed at the ranch. Elizabeth left Helen with the Venables, a visit Helen always liked because the Venables had fried potatoes and jam and things she could eat. The cowboys talked to her and played records on a Victrola. It was a ramshackle house, always messy, the rugs crumpled, and the tables stacked with old Sears, Roebuck catalogues. The living room smelt of grease and food and was smoky and noisy. No one bathed since water had to be heated on the stove and poured in a tin tub, and no one cared anyway. She played with Sister and Brother Venable.

"Let's ride the calves," Sister Venable, who was bigger than Helen, said that afternoon. "We can ride around the dung heap." They mounted the calves and went around the manure pile in a circle and Helen, who was still scared of riding, fell off.

"Ha, ha," said Sister, who was mean and bullied sometimes. But Helen could read much better than either of them and she hadn't even been to school, and she said that to Sister.

That night a blizzard came up. They waited until late expecting Elizabeth but the darkness and blinding snow were impossible to see through. Finally Mrs. Venable tucked Helen into bed between Sister and Brother. It was the first time she'd ever slept with anyone, or been kissed goodnight since her nurse had left.

Elizabeth came late the next morning after sleeping in the Ford until daylight and climbing through snow drifts to borrow a team of horses to draw the car out. Albert was quiet when they got home, and later that night Helen heard the sounds of a tremendous argument in Elizabeth's bedroom.

"I'm not staying in this godforsaken place with nothing to do and you being uppity all the time. You aren't going to succeed in anything out here because you're still acting Eastern."

"I will succeed, and it won't be because of any help from you," Elizabeth replied.

Albert took Helen aside the next morning and told her he was going away to the war in France.

"If we win," he said, "you can have butter instead of margarine."

"How will we get along without you?" she asked.

"Your mother's decided not to raise cattle anymore. She doesn't have money for the overhead. It costs too much. She's going to raise hogs instead, and keep one cow. She won't have to do this alone. I'm going to send my nephew Tom to help. Tom is too young to fight."

Albert went off to Miles City and so did one of the hired men. The hired man piled his wife and babies and furniture into a wagon and drove away. Helen and Elizabeth were alone with the exception of one man beyond the hill.

So they raised pigs and kept one cow. The lazy hogs wallowed in the deep spring mud and foraged for sugar beets, roots and mash and rot of all kinds. Helen helped feed them and ready them for market. One spring morning, she perched beside Elizabeth on the hard wooden seat, after they'd prodded the hogs up a plank into the wagon, and were driving into Miles City behind a double-team. They needed strong horses to get through the bad roads. They plodded through axle-deep ruts, jolting and rocking while the hogs grunted, pulling through places where even the light Fords were stuck. Down from the hills poured rivulets of melted snow and ice. From the deep drifts still frozen under the pines, torrents five and six feet wide swirled through the gullies and across the road. The gullies were too deep for Helen to cross and when the wagon got stuck, she held the reins while Elizabeth trudged to the next farm for men to push.

Helen didn't last the whole trip. When she was too exhausted from hanging onto the narrow seat edge, Elizabeth dropped her off at a ranch house. That was worth all the cold and damp clothing and aches, for the women let her sit in front of the stove and read and they filled her full of fried potatoes and tucked her in bed. They were comforting people, shouting at each other and laughing, and they hung red flannel in the windows to brighten them.

"Your mother is lovely," one of the women said. "She must be very lonely so far from the city. It's bad for people to have to be by themselves. It's a pity Albert had to leave."

"We aren't alone, really," Helen said. "He has a nephew and he's going to come and be with us."

"Well, that's good," said the woman. "Now let's get you to bed and make sure you stay warm."

Helen was beginning to wonder whether it had been a pity, or whether Albert was lucky. As she fell asleep she thought about her mother. Elizabeth was abrupt and moody, and either sat by herself reading, or rode up the road for the morning, and never appeared with a smile. Helen missed Albert, especially the support he gave her, not talking to her very often, but telling Elizabeth to stop beating her so much. She remembered another argument she'd overhead.

"You're taking your nervousness out on the kid," Albert said. "You've been doing this ever since you bought the ranch."

"That's not true," Elizabeth replied. "The kid is smug and lies and she's just like a Crosby, and if there's one thing I'm going to do, it's cure her of any Crosby traits."

Helen knew she lied. She'd never been able to explain things to Elizabeth and she tried to make up reasons. Then Elizabeth got furious and made her unbutton her union suit. She spanked her with a slipper.

But then, Helen remembered, one day she laughed because the slipper didn't really hurt, and Elizabeth changed to a horse whip. After that, it was terrifying. She did it again and again after Albert left. Things got more and more muddled. Helen was really afraid. She got whipped for stealing a piece of chocolate and lying about it, and she was whipped again the next day, when her mother thought another piece was missing. Helen hadn't taken it, and said so, and got a whipping that raised welts because she had apparently lied again.

Now Helen realized that Elizabeth wouldn't believe anything she ever said again. She was whipped for hiding, and for reading at night, and for not eating. The day Elizabeth had discovered the disgusting little bullets of food and had strewn her clothes and toys all over the floor and pulled the cot out and searched the mattress, Helen had been almost paralyzed by the neat, red lashes. She screamed and fought, but Elizabeth only snapped down the harder, shouting, "The more you cry, the more you get and don't you ever forget it. Someday you'll thank me." After that she had to eat in the kitchen, and Elizabeth stood over her, saying, "Eat everything on that plate because you're much too skinny. AND SIT UP STRAIGHT!" Helen was wearing a strapped canvas back brace that cut into her shoulder whenever she stooped but she still couldn't maintain the desired posture. "Don't answer back. Shut up. I'll teach you to be a sneak."

Helen sneaked more than ever. She shifted into a deeper level of self-awareness and vowed not to let her mother win. Food tasted like grey rags and wouldn't go down. She slipped it into the stove whenever she could and gave her meat to the cat.

Elizabeth felt sorry for herself. She was bored and lonely. A six-year-old daughter could hardly be a successful second in Elizabeth's desire for adult conversation. She couldn't discuss anything with a child who mumbled and couldn't talk. Helen's complete resemblance to Maunsell did not make it any easier to forgive or forget the past. It was hard enough for her to show affection to an acquaintance. She couldn't bring herself to give affection to Helen except as an acquaintance. All she saw in Helen's face was Maunsell. Elizabeth was so impersonal that Helen could not recall her face with intimate knowledge when she was out of sight.

But Helen was not lonely, because month in and month out she had learned to play by herself. And sometimes, like this night when she'd been left with neighbors, she felt she had friends. If anything, her play world was more real to her than the daily routine. She talked to herself constantly, living in a land of make-believe the way people in fairy tales did. It began to be more fun to read than to do anything else. Elizabeth, pleased at having her problem child taking more and more care of herself, encouraged her.

"That's good that you've finished your book," Elizabeth said back at their ranch. "Come to the bookshelf and pick another. Take it to your room while I finish what I'm doing."

Helen was not rebellious. She accepted her situation as entirely natural.

But she did begin to wonder if Albert had been getting the best of his arguments with Elizabeth, and if he had really wanted to go to war. That question was answered when Elizabeth came in one morning to say that Albert was never coming back.

"Write him a nice letter," she told Helen, "and tell him you're sorry the war was ended before he had a chance to get into it, and I'll mail it, and then, let's never hear you mention him again. We were not married very long and he is gone now."

They were shut in a worse silence than ever before. Albert's nephew couldn't come until the fall.

"Don't ask me about my concerns," Elizabeth said. "And I won't ask you too much about yours."

There was just one time when they were close at all. One morning Elizabeth threw a stick at a wild boar, which was trying to fight their hogs through the fence. It had whirled around and headed straight for Elizabeth, not stopping until its tusks had ripped a gash, inches deep and long, in her thigh.

"Mother, mother!" Helen cried as she saw the wild boar plunging into Elizabeth's leg. "Don't worry! I'll get the first-aid chest!" She ran to the house to fetch a towel and bowl to catch the outpour of blood. And for three days she got the meals, while Elizabeth lay stretched out on the couch. But after Elizabeth was up again, she was as uncommunicative as ever—and sent Helen away to pile sugar beets in a hole lined with potato sacks, in the garden.

Towards the middle of September, one morning Helen woke up to find a collection of little flags and books and handkerchiefs beside her bed, and was very pleased to learn that it was her birthday and that she could do anything she wanted to. She asked to drive the Ford, and managed to get five or six feet before going off the road into a gully. It was an exciting day, and a nice birthday and she liked being seven. Elizabeth asked her if she was tired of being called "Baby."

"Of course I am," said Helen.

"Very well, then, we'll call you Ruth," said Elizabeth. And she called Helen "Ruth" the rest of the year, explaining to Helen that it was due to sentimentality towards a friend who had just lost a little girl named Ruth, and now referred to Helen as "Ruth" in her letters. Ruth was a step up from "Baby" and Helen practiced writing "Ruth Crosby" instead of Baby. There was also a little confusion about her birthday. Elizabeth said, months later, "By the way, I was re-reading in my diary this morning, and I found out that your birthday is on the sixth instead of the eleventh. You'd better remember it for me." Helen agreed to, but for two or three years afterwards there was always a little argument as to which day it really was.

Tommy Oñativia, Albert's nephew, arrived and Elizabeth was beginning to brighten up a little. There was a new face in the house and Helen decided that it was the nicest face she had ever seen. The whole house sounded different. Elizabeth's sullen silence was broken, for he was good-looking, amusing, and an altogether gallant companion as well as a good worker. He slept in the bunk-house and worked at keeping the fences in order and feeding the pigs. He ate with Helen and after meals would ask her to walk down to the barn with him. Helen felt necessary and important on these trips and told him what she had read and why she didn't like canned tomatoes and one thing and another of equal importance. Tommy seemed to be taking care of her too. He taught her how to feed the pigs and change their water.

Then Elizabeth decided to sell the ranch. Even with Tommy's help, she couldn't cover her costs. Tommy persuaded her to let Helen go to Miles City for two days, with Judge Sherman, who was trying to sell the ranch for her. Tommy knew the Shermans were kind to Helen. They went after supper and Helen had the intoxication of getting out of a car at night and seeing the prairie showered with stars and rich, soft darkness. And she knew that for two days she would be safe.

Tommy tried to stop the beatings but Elizabeth said Helen was her child and it was her business, not his. "She's a Crosby," Elizabeth said. "She has hateful qualities. She lies and defies me. I will whip her when I want to and you will not interfere."

Helen knew her mother didn't like her. There was something about her that her mother hated—perhaps it was her hair, perhaps it was her round, Dutch features—at any rate her face should not be so round and stupid and smug. Therefore, when, a week or so after the visit to the Shermans, Elizabeth said they were going east again, she was glad. There might be more people and there would be new books to read.

In the summer of 1919, Tommy, Elizabeth, and Helen left the ranch. Elizabeth hadn't sold it yet, but she didn't care. Once again, she was certain a solution would come her way. They sold the pigs and team of horses to a neighbor. They left the curtains and furniture and books, and Elizabeth said Helen would have to leave her toys as well. All she could take was her suitcase and the clothes that would fit into it. Helen knew her toys would rot.

They drove into Miles City in the Ford for the last time. Elizabeth was behind the wheel with Tommy beside her. Helen sat silently in the back seat, suitcases beside her. She stared at the ravines and cottonwood trees and wondered if she would see prairie dogs again. She wanted her toys with her.

They went to a hotel and Elizabeth told Helen she would have to wait for them there. She could lie on the bed in their hotel room while they went out to the movies. They said they'd be back to catch the midnight train. She could hear the trains backing and whistling beside the hotel. She heard them come in and heard them go out holding her breath, she was so sure each one was their train and that they had missed it. She was supposed to be sleeping, but she was too tense and afraid. Men shouted in the next room, feet clumped outside the door, it was hot and stuffy. She hated the hotel. The big brown leather chairs in the lobby reminded her of hogs. Helen wished they would come back. They might miss the train. They were going back to New York. They were going to start all over again, Mother said. That was why they had to leave. They had built a house and barn and bunk-house and lost. It was too hot and then it was too cold and they had no more money. They had had the only bathroom for miles around and that was now gone. And her toys were gone too. Mother said they weren't sure of anything.

CHAPTER 6

Tommy and Elizabeth set up house in Manhattan. They rented a walkup apartment on Grove Street in Greenwich Village on a long lease. It had a living room with two windows facing the street, a hallway with a cooking alcove, a bedroom, and a small bathroom. They made a bedroom for Helen by dividing off a corner of the living room with a curtain. Helen understood that her mother now had a second new husband, or sort-of husband, because they weren't married yet. Still, Tommy and Elizabeth lived together. Tommy had a small amount of capital, enough to invest for income that he expected would pay the rent. His father, Victor Oñativia, owned an investment firm on Wall Street. He'd told Tommy that someday he would inherit a lot of money.

Elizabeth knew she needed to work full-time and that she couldn't keep "the kid" at Grove Street alone during day. She got in touch with Mary Haskell, her former headmistress and neighbor in Boston, to ask about boarding schools. This was the first letter in a correspondence between them that spanned thirty years. Miss Haskell sent Elizabeth's letters to my mother, after my grandmother was hospitalized, to make the case that Elizabeth wasn't insane. Elizabeth had kept all of Miss Haskell's. I have both sets of letters now.

Elizabeth's first letter was written in mid-August, late to be looking for a school for September. She explained what had happened in Montana. Ranchers were everywhere, she wrote, some making fortunes with the start of a bull and small herd, others sinking, as she had.

> We didn't save enough working capital for interest, taxes, etc. Albert wasn't able to trade cattle with the men there for several years. We just went into it stupidly, got no honest advice, didn't understand these people's psychology—they're a crooked lot—and now nothing can save us. Can you lend me money and help me find a school for Helen Elizabeth? I know it's late in the summer but truly I need your help.

Miss Haskell found an opening at a small boarding school in Framingham, Massachusetts and Helen, now seven, was sent away. Elizabeth took a series of undemanding jobs, none of which pleased her. She worked at *Vanity Fair* but was let go after four days. She found a position with a spark plug manufacturer on West Broadway but gave it up when she learned of an opportunity to sell hosiery at Hearn's department store.

Within a year, Tommy lost all his money. He left Wall Street and took a job as an assistant to a male interior decorator. His hours were irregular and he drank during the day. Elizabeth came home one afternoon to find him with two women, laughing. She wrote Miss Haskell about it, worried that alcohol was straining their finances, but pleaded with her not to tell. She'd joined the Colony Club, a socially important achievement, and didn't want any of the members to know how poor they were. With Tommy now drinking, and bringing in no income, she struggled to pay the dues.

"I have to retain my membership," she wrote Miss Haskell. "It's the only place I can meet people and be sure I'm in the right surroundings. It's gone Hellish in the apartment, loneliness and no furniture and bed-bugs mostly. The bed-bugs travel round with me all day. I'm paying the Bed Bug Lady 50 cents a week to clean and exterminate." Miss Haskell lent her money as often as she asked, and to her credit, Elizabeth paid her back.

It was now almost eight years since Elizabeth had left Grasmere. Maunsell had agreed in the divorce settlement to see Helen when she was eight, and Elizabeth decided it was time to tell Helen about her father. She chose to do so when Helen came home from boarding school that Christmas. She met her at Grand Central Station and they took a taxi to Grove Street. Here is Helen's short story describing what happened.

> They were hurtling between the Third Avenue El posts in a taxi, pitching and slipping on the leather seat, when Elizabeth said, "I have some news for you." Helen sat as she had been taught to do, not asking questions, waiting politely. She was seeing her mother for the first time since she'd been left in the boarding school. They had been together only a few minutes, Helen having been handed over by a chaperone. She was glad to see Elizabeth, pleased that she had a mother.
>
> "You have a father and he wants to see you so you are going to visit him next summer."
>
> "I have a father!?" Helen said excitedly. "I have? Where?"
>
> "He lives in a big house on a farm, there are strawberries."
>
> "Why didn't I know before?"
>
> "Because we were divorced and I had your custody until you were eight. You will have your eighth birthday with him."
>
> Helen had thought her father was dead, perhaps from the war. By the time she was old enough to ask questions, she'd learned not to. It was always safest to sit very still. She sensed displeasure in her mother's voice—already knew that she didn't want to tell her more.

They lurched across 14th Street and past the stores. "That's where I work now," Elizabeth said, "in the basement—selling stockings. It's Hearn's."

They scattered a game of hopscotch, and stopped at 8 Grove Street. "Also," she said, "I have married Uncle Tom."

Well that was good news too. Tommy was good to sit next to. He was very good-looking with a Spanish name. Helen knew she would have to ask how to spell it. Probably she would have to write her mother's name differently when she went back to school. She was used to her being Mrs. Cooley. She couldn't remember that they'd ever had the same names.

There was no further discussion of the marriage. Helen sensed it wouldn't do if she seemed too pleased that Uncle Tom would be with them. She should pretend that she preferred her mother alone. So when Uncle Tom greeted her at the apartment door, she kissed him diffidently.

The days were pleasant with trips uptown on the El, with a lady who was her "chaperone," to museums and Central Park. Christmas afternoon they went to the Hippodrome and stared at the dancers descending step by step into the waters of the unbelievable pool, until there was only a ripple meeting over their heads.

They were good Christmas days. At night, a curtain stretched from the ceiling to the floor, partitioning Helen's cot away from the smoke and smell of gin—which had been fetched from the bathtub. She slept through it all.

She didn't see her mother again until Easter, when Elizabeth was able to leave New York for the weekend and brought Helen to Cambridge for lunch where she was staying with a friend. Helen played with other children and was glad to get back to school in Framingham that evening.

To all effects and purposes, Helen was in a boy's boarding school—and she was a girl. Started by a widow, who had a farm and two sons to educate, it was meant to be a co-educational school. All but two of the boarders were boys. All of the day students were girls. When the blizzard of 1919 piled up the roads in drifts of snow eight and ten feet deep, the day students stayed home.

All winter long Helen and a boy had their lessons together with a plump comfortable teacher. They were the fourth grade. The three previous grades Helen had done at her mother's knee. There were few reading and writing lessons. Mostly she did a prodigious amount of leather work and made Christmas and Easter cards, carefully cutting out images and pasting them on colored paper. She didn't learn arithmetic well and couldn't subtract 9 from 15 without counting on her fingers to be sure.

With three other students, Helen bought baby pigs in the fall and every fourth day it was her turn to trudge with hot pails of mash and heavy loads of straw, in every kind of weather. Once when she had rolled a bale of straw to the barn loft edge, she lost her balance at the top of the ladder, and instead of the straw, slipped head over heels down through space. Seconds later she was looking up at the face of the farmer—they looked at each other quite a long time—until she finally realized she wasn't dead, and was completely unhurt. They were equally pleased.

They sold the pigs for just about what it cost to raise them.

Only in the spring did she ever come to suffer from being the only girl—in her mind—in a boys' school. She got too big for her britches and lined up the farmers, the cook, and the teachers in a war against the boys. And then she got scared. When she saw that the farmer had roped the biggest boy to a tree, she knew it was inevitable that when that boy got loose she would be practically scalped. So leaving the farmer and teachers fighting a fine battle of chasing and roping the boys, she hid terrified until nine o'clock that night in a coat closet—until she could sneak off safely to bed. The rest of the spring the boys contented themselves with forbidding her any entrance to their tree houses, mammoth affairs they'd carpentered.

There was one boy Helen thought was perfect. He was fifteen and his name was, appropriately, Lord. He helped her make skis and taught her to use them. She thought of him as a friend and didn't think of sex until the other fourth grader made a date with her in the loft to explain it. Helen didn't like him (his nose twitched and she called him Rabbit) and she thought lying down on her stomach with her pants pulled down while he fiddled around behind her just plain silly and not exactly right. He didn't want anyone to know. She stood it as long as she could and quit him. They raised hundreds and hundreds of real rabbits at the school and Helen thought them much more interesting. There was so much sex going on with the animals that she didn't think about it at all until the farmer married her teacher during Easter vacation, and all the students thought that the most wonderful thing that ever happened, and just what should happen in the spring.

It wasn't so good back on Grove Street in the June vacation that followed. The windows were open and the streets roared. The ice in the bathtub was welcome in the heat, but the gin drinking was loud. Uncle Tom didn't seem to be working and Helen just sat it out until it was time to go back to Framingham, for in summer the school was a camp and was to be really co-educational. There wasn't much to eat and there wasn't anyone to play with. There was just one cooling thought—the farm, and the strawberries, and her father on her birthday.

Helen wondered whether her father's would be just like school, with pasture and pigs, apple trees and horses, and what would the farmer, her father, be like? Probably sort of like Uncle Tom, good at fixing things. And his name would be just like hers. He was going to meet her at the end of camp. Would she say, "How do you do, Mr. Crosby? I am Elizabeth?" She still didn't know that part of her name was Helen.

Finally it was too hot to bear and Elizabeth took Helen to Grand Central and sent her back to camp a week early.

Elizabeth pretended she didn't know it was early but Helen didn't care. Whenever she got somewhere early she made friends with the cook, and she looked forward to showing new girls around. She preferred her mother by mail, and got some very nice mail from her that summer because she broke her collarbone playing "Statues" and Elizabeth wrote her letters beginning with "Dear Lamb" instead of "Dear Elizabeth." Helen liked all the extra attention she got. She liked all but the smell of the unchanged bandage, it being a hot summer. The last week of camp she went on an overnight hike. With her shoulder not yet completely mended, she was given special permission to lead all the way there and back. To top all this excitement there was, of course, that of counting the days left until her father came.

* * *

It was the last day of camp and parents were driving up to the front door in either their own cars or taxis. Helen had on her best lavender dress. She waited with a friend in a nearby sun-house. She wasn't going to take any chance of running up to the wrong father.

The day felt very long. There was a circular driveway past the farmhouse, the barn, and the bungalows, up to the main house. Helen sat on her suitcase a little beyond where the cars drove up and halted. A car approached with several people in it. Was her father coming with friends? Or alone? Was that man getting out of the car asking for her? No, someone rushed up to him and was engulfed. Then there was a car with two women—that was not what she was waiting for. It was getting hot in the sun-house and her dress was getting creased. More thoughts raced through her mind. She wondered where she'd be tomorrow. A car arrived with a man and a woman. Did her father have dark hair? Why didn't anyone run up to them? Was that her father, with a woman with him? No, a boy came to his family.

Then a car arrived with a man in it. He was very tall. The counselor meeting cars pointed in Helen's direction. The man followed with his eyes. The counselor beckoned to Helen. Helen looked aghast at the friend she was sitting with and her feet dragged. She could hardly look at him.

"Mr. Crosby, this is your little girl, Elizabeth." Helen curtsied and shook his hand. He had a moustache. He smelled of sandalwood. He picked up her bag and they got into the taxi.

"Does everyone call you Elizabeth?"

"Yes."

"Have you ever been called anything else?"

"Yes, I was called Baby until I was five years old. Then Mother asked me if I would like to be called Ruth instead of Baby and I said yes."

He looked startled and asked, "Why Ruth?"

"She had a friend who had lost her little girl named Ruth. The friend started calling me Ruth. Mother thought it would make the friend feel better if she changed my name. After a while Uncle Tom started calling me Squee-gee and Liz, so they stopped the Ruth. Sometimes I get called Lizzie."

"Well, your name is Helen Elizabeth. Did you know that?"

"No."

"I'm going to call you Helen. I cannot call you Elizabeth. That's your mother's name."

"All right," Helen said.

They took a train from Framingham and Maunsell told Helen they were going to Albany. "It's on the way to Rhinebeck where I live." Maunsell lifted his watch chain and a round gold watch appeared. He glanced at it. "Now let's go to the Pullman car and have something to eat."

They ordered dinner and had huge baked apples with cream for dessert. Afterwards Maunsell leaned back and took a cigarette from a gold case.

"How much do you weigh?"

"Almost fifty pounds."

"You need some cod liver oil. We'll get some for you at Grasmere." He had a little board for checkers in his pocket and they played checkers for a while and then cards. He drew pictures for her. And Helen began to think that he was truly wonderful.

It was a long trip. The train went slowly and they had to change at Albany. They got off the train at Rhinecliff, by the river, and were met by a man named Gerraghty who had deep cracks in his neck like train tracks and who seemed glad to see them. "This is my little girl," Maunsell said. Gerraghty looked surprised. Helen looked out the window of the taxi watching for a farmhouse, but first they went through Rhinebeck on the Post Road. There was a church and a hotel. She noticed late Victorian houses. They went down and then up a hill just outside the village, past a cemetery, and turned onto Mill Road. A hundred yards from the turn was a large gate. She kept looking for a farmhouse but there was just a long driveway, with another driveway coming into it, and another driveway coming in further on, and trees meeting overhead. "Those are locust trees," Maunsell said, "planted many years ago."

The house was not a farmhouse. It was red brick, with climbing ivy, and had marble trim. There was a large front porch with green wicker furniture, and a huge front door, twice as wide as any Helen had seen before.

Maunsell rang the bell and opened the door as a maid arrived. They entered an enormous room and followed a little path through a mountain of furniture, all under white sheets. An old lady with a cane and a red face, dressed in black, walked towards them to look at Helen, and Maunsell said, "This is your grandmother." Fanny Crosby looked at Helen but said nothing. Helen curtsied. Fanny left the room and Maunsell asked the maid to take Helen to her room on the second floor.

Helen had slept in so many places she wasn't afraid to sleep alone, and besides, the bed was big and comfortable. She heard clocks chiming. Her father came to kiss her good-night and she fell asleep quickly.

She had breakfast with her father in a small room over-looking the garden the next morning. The man who drove the farm's milk route brought the mail in a huge leather bag. Maunsell explained that groceries would be delivered also, by the grocer, although, he grumbled, "they charge more that way."

He told her about the estate. She was free to go where she wished. There was a farmhouse nearby; the superintend-ent, Mr. Burroughs, lived there, and had two daughters with whom Helen could play.

Then he explained about the house. Helen would have breakfast with him. She'd have lunch and supper alone, in the breakfast room. "Sometimes we'll spend the day together," he said, "and then of course on those days we'll have our lunch together. In the evening I am usually out." The food would come up from the kitchen on a dumbwaiter that rattled and banged. She would ring a bell by the dumbwaiter when she was finished. "You are not allowed on the third floor, where the servants live, or in the basement," Maunsell said.

Helen explored the house after breakfast. There was a fireplace in the dining room and two in the drawing room, and another in the morning room. There was one in every bedroom, including her great-grandmother Schieffelin's room at the end of the hall. Mrs. Schieffelin was a very old woman with a kind face lying absolutely still in bed. She turned her head towards Helen and said, "We will say our prayers together every morning you're here. You will be on your knees, here beside my bed. And you will say 'good morning' to me in a different language each time."

There were clocks on every mantelpiece and desk and two grandfather clocks in the downstairs hall. One told the day of the month and the other played marches every hour, which Helen liked the best. A man named Mr. Henry Grube with a wall eye came every Friday night to wind them.

Helen found the farmhouse and Mr. Burroughs and his daughter Laura. Laura said, "Let me show you the barn. It's the biggest barn you've ever seen," and it was. It was made entirely of stone. There were hundreds of cows and a stable with horses and a garage. The garage was so far from the house that Maunsell often didn't use it.

Helen stayed at Grasmere three weeks. When she was alone in the house, she could hear the maids, the gardener, and the cook laughing on the backstairs or in the kitchen below, but she never went to either place. Her father often took her to visit his friend Miss Merritt, who was almost as small as Helen. Maunsell and Miss Merritt played tennis and let Helen walk around on stilts. Then they had raspberry shrub. Miss Merritt lived in a big place too, and a butler served them.

On the way home Maunsell stopped in Rhinebeck for sodas. He took her to the drugstore and bought her anything she wanted, like Eversharps and flashlights and writing paper, dollars and dollars worth. He took her to the dentist. She'd never been before. The dentist said her teeth were perfect.

Then Maunsell took her shopping at a clothing store in Poughkeepsie and let her choose three dresses, socks, a hat, and a coat. She had only one dress, the lavender one—the rest of her clothes were school middies and bloomers.

"Can I have whatever ones I want?"

"Yes."

"This pink and white one with checks and a sash?"

"Yes."

"And this blue one, and this plaid one with six different colors, orange and yellow?"

"Yes."

It took an hour to drive each way, the road was so winding. Maunsell told her the names of his neighbors as they passed each gate.

Helen had her eighth birthday at Grasmere. Three little girls from neighboring houses came in cars. They played racing games—Maunsell told Helen he used to be on a track team at Harvard—and then the girls roughhoused. That night, Maunsell told her a bedtime story about a mole and a woodchuck before tucking her in.

The only bad thing about Grasmere were the bats and rats. Maunsell went out every evening. The maids were restricted to the third floor. Great-grandmother Schieffelin was confined to bed and Grandmother Crosby was scary. She shouted sometimes. One night she came into Helen's room with a cane in her hand and beat Helen's legs and chest as she curled in fear under the blanket. Helen didn't know about her grandmother's opium and her changes in mood. There was no one to call for help. The bats came in the window and Helen hid under the sheets so they wouldn't get in her hair. The rats scurried across the floor. Helen put on the light and threw pillows at them but then more would come. Sometimes it was so scary she sat in the hall for a long time waiting for them to settle down. But then she would hear her grandmother in the hall tap-tap-tapping with her cane and she wouldn't know where to go. Maunsell and his mother didn't believe in screens. "I'm immune to mosquitoes," Maunsell said.

No one ever mentioned Elizabeth while Helen was there. No questions were asked and she didn't feel there were any to answer. She forgot all about her mother's description of Grasmere as a farm. She went to church with her father, a distinguished person in the town, and literally rejoiced.

Two days before school opened, Maunsell took Helen back to New York. He handed her over to Elizabeth in Grand Central Station and said, "Goodbye, Helen."

"Come along, Elizabeth," her mother said. And they got into a taxi again.

There were plenty of questions in her.

"Who was living at Grasmere?"

"My father and his mother and his mother's mother. And farmers. And a girl named Laura."

"How many servants?"

"I don't know."

"Who did you visit?"

"Miss Merritt." Elizabeth looked annoyed.

"She must be a hundred now," she said. "Who else did you see?" Helen told her about the Astors and Roosevelts.

"How was your grandmother?" They were passing Hearn's department store again on their way to Greenwich Village.

"I don't know. There seemed to be something wrong with her. She didn't like me. She hit me with a cane one night when I was in bed." Elizabeth gave no sign she'd heard. Helen tensed remembering the event, then realized her mother didn't want to know more.

"Why did he call you Helen?" Elizabeth went on.

"I don't know."

"It's ridiculous. He's got to call you Elizabeth. You're entered in school as Elizabeth. Did they all call you Helen?"

"Yes," Helen said.

"How do you like your father?"

Helen paused. She wasn't sure how it was going to be with her mother. "I like him very much," she said.

"He's a fool. He doesn't work. He doesn't know anything about money. How much did he give you?"

"Five dollars."

"Give it to me. We need it. He doesn't send enough money to feed you. What he sends just barely pays for school and camp."

Helen handed her the five dollars.

"You're not going back to Framingham," Elizabeth went on. "We've found a better school in Waltham and I'm taking you up tomorrow. We'll get you two dresses for winter today, and have one made for good occasions."

They got two dresses at Best's—one Helen liked, with flowers embroidered on the collar, and one she didn't, with a sailor collar and dicky. She stood for an hour in a dress-maker's shop while a dark red, heavy wool dress was cut and fitted. The hem was kept long to allow for growing and the neck was kept loose. Helen felt as if she were drowning in it.

She was glad to see Uncle Tom again and felt good when he picked her up and called her Squee-gee. Then Elizabeth set about packing Helen's suitcase for the trip to school the next day. She held up the cotton dresses Maunsell had bought and appraised them. Then she opened the door of the apartment, walked to the incinerator in the hall, and dropped them in. "You won't need those summer dresses anymore," she said. "And there won't be room in your suitcase for your scrapbook, the one with your Easter and Christmas cards," she added. She took the scrapbook with all of Helen's care-fully cut pictures down to the stoop, and in seconds, it too was gone.

CHAPTER 7

IT DIDN'T TAKE LONG for Elizabeth's relationship with
Tommy to sour. They had lived beyond their means from the
start. Yet they managed to stay together eleven years. They
were masterful at self-delusion, and co-dependent. Elizabeth
found explanations for every misfortune, always attributable
to someone else. Tommy drank himself into his own alternate
reality. After he lost his capital, they found a sub-tenant for
the apartment on Grove Street and moved to a less expensive
one on East 40th Street. Then they moved to Waverly Place
back in Greenwich Village, and then decided to live in the
country. They lived in Chappaqua, New York and Litchfield,
Connecticut for two years, taking care of a farm and doing odd
jobs (Tommy worked as a constable raiding liquor stills). They
returned to New York, to East 37th Street, East 34th Street,
and East 60th Street. Elizabeth ordered new personal stationery
every time they moved. She didn't dare resign from the Colony
Club, though she always found the dues difficult to pay.

Elizabeth had been duped by Tommy. He'd allowed her to
think he had more money than he did. He, in turn, probably
thought that *she* had money. Neither of them had the slightest
clue about how money worked and how it needed to be earned.
Both of them felt entitled to privilege, and with rosy glasses in
place, saw a world in which they would be saved. In the back

of her mind, Elizabeth believed that Maunsell would never let her fall into poverty, since she was the mother of his child. She desperately needed a buyer for the ranch in Montana. She'd bought 1,280 acres for $15,000 and invested an equal amount in improvements. But it was a falling market. There were no buyers, only expenses. "Mother's telling everyone I'm incompetent," Elizabeth wrote Miss Haskell. "I'm not, but it's hard to find work that pays enough and I'm trying to reduce the kid's expenses."

Elizabeth continued to be quick and witty at social gatherings, and managed to reacquaint herself with Maxwell Perkins and John Hall Wheelock. She began to think that she could free herself from Tommy if she could write, or do research, or perhaps become a literary agent or editor. She found work as a reader at the American Play Company. "I'm reading not only in French and German, but also in Italian," she wrote Miss Haskell. "And it doesn't matter that the work doesn't pay very well. I've found a way to earn extra money as a mannequin at fashion shows for Best & Co. It's such fun to wear pretty dresses!"

Helen spent one year at the boarding school in Waltham. Elizabeth worried about the cost. She tried to find a family in New York that would take Helen as a boarder. She met with no success, and asked Miss Haskell for advice. The timing in this case was excellent. Miss Haskell wrote that she was at that very moment merging her girls' school in Boston with the Cambridge School on the other side of the Charles River. Would Elizabeth like Helen to go to the same school she herself had attended years before? The fee could be reduced and a place was available. Elizabeth at once said yes. "Miss Haskell knows our family," she said to Helen, "and I'll be happy knowing you're in her care. You can see your father in Rhinebeck during vacations." Thus Helen entered her third boarding school in as many years, once again leaving new friends behind. Fortunately, she liked Miss

Haskell's school. She liked being near Harvard Square, looking up to older girls and hoping that now, perhaps, she could stay in one school long enough to make permanent friends.

But even with the reduced cost, Elizabeth had trouble meeting her expenses. As quickly as she earned money, Tommy spent it. "I've tried to give him up," she wrote Miss Haskell. "There's this hideous lack of money. I shall go on working, but we have so little, we are having to buy a double bed on the installment plan. I've had to sell my earrings and got only $500. Tommy has hocked his watch and cufflinks. I am playing chess to keep from going mad."

"My friends are all very nice," she wrote in another letter, "but they're rich and I cannot trust them not to gossip. I'm so low I've wept today. The *Social Register* won't put in my name, because of my third marriage. I'm trying not to mind, only I do."

In another letter, she said: "I need to get absolutely normal physically, away from Tommy. What is bothering me is writing. I want to write. I want to be read. It's all I can do to get out a letter. When a man and woman are at it together, it's easier, like Max Perkins and his wife. Tommy hates the typewriter. He is so inarticulate. It's being cooped up day after day in one room and seeing few people. Tommy has made no friends."

One afternoon, Elizabeth came home to find Tommy sitting by the window studying a racing sheet. He didn't greet her. He smelled of gin. She put down the letters she was carrying, mostly bills she couldn't pay, and poured herself a glass of gin as well.

She knew that when she had a drink, she felt better. She poured herself another, and sat down to the silence of her home. In her papers, I found this:

REMORSE

Wondering if you'll ever be able to co-ordinate again. Blinking, to stop things from swimming. Remembering that your brain was clear, and that you felt well, once. Hoping that you will, in two days. Having a drink. Wondering if tomorrow will ever come. Wondering why something doesn't happen. Remembering that you've had nothing to eat. Playing the Victor. Having another drink after you'd decided you'd better not. Blowing your nose ostentatiously. Pulling yourself together. Brain going like mad, receiving subtle impressions, enunciation like melting snow. Having another drink. Saying coddlesel instead of codicil. Wondering if you're getting away with it. Fresh air. No improvement. 'Nother drink. Groans. Ribald story. 'Nother ribald story. Knowing they're ribald, but thinking they're funny. 'Nother drink, when you've sworn you won't. Airy. Nonchalant. Keeping moving. Swaying. Relapse. 'Nother drink. Affectionate. Relaxed. Bed. Stupor.

Feeling like Hell. Never drink again. Cocktail. Feeling better.

Several months later, she wrote Helen to say that Tommy wouldn't be living with them any longer.

* * *

Elizabeth had severed her ties with her mother, Evelyn, and her sister, Bertha, for eleven years. She was angry at her mother for interfering with her voyage to Liverpool with Albert Cooley, and angry at Bertha because Bertha had dared to criticize her choices of husbands. Bertha, with many friends in Boston, supported herself as a portrait miniaturist. When she was fifty, Marshall Perry Slade, seventy-two, fell in love with her, irritating Elizabeth even more because when Bertha married him, she became the wife of a man with seven million dollars.

But there was one person besides Miss Haskell in Elizabeth's life who could help. He is an enigmatic figure, known to me only because Elizabeth wrote to Miss Haskell about him. I recognized him as one of the men with whom Elizabeth often had dinner in New York in 1913, when private detectives made note of him. He was William Wallace Atterbury, a World War I brigadier general who, at the time about which I am writing, was president of the Pennsylvania Railroad.

An 1886 graduate of Yale, General Atterbury was twenty-three years Elizabeth's senior. I've concluded that their relationship was platonic, more like a father and daughter; though one can't be sure. He was often in New York on business and he knew a great deal about Tommy. He made an unusual proposal.

"You're making a mess of your life," he said to Elizabeth. "You've no sense of preparing for a future. You're talented but not dedicating yourself to something in which you'll find success."

"You've seen me working hard," she said.

"Yes, and I know you want to do well. But you're taking jobs in too many fields. What is it you want to be?"

"I want to write," said Elizabeth. "I want to read books, and write about them, and also write books myself. I like the literary arts."

"Then you need to sit down and think about how you're going to accomplish this. You must settle down, with or without a husband."

Atterbury proposed that Elizabeth take some time to plan her life carefully. He offered to support her for a year, while she determined if she could succeed on her own. He would stay away and make no demands. He had the money and wanted to help.

Elizabeth said she would consider it. No one had ever proposed such a thing to her before. Two weeks later, she wrote Miss

Haskell, "It is so annoying to keep going through this thing with all my husbands. There are these sequences of men and they are so disappointing. I think I will say 'yes' to Atterbury."

She decided she would think about what to do with her life while revisiting Europe. She might have been thinking about the concerts and plays she'd enjoyed at her boarding school in Germany. Perhaps she wanted to rewrite the script of her honeymoon with Maunsell. Miss Haskell warned her that Europe was not now as lighthearted as it had been before the Great War:

> The English are desperately poor. They travel no more, and their great estates, for sale, can't even find buyers. They are taxed to extinction. France is so obliterated, and the white chalk that has been turned up on top of the fertile loam of centuries won't grow even weeds. Italy is sad and depressed. So many hotels and theatres in Venice are closed, so many gondolas idle, such small stocks in the shops. The English are still handsome, full of character and distinction, whether well off or not, but you will not find them as happy as before.

She booked passage on a ship with a return voyage two months later. She was optimistic that she might still find a place in society. But on the return voyage she experienced a social rebuff: "A girl on board I know refused to speak to me," she wrote Miss Haskell. "At night I think I should let the kid go to Maunsell; during the day I change my mind. I'm taking a house at Waterbury, Connecticut for a year beginning next month. Atterbury, who said he'd be silent for a year if I agreed to take the money, is remaining silent."

Once back in America, she wrote letters to potential employers. She wasn't interested in entry-level jobs; she wanted a position that would allow her to advance. She composed a 'life history' and sent it to a dozen prospects. Here is how she described herself to the scenario editor at First National Pictures on Madison Avenue.

Dear Mrs. Strauss,

Here is the life history. I was born in 1889, maiden name
Coolidge. This explains a great deal. I was educated at private schools in Boston and in Europe, was married in 1908 to
Maunsell Schieffelin Crosby, bore him two children, one of
whom died, and left the ancestral estate at Rhinebeck, with
my little girl, in 1912. I studied in England, went on the stage
for a year, and then was the manager of the Stenographic
Dept. of the N.Y. Edison Company for two years.

I got a divorce in Richmond, Virginia, and soaked every
cent I had in a ranch in Montana. I came back, selling two
cows and a bull for the railroad fare, to New York in 1919,
worked for *Vanity Fair*, married again, moved to the country,
and then his family fortunes went bust. I did title-searching
for the town of Litchfield, put up jam, and finally became
the secretary to the President of a manufacturing company in
Bantam, Connecticut.

Then we came to New York again, I worked at Hearn's,
and then decided that books were my job, and I'd better get
at it. I started in 1922 as secretary to Otto Liveright at the
American Play Company. I became Miss Marbury's secretary, head of the foreign department, and wrote synopses for
Hubman. In 1923, I started reading for *Famous*. Now, upon
my return from a short trip abroad, I have decided that plays
and film interest me most.

I have always read a great deal, and having had a fluffy
education, know things like languages and books and music
and art. But my business experience has been so thorough
that I feel capable of coping with any organization's methods.

What I mind more than anything else is going as far as I
can and being obliged to stop there and mark time. I should
like to find an employer who would allow me to do that and
who, without jealousy or self-consciousness, would allow me
also to proceed a little in his service.

Mrs. Strauss replied:

Dear Mrs. Oñativia,

The 'life history' sounds more like fiction than biography. We haven't a job that is big enough for your talents at the moment, and I know of course that you don't want to go back to the small-time one of just reading. My suggestion is to allow things to remain in status quo and keep in touch.

Rebuffed by everyone to whom she wrote, Elizabeth finally realized she would have to work for herself. She took her problem to Miss Haskell. Miss Haskell had a practical point of view, honed by years of advising young women about their life choices, and wrote a cautionary letter of advice to Elizabeth; which Elizabeth chose not to take to heart.

Dear Elizabeth,

In general, a job that one can keep even if elderly, and that pays a fairly good salary, is the best thing to have, because it is the surest thing. To be so useful that one is invaluable to a firm or a wealthy man is best. And to achieve that, one has to be efficient and sensible and non-talkative, non-suggestive, inconspicuous, self-effacing, quiet, serene, pleasant and impersonal—just an ever-ready, ever-dependable mechanism that works to order and can be forgotten when not in use. One sees such women in successful offices, and they hold their jobs and get good pay.

Can you work into such a position if you become a stenographer again? If a man subsidizes you, it is but for a season, and at too heavy a price, and leaves you worse off than ever. A business of one's own is a poor thing unless one earns so much that during twenty years one can put aside a competence. I spoke with a clever financial friend about your case. I did not tell him your name, but put your situation hypothetically as that of an able woman in a big city trying to establish a business of her own, and having to create the demand for what she is especially well fitted to supply, but being without money enough to live and sustain her infant job through an infancy of unforeseeable duration.

He said, 'It's certainly in part at least a matter of salesmanship. The thing has to be sold. Can she sell it? Can she sell it and provide it too? If she can't, and can't pay for selling it, how can she succeed in making it go and in keeping it going?'

Elizabeth, are you a good employee?—loyal, quiet, willing to follow and not lead, discreet, not cocksure, gentle, considerate, inconspicuous? I ask that like a schoolmarm, but anyone to be the kind of employee that is retained when others are dropped, has to be each and all of those things. If your venture makes good, then if you should fall ill, would it not fall to pieces? Is not a one-woman concern of questionable dependableness for a businessman or a firm to rely on?

You may have worked each and all of these things out. You need to be making yourself solid with employer or clientele, in order to make your future at all secure. These are your last ten years of 'apprenticeship'—and you ought to be doing in them what you are to keep on doing to the end of the chapter.

I have always thought that when I got too old to be desired as a teacher, I would go into a family and learn to cook. Then I would apply for a high paid cooking job; and a fine cook can always get good pay, and has few expenses. It is not what one would CHOOSE, but CAN one choose? Only rarely. The work is hard, but takes brains, and is worthwhile. I am not joking, but serious. It has no social standing, but social standing matters little beside the means to live without anxiety; and social life too fails when one gets older; but nobody minds the age of a cook.

CHAPTER 8

SARAH SCHIEFFELIN, Maunsell's grandmother, died in 1921. His mother, Fanny Crosby, died four years later. Eleanor, Maunsell's older sister, had married Lord Huntingfield and moved to England. It was a marriage of both love and convenience. Eleanor brought with her a dowry, and in return became the chatelaine of Heveningham, a large Palladian house in East Anglia. Maunsell inherited Grasmere and he and Eleanor shared the remaining estate. Maunsell at last had money of his own.

Helen was now fourteen. From the age of nine, she had visited Grasmere often. Maunsell looked forward to her visits and gradually they became longer. He gave up any notion that she wasn't his daughter; he saw the shape of her cheekbones reflected in his, the proof of paternity his Aunt Grace had hoped for when she wrote, "Unless she looks like you I don't see how you can ever be sure." He gave Helen a bedroom of her own, to use whenever she wished, bought her a pony, and introduced her to more of his friends in Rhinebeck, including Daisy Suckley, who lived nearby at "Wilderstein" and had befriended Helen's mother in the early years of her marriage to Maunsell.

Maunsell's consuming interest at Grasmere was bird-watching. He organized the Rhinebeck Christmas bird counts every year until his death, published a dozen articles on the birds of Dutchess County and completed a draft of a book about birds that was published posthumously. He went birding in Panama, Mexico and southern Texas, liking the warm climate and often paying the expenses of others in the party. He was the first to see a particular hummingbird, afterwards named for him. He spent time with Franklin Roosevelt in Florida, plying the waters on Roosevelt's boat, *Larooco*. In the summers, he visited his sister in England, looking for birds in Suffolk and Norfolk. I have photographs of him sitting in a rowboat with the keeper of Hickling Broad, at the time the largest expanse of water in England; they were hoping to see the elusive bittern.

When he was in Rhinebeck, he invited bird-watchers to join him at Grasmere. His weekends became almost an institution, with one or more ornithologists staying overnight. Florence Jacques, visiting with her artist husband, Lee, recounted her experience in Roger Tory Peterson's *The Bird Watcher's Anthology.*

> When I married a bird artist, I had not realized how continually I was to flock with birds. But now, I said to myself in slight alarm, wings seemed to be closing in all about me. Here was a whole weekend approaching, threatening me not only with birds but with bird lovers; for Maunsell Crosby had asked us to Grasmere, his place in Rhinebeck on the Hudson River, to share in one of his famous birding weekends. . . .For years he had kept careful census lists of the birds which appeared at Grasmere, month by month, and he thought nothing of traveling a hundred miles to attend an ornithological meeting. . . .Every weekend in the spring and fall he filled his house with guests who went with him on his all-day field trips.
>
> Maunsell, a big man full of life and cordial charm, met us at the station and drove us through country roads. . . to a pleasant old mansion surrounded by thorny locust trees whose trunks were veiled in pale green. On the steps we met the other guest, Ludlow Griscom, a square man with black

and silver hair, strong decided features and equally decided opinions. . . Mr. Griscom was supreme in identifying birds in the field, 'all known sub-species at ultimate range.'. . . After dinner, we had coffee in a yellow drawing room and Mr. Griscom played Bach for us, while our host showed us his daughter's poetry.

People sometimes wondered why Maunsell never remarried. He was a good dancer, an engaging raconteur, and a gracious host. He never said much more about himself than this, his contribution to a Harvard bulletin on the occasion of a Class of 1908 reunion: "I am mainly in agriculture and ornithology, with little public service except local committees. My New York clubs are the Union, Racquet and Tennis, Army and Navy, Explorers', and Harvard. My memberships are the Sons of the Revolution, the Ornithologists' Union, and the American Museum of Natural History." His reference to "little public service" was to his serving as a captain in the National Guard beginning in 1917, and in the Army until the summer of 1919.

One summer afternoon in 1924, when Helen was thirteen, Maunsell was reading in the garden at Grasmere while Helen sat nearby. He thought she was writing a friend. He was going to New York later in the day, and Helen decided to write him a letter secretly.

Dear Daddy,

I decided you might like a letter waiting for you when you got back, to cheer you up if you felt lonesome. So I'm writing you right now. You are out in the hammock reading *The Avalanche*, and wondering who I'm writing to. I'm writing you for another reason. I want to thank you a great deal for everything you've done for me, and for the lovely time I had this summer. I had a grand time, and I hope you have. I'm truly, awfully sorry to leave Grasmere, and you most of all.

Do name the little colt. It's such a darling and I've had great fun with it. Thank you for taking me swimming whenever you could and to lots of other nice things. I've had simply packs of fun from one day to another. If I have been very naughty I certainly didn't mean to be, and I hope I haven't given you more trouble than necessary. Thank you, Thank you, Thank you—for everything. Please give my love to anyone who mentions me. Say I sent it to them—but keep a lot for yourself.

From your bad, naughty, loving, mischievous
Helen
—alias Spider Monkey!

P.S. I love you <u>lots</u>! You are still reading *The Avalanche*!

She sealed the envelope and drew a heart where the stamp should go. She wrote her father's name and address on the front. On the reverse side she wrote, "Not to be opened till Squire Crosby gets back from New York—please."

All Maunsell's friends had known Elizabeth. They talked among themselves sometimes, concerned about her influence on Helen. Edward Sheldon, the playwright, brought up the subject with Maunsell one day in the spring of 1925.

"I'm wondering," he said, "what it's like for Helen to spend so much time at Grasmere, with its thousand acres, and then return to Elizabeth's small apartment in New York."

Maunsell wasn't concerned about the contrasts in Helen's life. "A daughter belongs with her mother," he said.

"Helen tells me she's in another school," Sheldon replied. "This time she's in Cambridge. She tells me her grades aren't very good. I'm wondering whether she's making lasting friends. It seems she's being uprooted a lot."

Maunsell had only a rudimentary understanding of how girls grew up, counseled mostly by his unmarried virgin Aunt

Grace Crosby, who'd told him what she remembered of her own growing-up experience. (Aunt Grace now lived with a Miss Bigelow in what was called a "Boston marriage.")

"I'm thinking about the importance of lifelong friends," Sheldon continued. "If she stays at one school, she'll make friendships that last. Maybe staying in one school would allow her to concentrate on her grades."

Maunsell considered the question. While he and Elizabeth were happy not to be married to each other, they did in their own ways care about Helen's welfare. There are many letters they wrote each other attesting to this. Maunsell knew about Helen's grades.

"Helen's meeting young people here," Maunsell said to Sheldon. "And she'll meet other young people in New York when she has her coming-out dance. These will be the friends who count."

Sheldon persisted. "Remember how you and Wheelock became friends at boarding school, and entered Harvard together? With whom will Helen go to college?" Sheldon proposed that Maunsell assume financial responsibility for Helen's school and find a place where she could stay for several years. "I know the founder of the Ethel Walker School in Simsbury, Connecticut," he said. "If you like, I'll inquire about a place. It's a beautiful school with riding trails and strong athletics. And the graduates go on to good colleges, like Bryn Mawr."

Maunsell wrote Elizabeth to ask if he could see her in New York. They met at the Colony Club. They'd both been bred to show good manners and they were cordial with each other. Maunsell offered to pay for Helen's education from this time on, if Elizabeth would let him choose the school. He asked Elizabeth to share the expenses of summer camp and Helen's clothes.

"I'm not sure about this, Maunsell," Elizabeth said. "You'll groom her to be a socialite and not a thinker in her own right.

Ethel Walker's is for rich girls. I'm not an appropriate mother for a young girl in a school like that. There's no way I can afford to give her the extra things she'll need." Elizabeth was thinking of fur coats and evening dresses and subscription fees for dances, not to mention the cost of a coming-out party in Helen's honor.

"Parties will happen for Helen because of who she is," Maunsell said. "Invitations will come because she's well-connected. The parties will take care of themselves." He had no idea that a débutante's season actually cost money. He didn't know that invitations were sent to those who gave parties in return.

Elizabeth said she thought Maunsell now had enough money for everything Helen needed. She was deeply worried about losing her investment in Montana; she was negotiating to sell the ranch but it carried $2,000 in debt and the most she'd been offered was $3,500. She countered and asked Maunsell to pay for summer camp as well as school. When he said yes, she said, "Very well, I will agree, and I'll do what I can as a mother."

A letter of acceptance arrived from Ethel Walker's shortly afterwards. It included the requirement that Helen repeat a year to improve her grades. Maunsell told Elizabeth not to worry about the expense. He told her he'd explained their divorce to the school, and that Helen wouldn't need expensive clothes. "They told me not to worry about the clothes," he said. "No one will know who's rich and who's not. All the girls wear uniforms and there's no way of knowing the difference."

Elizabeth showed the acceptance letter to Helen and Helen hardly noticed the requirement that she repeat a year. What caught her eye was the first sentence:

My dear Mrs. Oñativia,

I cannot let our form letter of acceptance go without just a word to say how glad I am that we have been able to make a place for Elizabeth. . .

Helen understood, once again, that she would be sent to school with her mother calling her "Elizabeth" and her father calling her "Helen."

* * *

In the summer of 1926, before she went to Ethel Walker's, Helen went to a summer camp in Center Harbor, New Hampshire. Recommended by one of Maunsell's friends, Camp Asquam was different from any place Helen had been before. She immediately noticed new accents and ways of speaking and wrote Elizabeth: "I met the mother of one of my cabin mates. She came today to visit—beautifully dressed, grand car, etc. Know how she talks? Through her nose, and she says 'that's real cute.' I do seem to slam parents every time I write you, but I get such satisfaction out of knowing you're nicer."

There were many things about the camp Helen loved: walking in the woods, being on the water in a boat, and swimming; but the camp's greatest attraction was the expectation that every camper would write. Each summer the girls produced a hardcover volume of poetry and essays. Helen was inspired by the head camper who said, "If some funny incident happens, write it up in a little poem or story. If some place around camp is particularly lovely, write about it so we will know of it too."

Helen, who'd been writing poetry for as long as she could remember, decided to participate. She submitted five poems, giving as her address the address of her school in Cambridge. She didn't submit the poems with either of her given names: she signed them "Peter Crosby." She didn't explain anywhere in her diary why she chose the name. There were no "Peters" on either side of the family. For the next thirty years, when she was introduced to someone, she said her name was Peter.

All five poems were accepted. Here is one: *Asquam's Pines*. It's about an orphaned pine tree, clearly suggesting that Helen must have been feeling she was an outsider.

Way down by the lake many years ago,
A pine tree lived, desiring to grow.
By him were groups of elm and oak,
But no one of his own pine folk.

Each day he prayed unto the sun,
'Light me 'till heaven and I are one,
And give me strength to grow so tall,
That I will bring sweet peace to all.'

His seedlings grew as years went by,
'Till someone saw the pines and sky,
And brought their children down to stay
Among the aisles of pine all day.

Then as he saw they loved it there,
He found the answer to his prayer
Was granted him; that children knew
The pines were one with God and heaven's blue.

Helen returned to Elizabeth's apartment in New York at the end of the summer. Her first evening home she tried to show the book of poems and essays to her mother. Elizabeth was sitting by the window reading letters, with a cat on her lap. Helen handed her the book and said, "I have some poems to show you that the camp printed."

Elizabeth glanced up from the letters she was reading and said, "Oh, do I have to read them? I hate poems. I'll look at them later when I have more time."

Helen instantly knew now that she'd have to keep her desires and thoughts to herself. It didn't matter that she'd said nice things to her mother in her letters home. She wrote in her diary that night: "My mother doesn't love me." She recognized that she was afraid to ask certain questions, like where Uncle Tommy went, and where the cat had come from.

From then on, Helen used her diary to write out the questions she had and to try to figure out their answers by herself. She needed someone to talk to. "I'm sick and tired of asking her things and having her treat me as if I am stupid," she wrote. And then, addressing her mother directly in her diary, she wrote:

Can't you understand that as you are my mother, I should be able to talk to you, and tell you anything within reason? Instead I have to work it out in a diary, questioning, and getting no answers, merely doing what I would call trying to get rid of it on paper.

You wonder why I always look dumb, stupid and unsympathetic. Why? In reality I feel all your sarcasm just the way I ought to, hurting like mad. I feel driven to stupidness by you, because you won't come in contact with me. Every single emotion is hidden from you. If I ever should come crying to you, you would be embarrassed.

You give more affection to your cat in one day than you give me in a month. You think I'm stupid? Not so much that I can't feel that. I'm sick of it and I want that which is yours to give me. That is why I am so stupid. Isn't it your fault too?

She went to bed that night determined never to reveal herself to her mother again.

* * *

The Ethel Walker School in Simsbury, Connecticut was one of America's best and most exclusive schools for girls. The campus sat just outside the town, on sprawling acres of fields and woods. Its horse trails were renowned. Girls came to the school from across America, most from wealthy families. When Helen entered in the fall of 1926, the cost was $1,850 a year. This included tuition, room (a bed on a sleeping porch shared with other girls), meals, laundry (up to eighteen items a week, and three shoe cleanings), mending, and a shampoo every three weeks. At additional cost, students could study studio art, piano, voice, and violin. For fifty dollars, they could have seventeen horse rides a term. Maunsell paid for riding and provided an allowance for teas and meals at a local inn. The school didn't allow more than this, and the girls were not permitted to do individual shopping.

Helen didn't know until she arrived that she wouldn't be allowed to read a newspaper. She'd read the New York papers every day with her mother and father. Even a glance at the front page was prohibited. One of Helen's roommates, Beulah Parker, wrote about the punitive atmosphere in a memoir, *The Evolution of a Psychiatrist*:

> To give credit where credit is due, I never met a nicer bunch of girls anywhere. . . (But) except for the long Christmas and Easter vacations, I cannot think of anything good to say about the school as it was then. Under a self-government system stricter and more puritanical than any I can imagine even in a convent, any infraction of rules was reportable on an honor system as a "sin" at Sunday morning assembly, presided over by prefects in black caps and gowns. "I have done thus and so; otherwise I have done nothing to my knowledge contrary to the laws of the school." One by one we stood up and said it. We were not punished physically, but we might as well have been. It was a "sin" to speak a word in the hall between classes, to whisper in study hall or even to say "good night" after the last bell. Two "sins" in a week put you on bounds for two weeks, and three or more very likely got you on bounds indefinitely. I was once severely reprimanded for fiddling with my hair in chapel, and when my brother once came along with my parents on a visit, I was told that he would have to sit at a separate table if my roommate joined us for lunch at the local inn.

* * *

The girls wore wool separates in the winter and green gingham dresses with white collars and cuffs in the spring. Cardigans had to be entirely white, with no bands of color at the neck. Leather sport shoes had to have black saddles; otherwise, the girls could wear white tennis shoes. Many of these items were ordered by the school. For the rest, the girls went to Best's or B. Altman in New York. While uniforms helped foster the notion that all of the girls were equal, there were subtle indicators of who had money and who did not. It was recommended that each girl have six changes. Some parents provided more than six. Other families bought one uniform to be copied by a seamstress at home.

As opening day approached, the school sent instructions about travel:

> All girls' temperatures should be taken on the day and those whose temperatures are even slightly above or below normal we ask to have kept at home. The girls may not bring any food, fruit, candy, magazines, books or clothes except those on the clothes list.
>
> Our safe is full of bracelets, expensive wrist watches, diamond bar pins and so on, and we really cannot accept the responsibility for these. We ask particularly that no girl bring any jewelry back with her other than a simple seal ring, a simple bar pin and a pair of cuff links.
>
> Since our arrangements for the return of the girls necessitate their being on the train during the usual lunch hour, we ask that they eat a light lunch at home before taking the train and that they are not given anything to eat on the train. We shall serve afternoon tea here, in all houses, at half past four; by which time we expect to have back at school all the girls taking our special train from Hartford.

Elizabeth decided to drive Helen to Simsbury rather than put her on the special train. She reasoned it would be easier to take Helen's suitcases by car. Maunsell gave Helen a raccoon coat that had belonged to his mother. Elizabeth wanted Helen to arrive in style and make a good impression. She wrote Maunsell afterwards to tell him how it had gone.

Dear Maunsell,

We hired a Hupp, as a Ford seemed a trifle too democratic, and deposited her among the younger scions of noble families. I was sort of cheered when Miss Walker greeted me as Ned Sheldon's friend, and said that any child of a friend of his would be welcome, because I felt it gave her a very fair start. It seems to be a good school, vastly different from anything she has encountered, and I think she's on the right road, if her cursed brains don't interfere. Her prefect is Barbara Litchfield, daughter of Bayard Litchfield, who, Bertha always claimed, was one of the 587 people she refused to marry.

I find myself absolutely worn out, so for a little while I can't earn any money, and shall be my usual poor. Then, no doubt, I shall do something.

Sincerely yours,
Elizabeth C. Oñativia

One of the reasons why Ethel Walker's was so highly regarded was that it got girls into the best colleges. Miss Hewitt, the headmistress, took Helen aside and told her the school knew she was intelligent. It was her poor marks in other schools that led to the requirement that she repeat a year. "We're sure, with private tutors in the summer, that you'll be accepted by Bryn Mawr along with all the others," she said.

Helen wasn't sure about Bryn Mawr, or about even going to college. She had real difficulty studying. Her eyeglasses always seemed to be one prescription behind. There were far more hours of class and homework than she was used to. She preferred to read what she wanted to read. But she recognized that her life now promised some stability, because her father was taking an interest, and she tried to fit in.

She quickly noticed that her classmates came from intact families. They talked about their fathers and mothers and their summer houses in Maine, northern Wisconsin, and Massachusetts. Many of the students were intellectually curious; her three roommates shared her love of books, and she took comfort in believing she was better read. She used her eyeglasses to good effect, lowering them on her nose when reading aloud.

One thing that disappointed her was the absence of any classes in poetry. She couldn't understand why this was so, and continued to write poems despite her teachers' lack of encouragement. The greatest admirer of her poems was Jean Parrish, daughter of the illustrator Maxfield Parrish, who lived in the same dormitory. Jean had a nickname, "Pig," and sometimes "Piglet."

Helen wanted to play field hockey; she had the same love of running as her father. But she couldn't find pleasure in the game because the hockey coach wouldn't let her wear her glasses on the field, and called her "One-Way Crosby." This same coach kept her from playing competitive tennis, at which Helen was sure she would excel.

When Helen returned to New York for Christmas, Elizabeth had a terrible reaction to watching all the girls disembark from the train. Many were wearing smart winter coats and carrying leather suitcases. She took Helen shopping the next day. The plan was for Helen to go to Maunsell's several days later, and she wrote Maunsell that night seeking more financial help.

Dear Maunsell,

I hope you won't think I've been extravagant, but I think you
would have done the same thing.

First place, I got a kit bag, charged at Brooks, the bill to
be sent to you, $38. The suitcases made of good leather are
anywhere beyond $50, and very heavy, and I will lend E. my
bag for this trip and teach her to pack a kit bag, and I think
she'll like it. I do like things to look well, in this shoddy age,
and it's very difficult to find anything that looks well at a
Christian price.

Second place, that coon coat of your mother's looks like
thunder. I saw all the girls coming off the train, and I said,
"Well, _this_ time she'll look like other people" and then she
appeared with the coat draped about her waist, as it were.
She was so proud of it, poor kid, and it's a nice coat, but it's
too big. I expect it will be all right next year. So I tried her
last year's coat, and that's too small. It makes her look like
an Irish kitchen maid. So today, after I'd been conscious of
her for some time, I set out to get a new winter coat. Jaeger
would have to make one up, take two weeks, for $95 or
more, so I just got one for $125 at Abercrombie, that at least
will always be good. You see, she has no flair for putting _on_
her clothes, so the only thing one can do is to get as foolproof
ones as possible. I HATE having her ALWAYS look so oddly,
because she is fundamentally good looking, but difficult
to dress.

We had an awful time about her hair, she wore it loose,
pretty but unpleasant at meals, and wept through lunch
because I was cruel. Oh, dear, oh, dear. I suppose she'll just
have to look intellectual.

Anyway, I am sure the bag and coat will not be wasted,
and I hope you don't mind. I think that school is dreadful
about clothes, but it may work out. The girls are all rolling,
you see.

Merry Christmas, though I can't say I feel that way at the moment.

Sincerely Yours,
ECO

Helen's grades her first year were poor. She did badly in algebra and French and only slightly better in Latin. Her only good grade was an 86 in English. Miss Hewitt sent the report card to Elizabeth with a personal note:

She's an interesting child, excellent in English. She has a difficult disposition and makes things harder because she has the old fashioned idea that all in authority are her natural enemies. She has not caught the spirit of the school. She does not want to do what she is expected to and loves singularity, when it is her own. Perhaps next year she will do better.

Elizabeth was fierce in her questioning of Helen about her grades. "Why didn't you do better when your father has given you such a splendid opportunity to learn? Will you apply yourself more next year?"

"I don't know," Helen said, this time not feeling timid. "I don't like studying. I'd rather finish the book I'm reading or write a poem or play the piano." She wasn't sure her mother was listening or that she should try to explain, but she continued. "I want to watch a sunset or listen to people talk. I want to hear music, write fairy tales, make cloth dolls or paint tiny pictures. But most of all, I don't want to study."

"What about college?" Elizabeth demanded. "You'll need college if you want a proper job. I didn't have college and look what's become of me."

Helen thought about that. She knew the difference between her mother's tiny income and the way her father lived. She knew about her mother's constant searches for work. She didn't think she wanted her mother's life, but she didn't yield.

"That doesn't make me want to study. I don't want to concentrate. I'd love to go to college but I don't want the routine that gets you there."

"What then *do* you want?" Elizabeth persisted. "You have to be interested in something practical."

"I want to learn why some clouds go one way and some the other. I want to know why the frost turns the leaves. I want to know what makes rain and snow and hail. I know I'll never get a job without a college education, but why should I get a job? Why can't the men do the work for once? I don't want a nine-to-five-o'clock typewriting job. If you say I can't do what I want, I'll stay with my father." She'd already been daydreaming in her diary about the possibility.

Then she changed the subject and talked about her eyes. Neither of her parents understood that she was actually frightened of losing her eyesight entirely. She reminded Elizabeth that she couldn't see well, that her eyes got tired. "You think this is a romantic imagining but it's not. If your eyes hurt you when you'd been reading all day and you knew there was nothing but more reading in front of you, you'd go mad!"

The question wasn't resolved. Helen had two more years to improve her grades. Maunsell was offering her wonderful new entertainments in Rhinebeck and she concentrated on those. Interesting Crosby cousins came to visit. Maunsell's friends liked her. She especially liked his neighbor, Daisy Suckley, who'd known Elizabeth and intuitively understood that Helen needed an older woman friend. Miss Suckley invited Helen to write to her and Helen did, sometimes twice a week, addressing her as "Dearest Aunt Daisy" or "Dearest Aunt Dee."

* * *

One Crosby cousin she especially liked was Alice Nelson (not her real name). Alice had five children younger than Helen and seemed to behave the way a mother should. She visited Grasmere every summer on her way from New Jersey to a farmhouse in New Hampshire. On her most recent visit, she'd given Helen a photograph of herself, "solely for your love of me," she'd said. She visited Helen during her first year at Miss Walker's and brought chocolates, something Elizabeth had never done. Helen looked forward to seeing Alice again later in August, before she began her second year.

Before that, however, Maunsell had a surprise. Helen wouldn't go to summer camp in 1927; she'd go to Europe. He wanted her to meet his sister, Eleanor, who lived a hundred miles from London. Eleanor and her husband, Lord Huntingfield, had four children close in age to Helen. The children, Helen's first cousins, were her closest Crosby relations. Maunsell thought it was important that Helen feel she had family.

Maunsell discussed the trip with Elizabeth, pitching his desire to take Helen to England in terms of its being good for her. "She's sixteen now," he said. "She should know that she has cousins. Otherwise she'll feel like an only child. When we come back in August, we'll think about a tutor. This is more important now."

No one in Helen's class at Walker's had been abroad. This excited Helen. She felt special because she'd already been to Europe once (though she couldn't actually brag about it, because it was the time she went with Elizabeth and Albert Cooley and the authorities turned them back). Now she could tell her friends that she was going with her father, and she was going to meet her English cousins.

They sailed July 7th on the *Mauretania*. Before going to sleep that night, Helen wrote in her diary, "I'm with Daddy! I'm to have breakfast in bed and we sit at the Captain's table."

* * *

Helen's introduction to the luxury of Grasmere was nothing when compared to her introduction to upper-class life in England. Charles Vanneck, Lord Huntingfield, had inherited Heveningham Hall in Suffolk. Built in 1779 for his ancestor, Sir Gerald Vanneck, it is still today one of the loveliest Palladian houses in England. The interior was designed by James Wyatt. The grounds, including a lake, were laid out by Capability Brown. The approach was through miles of softly undulating agricultural land. Helen wrote Elizabeth:

> Thursday, I came out here, to Aunt Eleanor's house in the country, and Aunt E. has sent us to see something every day. Yesterday it was Norwich, the day before a sheep auction. And I love England. All the tiny houses with thatched roofs, and the tiny cars, and big parks, and the queer trams.

Her cousins, Gerard, Sara, Anne and Peter, were welcoming, though she didn't see a lot of them. They came and went, visiting their own friends at other country houses. She was often left alone. She was told she wasn't old enough to eat with the adults. She ate in her room when there were house parties. She wrote Elizabeth:

> It was rather awful, as there are no other children here. I had dinner in bed. There were Dukes and Marquises, etc. and they all played Ping-Pong as there wasn't anything else to do. The butler's name is Reeves and he is absolutely perfect, the kind you get in detective stories! Tells Daddy where all the birds are. And there's a grand lot of maids, who do "everything for you, miss!" and bring my tea at eight and lay out my clothes, etc. Aunt E. thinks I'm very well dressed—in my school uniform!

Two weeks later she wrote Elizabeth about a visit to London:

On July 22nd, Her Ladyship, her maid and chauffeur, and two non-descript Americans (Daddy and me) motored from 7:30 a.m. on into London. We got there for lunch. Then Uncle Charles and Aunt E. went to the King and Queen's Garden Party, and as about seven thousand other people went, London was full of top hats, chiffon frocks n' bishop's gaiters. So Daddy and I went to the National Gallery where I dragged myself about, and liked Rembrandt, Velasquez and Turner. I had dinner at the Savoy in the Grill Room where all the detective stories begin, and then went to Leslie's "White Birds" in which a darling Frenchman was duly clapped, Maurice Chevalier.

And the next day, I really enjoyed myself. Aunt E. and I went to Marshall and Snelgrove's and got a tan coat, a tan felt hat, and a tannish washable dress. Then a green evening dress, and a navy blue silk dress like yours, long sleeves and very respectable, I thought it would be grand for New York City. Then, instead of a blue sweater, I got a navy blue "blazer"—what all the little school girls wear, which goes with my blue skirts. And all of these things are as simple as we could get them. I picked the plainest every time, as I'm petrified of your veto.

On Wednesday I went through the Natural History Museum with Daddy and after lunch we took a bus to Ranelagh, and watched my first polo there. And the next morning Daddy departed London before I was up to a girl's place at Yarmouth to look for birds for three days. So I toddled back here with Aunt E. to consume all available books.

Early in August, Helen and Maunsell flew to Paris in a small plane. They crossed the Channel in twenty minutes, but it was up and down the entire time. Helen took writing paper from their hotel, the St. James, and wrote Elizabeth:

My insides were somewhere under the seat, but Paris was wonderful. We went to Versailles and Le Petit Trianon, where we walked through the woods, and visited the Tuileries and Arc de Triomphe, and saw Lillian Gish in *The White Sister*.

She didn't write Elizabeth about something else she did. She confided only to her diary that she'd spent an afternoon by herself browsing among the bookstalls along the Seine. She innocently bought a French edition of *The Well of Loneliness* by Radclyffe Hall. Its title, she thought, spoke to something about herself. What she didn't know was that the book was banned in England, where Radclyffe Hall, a lesbian, was living openly with Una Troubridge, the wife of a naval officer. The book depicted the difficulties of being attracted to someone of the same sex. It pretended to be fiction but everyone in England knew it was not. Helen put the book in her suitcase and thought nothing more of it. Her trip to England was drawing to a close and she sent Elizabeth a short note:

> Aunt E., my cousins Sara and Peter, Daddy, the chauffeur, and I motored three hundred miles straight into Wales. At the end of that week I had the worst case of mental indigestion. We sail the 20th from Liverpool on the *Laconia* unless Daddy gets cabins on the *Berengaria* the same day. Will cable if we do.
>
> Ever and ever and ever so much love, I do want you here so!
>
> E.

CHAPTER 9

ALICE NELSON, MAUNSELL'S COUSIN who traveled every summer from New Jersey to a farm in New Hampshire, arrived at Grasmere shortly after Maunsell and Helen returned from Europe. The night of her arrival, Helen showed her some of her poems. Alice told her they were beautiful. Helen told Alice about buying *The Well of Loneliness* in Paris and how much she'd enjoyed reading it. She showed the book to Alice. Alice departed the following day. Helen returned to Ethel Walker's in September, leaving the book in her bedroom at Grasmere.

In December, Alice sent several books to Helen as a Christmas present. She addressed them to Helen in care of Elizabeth's address in New York. One was *Dusty Answer*, by Rosamund Lehmann, whose protagonist, named Judith, is a lonely girl who idolizes the older children next door. Helen began to read the book at once, feeling an affinity with the heroine. She hadn't yet been touched sexually, except by the fourth grade boy at her school in Framingham, so it never occurred to her that Judith might be feeling sexually aroused. Helen didn't know at this time that she had a vagina. She'd had no sex education of any kind.

The next day, Helen took the books to Grasmere to continue reading during her Christmas vacation. Maunsell saw them and was furious. He believed Helen should read only the books that were on the official Ethel Walker school list. Helen didn't care. She packed Alice's books in her suitcase, along with *The Well of Loneliness* she'd left at Grasmere, and took them back to school at the end of the holiday. She knew that all students' suitcases were opened and inspected when they returned to school, so she must have believed no one could find fault with these. She was wrong. Miss Hewitt, the headmistress, retained them without explanation until June. For the balance of her second year at Ethel Walker's, Helen was unaware that the books were circulating among the teachers, virtually all of whom were spinsters, and that Helen was suspect from then on.

Alice wrote letters to Helen throughout that semester. In one of them she said that her marriage was a mockery. "She wrote it naturally," Helen wrote in her diary, "but it's the first time she's said anything to me which fitted in with what the family says of her, that's she's remote, and that Crosby marriages turn out badly."

Helen was attracted to Alice because Alice liked her poems. Alice was the first adult to say they were good. Encouraged by this praise, Helen now began to show her poems to the teachers she liked. She left them on their desks. Most of the teachers remained silent; poetry wasn't in the curriculum and perhaps that was the reason why. But it could also have been because the teachers feared Helen was developing attachments. Only her English teacher, Mary Underhill, responded openly and told Helen she had talent. Miss Underhill's praise unleashed a flurry of new poems. Helen found opportunities to be with Miss Underhill when she felt depressed. "She knew I needed to talk," she wrote in her diary, "and she let me. I talked myself down and out."

Valentine's Day arrived and Helen asked Miss Underhill if she'd mind if she gave Miss Walker, the founder of the school, a valentine directly. Helen didn't want to hurt Miss Underhill's feelings and Miss Underhill seemed understanding. "There's candy for me in knowing you're giving Miss Walker one," she said. "I'm too old for such things. But do keep coming to my room to show me your poems when you want."

Later, Miss Underhill told Helen that Miss Walker had shown Helen's valentine to her. "It was so good you could almost sell it," she said. "I shall beat you if you don't keep on writing. You're getting better every day." Helen was excited by this unexpected encouragement. She now began to write daily notes to Miss Underhill, to which Miss Underhill replied. Miss Walker wrote a note also, and Helen began to feel dizzy. Two of her classmates told her on a single day that they were thrilled sitting next to her. "What *is* the matter with everyone?!" Helen asked her diary. "People like me!"

She was sixteen and her hormones were surely stirring. Pheromones may have been in the air. For some reason, Miss Underhill became agitated.

"You're making me nervous," she said to Helen. "You're always running up to me."

Helen decided she could have just as much fun keeping out of Miss Underhill's sight. "But," she wrote to herself, "I'm physically and mentally a wreck. I sat alone on the stairs reading Willa Cather's *The Lost Lady.*"

After lying low for a week, Helen sent another poem to Miss Underhill, who wrote back: "I lay awake thinking about you. I can't look you in the face. I see that you are writing your poems for me." And Helen wrote in her diary, "I have her number. A marvelous letter, as letters go, but I've laughed at her ever since. She jumped to too many conclusions and undoubtedly thinks that she seems more wonderful to me than she really does."

Then Helen felt disgusted with herself. She wanted literary recognition but didn't really like playing games. "I gave a poem to Miss Walker very shamefacedly and fled. Why I do things like that I wouldn't know. It's a fiendish desire for sympathy and contact." She had been touched affectionately only by the Shermans at their ranch in Montana. Everyone in her family and at school curtsied or shook hands, and didn't touch at all.

She immersed herself in extracurricular activities to take her mind off her encounters with her teachers. She finally found a sport in which she was welcomed: track. She made the team and went off in April with fourteen classmates to Rosemary Hall, a girls' school in Greenwich, Connecticut, to compete.

* * *

In early June, Maunsell came to Simsbury to collect Helen for the summer. She'd now completed her second year and would be a senior in the fall. They loaded his car with the help of seven girls: two heavy suitcases, two 'dressing bags,' a duffle bag, a bright pink laundry bag, her typewriter and tennis racket, and a pile of records. It was the first time she'd motored home, and she underlined the word "home" in her diary. This time, her belongings were going to Grasmere. The trip, a distance of seventy-four miles, took three hours.

Maunsell hired a spinster, Miss Green, to tutor Helen at Grasmere. They worked together mornings. Helen found it difficult to be agreeable. "I want to be alone," she wrote in her diary, "and not have to be nice to people who are being paid, and who are people I didn't choose." Miss Green told Maunsell about Helen's moodiness. They agreed to wait and see if it smoothed itself out.

The afternoons were more fun. Helen was almost seventeen. She joined the grownups for lunch. She played lawn tennis at a nearby club in Tivoli. Maunsell gave her a full-grown horse and bought a jumper for himself. They rode together. She changed for dinner, into an evening dress.

Alice Nelson came to Grasmere in July, on her annual trip to New Hampshire. This time, she brought her daughter Betty, then twelve. They stayed several nights. Helen wrote in her diary about the first evening, "She read more of my poems and talked to me, and once again came the old feeling of talking to someone who understood everything and who was wise and courageous."

The following evening Alice and Helen listened to "Liebeslied" on the Victrola before going upstairs. Betty had gone to her own room earlier. Alice invited Helen into her room to look at the full moon. Helen curled up in a red wrapper on the window seat. Alice stood where she could watch her face. "I tried not to show anything," Helen wrote, "and only ached inside." At 1:00 a.m. Betty slipped out of her bedroom down the hall and came into Alice's. Alice held her in her arms, and Helen never felt so lonely. Alice took Betty back to bed and then came to Helen and put her arm around her, the first person ever. "She who is so shy dared to do it," Helen wrote, "for it takes courage to give yourself away. And I, all hot and chokey and rigid, leant back, not at peace, for my whole self was aching, but I should have liked to pray. Her hair was that soft, and her hands so still."

Alice suggested bed, and Helen never opened her eyes. They walked down the hall together to Helen's room and Alice tucked her in. At Helen's suggestion, Alice took some of Helen's letters from classmates to her room to read in bed. Helen suffered supremely in her own bed. She crept back to Alice's room. The second Alice saw her, she turned off the light and Helen went to her bed, and Alice gave her more than anyone else had ever given.

"She put her arms around me, and gave me my first kiss on the mouth. I have never had such an electric shock since." Helen went back to her room at 4:00 a.m. and shivered in her bed. She was aching and burning, and asked in her diary whether it was natural or bestial. She didn't know.

The following day Helen avoided Alice, but every time she shut her eyes, she could feel her at her shoulder. She couldn't eat lunch and Alice seemed to know how she was feeling, for she asked whether it was because of her. The next morning Helen went out for three hours with a young man in a two-seater Packard roadster, while the others were in church. They talked about marriage and of his view that after initial love, it becomes a practical arrangement of living with someone who has the same outlook and views. Helen thought of Alice's confession that her marriage was a mockery and that she was tolerating it for the children.

Alice and her daughter, Betty, left the following morning. Helen waited for her letters. When her father went again to New York, as he did every week, she slept in the bedroom that had been Alice's. She worried about writing in her diary. "I can't read a single page of any diary I've written without wanting to tear it up, and throw it far, far away. And yet, it steadies one so to write things down. I wish life were more elemental, like the river, which in spite of brickyards and railroads is supremely unaware of civilization and remains as primitive and beautiful as in the year of creation."

Several letters arrived, and then an invitation to visit Alice in New Hampshire. Helen was incredibly naïve and showed it to Maunsell. She noticed his strange expression. Nevertheless, he said she could go. The tutor was given the week off and Helen went by train.

There was a long, careful packing of certain books and dresses and wrappers, a drive to Millerton station, and then an endless hours-long ride on a stuffy train. I worked over my poems and read "Not That It Matters" by A.A. Milne and checked off stations on the map and wondered if I ought to

WOMEN IN HELEN'S FAMILY TREE

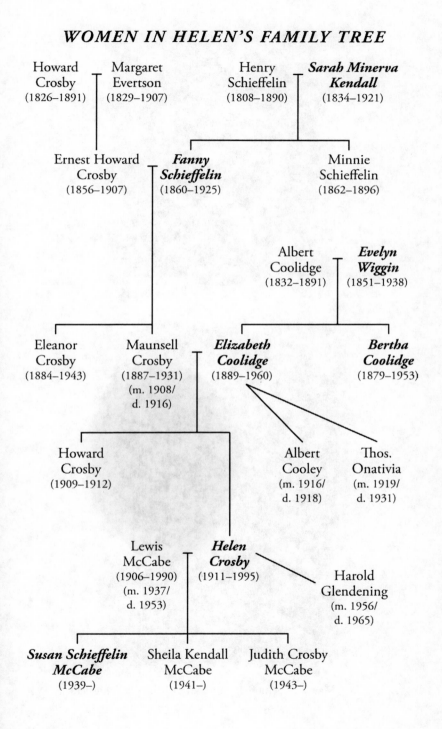

Henry Maunsell Schieffelin and Sarah Minerva Schieffelin

Minnie (left) and Fanny Schieffelin, 1870

The NYC house in which Howard Crosby, Ernest's father, was raised

665 Fifth Avenue, New York

Ernest Crosby and Fanny Schieffelin

Ernest Crosby with
his daughter, Eleanor

Fanny Crosby with her children,
Maunsell and Eleanor

Fanny Schieffelin Crosby (standing), Maunsell Schieffelin Crosby, Minnie
Schieffelin, Margaret Eleanor Crosby (seated left to right), circa 1894

Albert Leighton Coolidge and Elizabeth Evelyn Wiggin Coolidge

Elizabeth Coolidge

Elizabeth and Maunsell Crosby on their honeymoon

Maunsell Crosby with his Dutchess County neighbor Franklin Roosevelt

Helen Elizabeth Crosby, New York City,
before she went to Montana

Helen Elizabeth Crosby, 1920

Grasmere, Rhinebeck, New York

The Italian garden at Grasmere

Helen Crosby at Grasmere

Helen Crosby

Helen Crosby with Lewis McCabe
during their courtship in 1936

Lewis and Helen on their honeymoon in 1937

Elizabeth Coolidge
Oñativia in her last
passport photo, 1937

Bertha Coolidge, Elizabeth's sister, with her husband, Marshall Perry Slade,
at Woodston, their house in Mount Kisco, New York, 1941

Helen with Sue, Judy and Sheila, at 117 South Van Buren Street, Rockville, Maryland in 1945

Helen with Judy, Sheila and Sue in Stockholm, 1954. Sheila and Sue had their hair cut in Paris two weeks earlier

Sue with Helen at Sue's coming out dance in Washington, 1956

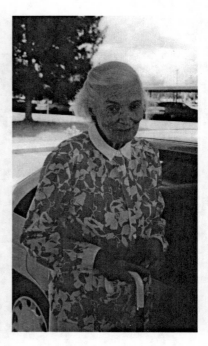

Helen in her apartment at 550 "N" Street, S.W. in Washington, D.C. in the late 1970s

Helen in 1994

Helen with her son-in-law, Al Gillotti, in Florida in 1994

get off the train at North Adams and run to a train returning home. Never have I known such misgiving. It wasn't my faith in Alice that was ruffled, it was my faith in me. I was even hanging back when it came to leaving the train. I was almost last getting off and saw her miles before she saw me. Then she led me into a taxi and talked all the way up the Mohawk Trail and the "hairpin turn," for of all wondrous places, they live at the top of it and crawl up and down it everyday.

Helen's tension ended when she found herself sitting on a porch listening to an English governess reading *Daddy Longlegs*, her favorite book from the Waltham School. Alice was sitting in the sun with her youngest son in her lap and her two older daughters at either shoulder. Then the two smaller boys came rushing up to whisper secrets in Helen's ear.

Supper was at six, the simplest farmhouse life, a Mr. Hoskins doing the farming and Mrs. Hoskins cooking. Alice and Helen walked afterwards. Alice kept trying to drop the children, who refused to be dropped, but Helen enjoyed the children's company. There were motionless aisles of pine and, a little beyond, birch trees glimmering through, while everywhere the ferns were tall and green. And then, wrote Helen, "came moments incognito—the moon just coming up, reflecting dimly through the corners of our room on plaster ceilings and low walls, the darkness—and my achings were almost beyond control. I was set off by her touching fingers."

Alice drove Helen to Cornish, New Hampshire, to visit Pig Parrish, Helen's Ethel Walker friend. Pig had an art studio, given to her by her father, Maxfield Parrish, and had begun to work in soapstone. Her father's studio was nearby, filled with paintings in its nooks and crannies. His bedroom was next to his studio. There was a room jammed with machinery downstairs, where he also worked. Helen came away dazzled by the vibrant colors and exotic lifestyle.

Another day they motored through Lenox to Stockbridge with Betty, Alice's oldest daughter, sitting between them. Betty was oblivious to any by-play. "Scenery had no thrill for me whatsoever," Helen wrote, "though those lovely suburban estates deserved it." They drove slowly, Alice wanting to go at as leisurely a pace as they could.

That night, Alice said, "What we are doing is wrong." But Helen didn't think they were doing anything wrong. In her diary she wrote, "We weren't *doing* anything. Her arm was around me and I was close to her bosom. And there we lay. Night after night we lay. And when we drove about in her car, I put my hand on her shoulder or on her leg, and she put hers on mine."

Then Alice took the subject further. "You don't know what you're doing. You shouldn't be doing this without a vision beyond."

"I do know what I'm doing. I love you and love being with you," Helen said. But she began to worry about whether Alice loved her more than she loved Alice, and she didn't want to hurt Alice.

Then the week was over, and Helen was thankful to escape. On the train she tried to sort it out in her diary:

A crush is one-sided love. A crush fulfilled is two in love. It ceases to be a crush. Now I at least know what I unconsciously wanted all last winter. And I know why it is wrong to have a crush, because that sort of love should be between man and woman. Isn't it wrong for two women to love each other physically? I'm too young, too inexperienced to know. I've never known a boy. Until I get away from women, get balanced, and can go back to them with the right proportions, I should stay away. Alice took something she shouldn't have. She knew what it was she was taking and thought that because I had mental knowledge of what was right and

wrong, and thought it all right, she could give and take. I
didn't know what she was taking. I won't ever really know.
Mother would turn over and die, because she is so attractive
to men that this happening to her daughter never occurred to
her. Stupid I have been. I reassured Alice so much that I can't
possibly blame her. I don't blame her. She was O.K. I was,
too. But my mind is working now, instead of my feelings.

When Helen's tutoring resumed, Miss Green seemed mysti-
fied by what appeared to be a sea change in Helen's tempera-
ment. From a moping adolescent, she'd become a wildly ener-
getic, reasonably sane child. Helen understood the change and
was happy about it. It could have marked the beginning of an
improved relationship with her father, for she was beginning
to understand the value of being kind. What happened next
became a turning point in her father's acceptance of her.

Miss Green told Helen that she'd noticed a difference in her.
What had happened in New Hampshire? Did Helen know what
the word homosexual meant? Helen did not. "Then, look it up
in the dictionary," Miss Green said, handing one to her.

Helen looked it up and it said, "The love of one member of
a sex for the same sex." Then Miss Green asked if Helen loved
Alice. Helen said she had. And then, Miss Green went downstairs and told Maunsell that Helen was a homosexual.

When she came back she told Helen she knew how she felt,
that she had had a choice so to be, but had decided against it,
and she advised Helen to do the same.

"It" couldn't have mattered less to Helen by this time. She
was totally bored, or else wrung out, by Alice.

The finale came when Alice returned to Grasmere at the
end of the summer. She waited in her room for Helen. Bolstered
by Miss Green's continuing advice, Helen knocked, entered, and
announced in what she described in her diary as her best ham
actor fashion, that she thought it best that they discontinue their

relationship. Alice smiled tenderly and said she understood. In due course she divorced her husband and went on to a more active lady in Washington.

Meanwhile, Helen was stuck, until her father's death three years later, with his mistrust. He suspected every visitor she had—but she didn't know this until after his death. Worst of all, he'd written Aunt Eleanor, in England, that Alice had seduced his daughter, and that she could never enter his house again. To her credit, Aunt Eleanor seemed not to be perturbed. She looked forward to introducing Helen to eligible young men from then on, whenever she could.

Helen, not aware of these behind-the-scene concerns, continued a desultory correspondence with Alice until Christmas, when a present arrived. Whatever bad thoughts Maunsell might have had could only have worsened. Alice sent the equivalent of a diamond necklace, only in sapphires. At his request, and quite willingly—she was shocked too—Helen bundled it into a little box and returned it—and never heard from Alice again, until she sent a wreath to Maunsell's funeral.

After returning to school in January, Helen wrote a poem, *Disillusioned,* in which she excoriated Alice:

> God damn your rotten love, I know it now.
> No one can break this knowledge from my hands
> And with it as a passive sinecure
> I will refuse your hurtling, free demands.
>
> How stupid you must be to hope I care.
> My half-gods you sent rolling to the earth
> But as for whole gods, do not dare
> To think you lit their flaming birth.
>
> You left me often making good excuse
> But I have wits at least and I could see

You played my love against another's waiting—
So suddenly I fled you, and went free.

I rather had you, much against your will.
In summer, loving me you lost your way
You seemed a trifle dazed when I preferred
Not prophecies of night, but bare-faced day.

There's no use asking me for old response.
I'm grateful for the things you taught so well
Which never should have been, but have not hurt
Because I have consigned your love to hell.

She didn't send the poem to Alice. She showed it instead to her teacher, Miss Underhill, who immediately assumed Helen had been raped. Helen gave Miss Underhill a second poem at the same time, called *From Thinking Oddly of M.U.:*

The wind had been flicking my face with frost
The moon had been hurtled high
The stars had been riding the gallant night
They swirled in a falling sky.

They seemed to be braving the universe
As I stood in the driving frost
And hate and love were an abstract thing
And Time was a word I lost.

And so as I stood, I lost desire
To stab at your eyes today.
The knowledge they bear are grievous swords
You prick at my wonted way.

When you used them last, they were torture things
That dragged me into your hell
But whatever you do from this time on
Is nothing that is not well.

I hated you once, I could love you now
I am free, I am free, I am free
For your words, and your eyes and your hands,
My dear, were lost in eternity.

Miss Underhill now believed that Helen had feelings for her
that went beyond the normal feelings of a student for a teacher,
and she became frightened.

* * *

Helen spent her final months at Ethel Walker's studying hard.
She was genuinely nervous about her grades. Maunsell and
Elizabeth were both insisting that she go to Bryn Mawr. Bryn
Mawr had already assured some of her classmates that they had
a place. Helen still wasn't sure, herself, about Bryn Mawr; she
thought she'd prefer Smith. She was counting on her extracurricular activities to help. She was editor of both the school
newspaper and the class of 1929 yearbook. She was voted "most
intellectual" and "most original" by her classmates—the latter
because of the French beret she now almost always wore.

Helen earned an honorable mention in English and Ancient
History, but was advised by Bryn Mawr that they didn't antici-
pate accepting her. Maunsell took an unexpectedly relaxed
attitude towards the situation but Elizabeth was upset. She
called Helen ungrateful and lazy and said the time had come
to wash her hands of her. She came to the school's "Certificate
of Completion" ceremony as a dutiful mother, in a Rolls Royce
borrowed from a client, and wrote Miss Haskell afterwards.
"Helen is all mixed up about rich and poor and brains and society, and why her father can't be like other fathers."

A "Certificate of Completion" was given to seniors when
they finished their course work, but the final Ethel Walker
diploma wasn't awarded until after College Boards were taken

two weeks later. During this period, the seniors were required to stay on campus. The regulation applied even though the students had technically graduated. They were not allowed to leave their dormitories after "lights out."

That June, in 1929, the days and nights were hot. The girls were eighteen years old and the taste of freedom was in their minds. Helen's bed was on a first-floor sleeping porch beside a window. One night, she'd gone to bed early. She woke up to find, one after the other, ten girls climbing over her bed and out the window. They were in their pajamas and giggling as girls do when they're suddenly deciding to be daring. They had one box of Hydrox cookies and were going to eat them in the hayfield. So, Helen followed.

Miss Underhill saw them. Helen saw her as well. She'd never seen Miss Underhill with her black hair down, and thought she looked like a witch. Miss Underhill begged the seniors to go back. The feeling of freedom was contagious and the seniors fled in every direction, further into the fields and down the main road. The plea from Miss Underhill was unheeded. The French teacher also saw the mayhem, and immediately told the headmistress, Miss Hewitt.

In her memoir, *The Evolution of a Psychiatrist,* Beulah Parker described what happened next:

> You can imagine the giggly excitement with which a group of nearly adult women enjoyed this delicious chase, but I don't think you can imagine what happened the next morning. We were called together in solemn ignominy, and told that what we had done was a heinous crime. We had no honor, we had no decency, and we were a disgrace to the school. For this reason, we would not receive our diplomas.
>
> Most of us had already been admitted to college, and lack of a diploma mattered to only a few, but the only girls who

actually graduated from the school that year were a few prefects and those who for some reason had gone home early.

That is why no money from the class of 1929 has gone into the alumnae fund for over fifty years, and that is why no money ever will.

Miss Hewitt believed Helen was the ringleader. "You were sent to Ethel Walker's to be sure you'd get into college, and that's the end of that. No college will accept you now," she said. Helen held back a smirk and didn't let on how much happier she was that this was the case. She didn't argue about being the ringleader, even though she'd been the last to leap through the window.

Helen was now free at last, and she burst out of the school with a desire for fun. It was her first summer without a tutor. She was accepted by Smith. She enjoyed a constant round of parties, dates, visits with friends in Maine and New Hampshire, and outings to New York with her father. The summer was marred only by one more set of misunderstandings—her father still not certain of her sexuality after Alice Nelson's visits, and letters from Miss Underhill now arriving at Grasmere. Maunsell knew Miss Underhill's name. The year before, Helen had mentioned her, seeking her father's advice on how she could avoid a teacher who seemed too interested in her. Maunsell didn't know that Helen's feelings for Miss Underhill had softened.

At the end of the school term, Miss Underhill went to New York where she had a job correcting College Board tests. She was a large Trojan woman, immensely intelligent, supporting her widowed mother on a miniature salary, and totally bitter. She wrote Helen that it was sweltering in the city, but she needed to be there for the work. Maunsell went, as he always did, to New York for two nights. Not thinking through the possible consequences, Helen invited Miss Underhill to Grasmere while he was away, without telling him. Miss Underhill sent a telegram, "Leaving on 3.13, breathlessly." Helen was so scared and excited she could hardly stand up afterwards.

Miss Underhill had grown up in a comfortable house in Boston. Her family fell on hard times, but before then, she'd had an opportunity to live in a cultured atmosphere. She got off the train wearing a neat brown ensemble, looking to Helen far from school-teacherish. She appeared to be completely at ease exploring Grasmere. She knew far more about Dresden china, rock gardens, and heart-shaped photograph frames than Helen. So they went peacefully from room to room, smoking, talking, sitting and being happy. Helen's hostile feelings toward Miss Underhill disappeared as she became more and more natural. "She loved my playing the piano," Helen wrote, "but then, she loved me."

Miss Underhill knew about Alice Nelson's relationship with Helen the year before. She understood the angry feelings expressed in Helen's poem condemning Alice to hell. She was certain Alice's overtures had been forced. Her desire was to free Helen from the "crust" of Alice.

"And glory be to God," Helen wrote after Miss Underhill's visit, "she did. Fingers light and impersonal, she gave me tenderness unlimited and quietly, and for the first time since last summer, I can't remember Alice, and feel clean and basic again. I learned her father was a surgeon, and all her life people have found that she had 'electricity' in her fingers, inherited from him, no doubt. I had cramps, headaches, one after the other, but the second she touched my forehead I could feel myself being drawn into her fingers. I doubt if she knew it—a pity—for it really is a gift, and an explanation of her."

During part of the ministrations, Helen went to the bathroom and tried to relieve her cramps by splashing in hot water in the bathtub. She kept the door open so they could talk. There was obvious tension, Helen realized, and she didn't want Miss

Underhill to see her; but on another level Helen also didn't know what she was coping with.

The following morning, Maunsell telephoned and said he was staying in New York one more night. Miss Underhill was packed to leave. Helen invited her to unpack—and although she resented the sudden knowledge that Helen's father didn't know she was there—Miss Underhill stayed. There was "none of the maudlin night time Alice business. This was affection suitable for daylight and a child, and did me so much good! I do feel so unutterably clean again."

Miss Underhill told Helen all about herself, of having spent two days in a convent with the intention of taking the veil, until she saw a young nun beating hysterically on the bars before an altar, and an old one dragged against her will to chapel. She spoke of her bed in her room on Dartmouth Street in Boston in back of her father's office, with a grand piano, and her mother whose Puritanism forbade her music lessons. She spoke of the fire engine house three doors away with great horses rushing out, and the street lamps shining all night. She spoke of the night the man she was going to marry broke up with her, and of the house in Brookline where she now had a room. And when she had finished speaking of these things, she read poetry to Helen, Emily Dickinson and Robert Frost, "and it was bliss."

After Miss Underhill left, Helen knew she couldn't "drop" her for anything. Why not have a sure haven once in a while, "someone who would treat you as, and only as, you wanted to be treated, and otherwise, not bother you or intrude?"

What never occurred to Helen was that the servants would tell her father that she'd had a guest. Maunsell never told Helen that they had told him, and the fact that she hadn't told him herself made it all the worse. Helen found out from the housekeeper at the end of the summer.

*　*　*

Many years later, Helen thought deeply about these experiences, as part of her psychoanalysis. She wondered whether her relatives weren't loaded for lesbianism, and somehow passed it on. She remembered her great-aunt Grace stroking her hair and saying, "How like a little boy you look." They were terribly isolated, intellectual women, Helen understood. She granted that they were far better educated by their fathers in those days than she was in college. She wrote in her journal that if *any* one of these adults had explained, specifically, what they had in mind, she would have become less and less interested in relationships with women and wouldn't have become, finally, a sitting duck for college lesbians, who went further than reading her poetry.

It was Helen's conclusion that if her mother had left her with Miss Haskell at the Cambridge-Haskell School, five blocks from Harvard Yard, she would soon have been going to dances just as the seniors did. She'd even made her first dress, for $1.50, out of brown silky material and an orange scarf, so that she could sit on the sidelines and watch the seniors with their favorite beaux. Not only had her mother forbidden such a dress, but subsequently, after two years of immersion in Boston culture, of every kind—with full access to the *Boston Transcript* (Helen cut out the poems and put them in scrapbooks)—and the symphony and the bookstores—she was removed once again, in her words, "to my fourth boarding school, the best, the most exclusive and the most isolated in the country."

In a small spiral notebook, Helen penned additional thoughts about her upbringing:

> While I was pulling sugar beets, and digging for potatoes, changing the chickens' bedding, collecting the eggs, and sitting on the wagon bench driving the horses as the corn was tossed into the wagon—in Miles City, Montana—my father

was sitting down to a three course dinner in a house with six servants.

My father, in his Victorian way, never realized that his daughter was longing for a mother's affection, which she never received. Instead, he let her stay in her mother's legal custody. Under my mother's spell of brilliance, and the camouflage of her charm, I never told my father, not once, of the beatings and constant humiliation I had received. I desperately wanted to be like her. I desperately wanted her approval. But whenever I succeeded in school, she denigrated and humiliated me.

He never questioned me about my mother. Silence was easy. But once he said, and it was the only time he mentioned her, "Never be like your mother." I didn't ask why.

My mother was so seldom kind I can remember every kind thing she tried to do for me. They number about a dozen. Or maybe, two dozen.

When my father said, "Never be like your mother," he had meant to be educating me about sex by warning me not to sleep with men injudiciously. To be sure I wouldn't, he drove his car forty feet behind a young man who came to drive me out, to see the camp where he was a counselor. Out and back. He did it with other suitors too. That didn't help either.

CHAPTER 10

Two weeks before Helen was to enter Smith, Maunsell called her into his study and showed her a letter he'd received from her mother. During the three years Helen had been at Ethel Walker's, Elizabeth had attempted to create a money-making news clipping service. Her idea was good: she planned to subscribe to more than twenty newspapers and provide her clients with news about their competitors. She'd persuaded a number of business executives to sign up, and for a while she seemed to be doing well. But gradually the clients fell away, deciding to hire in-house librarians, and Elizabeth once more was without money.

In her letter to Maunsell, Elizabeth said she no longer cared what Helen did with her life, or who "governed" her. Maunsell wanted to know Helen's feelings about the matter. He told her he would like to be her legal guardian. Would Helen agree? Helen said yes, and they went to New York the next day for hard bargaining with Elizabeth. Helen wrote of the experience, "after nineteen years, I sold myself to father. Mother was sweet and very pathetic."

After the meeting, Maunsell and Helen joined one of Maunsell's friends for an evening in New York. They tried four closed speakeasies, went to the friend's apartment for cocktails, then to the St. Regis roof "which was heavenly." They watched the German zeppelin "sail into view over lower Manhattan, and come straight towards us, apparently between skyscrapers. Then, turning towards Long Island, it grew bigger and bigger, and with a searchlight on its bottom, was unearthly and a stirring sight." At 11:45 p.m., Maunsell put Helen on a train to Windsor, Vermont. She crawled into an upper berth and slept.

Helen's Ethel Walker friend, Pig Parrish, lived in Cornish, New Hampshire, across the Connecticut River from Windsor. Pig met her at the station. Helen slept that afternoon. But then "life became real again. We looked at her father's paintings and had tea in a cubbyhole. After dinner a group of us went to a movie and drove sixty miles, too glorious for words! Shoulder to shoulder, humming, talking, silent, we went shooting head-long over roads, under a divine sky, then home and to sleep on a wide open porch." When she left at the end of the week, "Pig's father kissed me goodbye, privately and firmly, which pleased me, and I got on the train at White River Junction and Daddy met me in New York."

The following evening, Helen and Maunsell boarded a sleeper for Maine. They were to be the guests of Oliver Wagstaff, a distant cousin who had a summer house on Mt. Desert Island. Helen discovered some of her boarding school friends in Northeast Harbor, and bought a yellow evening dress to wear to a party with them one night. The following day, the parents of one of her friends hired a boat and invited her to come along.

> It was wondrous peaceful. We started at ten and came back at six, and never for a moment were we near enough other people to speak to them, or far away enough to be out of sight of land. We circled islands, with mountains always in sight, and other sailboats, and the water, grey like a hippopotamus skin, and open, like tiny fish mouths. The sun was seldom out, but when it did come shoving through, it formed rain-rays of light, and the sky was forever a changing sheet of greyness. We landed on Cranberry Island and built a fire,

scrambled eggs, let bacon splutter, and munched brownies. Wild roses grow in thickets of raspberries and goldenrod mixes with Queen Anne's lace and clover—for there seems to be only one month of real summer and everything comes out together.

The smell of black seaweed, and grasses, and paint and old wood is the most satisfactory one I know, and I'd like to live by the sea for that alone. Our captain was born of a novel. He had a paunch, and blue eyes, heavy red cheeks, old shoes, and a timeless expression, as he snuggled the tiller under one arm. I've never been so contented as I was, watching the gulls over his shoulder and the sail swelling above, tall as a house, and its tugging on the ropes and smooth beam. It gave me the same feeling as I had on the top of the hill at Cornish, of being over everything, and a part of it, and in an allotted, impersonal place, no need of anyone else, as if it were some sort of fulfillment of myself.

Gosh, how pleasant it is to shed inhibitions, and be able to say what one does or does not like. I think a picnic that is posted for a petting party is the only thing I didn't like. It's like putting male and female dogs together.

And then the summer 1929 was over, and it was time for Smith. Maunsell drove her to Northampton, over much the same route as she'd driven with him from summer camp the first time they met. Helen immediately fell in love with the town and campus. She had a room at 150 Elm Street and wrote about her first weeks with enthusiasm. How different it was from Simsbury! She could walk to bookstores again. Her first purchases were Blake's poems and Voltaire's *Candide,* and "piles of expensive history books." She tried out for the freshman choir and was invited to join, but resigned two months later. "I want to spend all my time reading," she wrote in her diary. "I've read Willa Cather and W. Somerset Maugham and Aldous Huxley—and fifty pages of history, and I liked it!"

There were ample opportunities to explore the country-side surrounding Northampton. "We drove along the river and found it incredibly lovely." She was introduced to alcohol. She'd known her mother drank, but had not drunk alcohol herself. Now she drank with abandon: "cocktails and sauternes," "whisky with Eileen," "sauternes in Kate's room," "much liquor, much smoke," "cocktails, sherry and apricot brandy at dinner," "Chablis, burgundy, rum, and rye." She also noted in her diary: "Hangover."

Helen was once again surrounded almost entirely by women, both students and faculty. She was attracted to some of her classmates. Towards the end of her freshman year she wrote in her diary of an incident with a classmate named Edda. "I walked with Edda. Stopped for view. Too much of a goodbye kiss. Upset. Soap & water."

Elizabeth, all this time, was arranging a coming-out party for Helen in New York. Maunsell now recognized the need to help financially, and paid for several evening dresses and earrings made to order. Helen traveled to New York many times that winter and met many young men. Some came to see her at Smith, mostly from Yale and Amherst.

Pig was still at Ethel Walker's, finishing her senior year; but she and Helen saw each other often. She was accepted by Smith and they spent much of the summer of 1930 together. By the time Pig arrived in Northampton that September, they were inseparable.

Helen's relationship with young men remained chaste, but they nonetheless bothered Pig. "P is furious when letters come from beaux," Helen wrote. And then, "P came across." "No P until 10pm." "P came in the evening. Neither my feelings or brain involved. I am trying to fight it through, to what I don't know." "Kiss, can't you?—Relax, won't you!" "P feeds me.

Kept woman." "Wonder if I'll ever be ashamed of myself, if I'm not now?"

* * *

Early in the winter of 1931, during Helen's sophomore year, Maunsell went to the Rhinebeck hospital for what he thought would be a simple appendectomy. He was discharged shortly afterwards. A week later, he contracted pneumonia. His condition worsened and he was readmitted. Helen, who hadn't known about the operation, was summoned on February 10th. "He was in a delirium. Ghastly breathing." The following day he took another turn for the worse. Daisy Suckley, the long-time Rhinebeck family friend, stayed with Helen throughout, and Ludlow Griscom, Maunsell's ornithologist friend, came from Boston. On February 12th at 5:30 a.m, Maunsell died. Pig arrived from Smith and Helen "slept, and slept, absolutely exhausted." Daisy and Pig helped her choose prayers and hymns for the service, which took place on February 14th, Maunsell's forty-fourth birthday. Helen was nineteen, and had known her father for just eleven years.

The following day, the will was read and Helen learned that her father had left all his money to Oliver Wagstaff, the Harvard bachelor whose house on Mt. Desert Island she had visited the summer before. Maunsell had never felt comfortable about his financial arrangement with Elizabeth. He'd concluded that the only way to prevent her from obtaining his money would be to assure that it went to someone other than Helen.

The will consisted of just one paragraph. Maunsell left to Oliver Wagstaff all his stocks and bonds and rental properties in Lower Manhattan. Helen inherited Grasmere, but no funds to manage it. If she needed money, she would have to have Oliver Wagstaff's approval. She was left not even the proverbial one dollar which would have made the will legal. The newspapers went wild. Greatly exaggerating the size of Maunsell's estate, putting it in the millions, they reported that "Boyfriend Leaves Boyfriend All."

Besides the will, there were three pages of secret instructions to Wagstaff. These proved more shattering to him than they did to Helen, accustomed as she was to her divorced mother's three ex-marriages. There was, finally revealed now, a common law wife, living on Riverside Drive in New York, who had been promised a lifetime income. No one had ever had an inkling of her fourteen-year existence; but she was on the telephone with her demands and proof even before the funeral. So was Elizabeth, who wanted it all, because Helen was the presumed heiress and still a minor. Because they didn't want another headline, "Girlfriend Gets One Third," Oliver Wagstaff agreed to send the common law wife a large monthly check, twice what Helen was to get as an allowance.

In the three-page letter, Maunsell wrote that he had reason to suspect Elizabeth was capable of injuring Helen, hence the unprecedented bequest to Wagstaff whom he trusted to care for his daughter. Eventually, Maunsell's sister, Eleanor, came from England and talked Elizabeth into letting the courts handle it without a confrontation from her. At a cost of $8,000, four Harvard lawyers escorted Helen to the Poughkeepsie Court House where the judge in approximately sixty seconds threw out the will and set in its place a trust for Helen, with Wagstaff as executor until Helen was adjudged fit to assume ownership. The agreement stipulated that Helen was to have no communication with her mother.

Helen was uncomfortable with Oliver Wagstaff but there was no way to be free of him. Of all her father's friends, she felt he was the least suitable. He was heavy-set and unattractive, with a falsetto voice and on his way to alcoholism. To his credit, Wagstaff himself thought the appointment was wrong.

He unloaded the responsibility of sending money to the common law wife onto Helen; and in all the years this arrangement lasted, Helen never met her.

Helen returned to Smith after Maunsell's funeral but found it hard to concentrate. She was faced with immediate questions about Grasmere. It was the middle of the Depression, and impossible to make ends meet. Even the apple orchard had ceased to earn money. She sought advice from a professor at Smith, telling him the circumstances of her life, that her father had died, that she had a mother who worked in New York, and a paternal aunt who lived in England. After the conversation, Helen, who'd decided she couldn't entirely agree to the trust's stipulation that she not be in contact with her mother, wrote Elizabeth.

> I went to the head of the Government department and asked him what to do with my life. He'd never laid eyes on me before, so he assumed that I was emotionally irresponsible and told me I should live with my aunt in England. When he then saw me with glasses on, he told me to finish here. I was trying to get back to France but there's no use playing that game anymore, because there's no money coming in.
>
> After a great deal of talking with "college authorities" I've decided not to come back next year. It's no good sitting here and worrying about Rhinebeck. I'm going there, and I'm going to settle it once and for all. And give myself two years to get farm and education on a financial basis. It won't interfere with my finishing here, or at a university year after next. But I am just getting into such a state that my sentences run backwards, and finally the authorities told me to clear out with their blessing. It didn't do me or the farm any good to have to be back here at 8:30 am on April 6th, when I had an offer to sell 150 acres on April 5th, and couldn't do anything about it.

Helen left Smith at the end of her sophomore year and spent the next two years living on the estate. She kept up with several close classmates but also began to go out with young men from Rhinebeck, who presented themselves as suitors, but didn't arouse her romantically. They took note of the large house and the acres of land, and proclaimed she must be rich. Helen protested she wasn't, but they didn't believe her.

Grasmere was in serious trouble. Some of the ponds had become polluted. The cows developed Bang's disease and had to be auctioned off. Her main companions, the ones she valued most, were the workers on the estate, who could offer advice but not money. Dexter Burroughs, the superintendent, told her Maunsell had been reluctant to invest in new equipment. She worked with Mr. Burroughs and the others in the gardens and on the land, and she gave up caring about the condition of her hands.

Oliver Wagstaff wasn't entirely unsympathetic and saw the difficulty of the situation. He advised Helen to visit her aunt, Lady Huntingfield, in England, to get away and have a rest. He offered to write a check from the trust. Lord Huntingfield proposed a cruise along the eastern coast of Africa. Helen agreed to both, remembering how happy she'd been when she traveled with her father. She was ready for a change of scene. She left Grasmere in the hands of the superintendent and sailed in January of 1933. She sent Daisy Suckley a postcard from Mombasa: "It's the most exciting part of the world I've ever been in—tremendous stretches of sea and land and people." When the Africa trip ended, she returned to England. It was spring. She was twenty-two and an attractive young woman, with soft brown hair, high cheekbones, a slim figure, and a fashionable style of dressing, learned from college friends. And while she'd been aroused by some of these women, she was still technically a virgin.

CHAPTER 11

HELEN DOCKED IN SOUTHAMPTON and went by train to her aunt's large house in East Anglia. They had a good visit together, but Helen didn't want to linger in the rural countryside. She wanted to explore London. Lady Huntingfield found her a small flat at 9 Park Place near Green Park in Mayfair, and arranged introductions to young people.

It was a beautiful spring, with trees coming into leaf and white clouds scuttling across the open blue sky, and Helen walked in London every day. She found herself sought after, and enjoyed night after night going to the theater and dining in restaurants. For the rest of her life, she would wonder whether, if she made one fateful mistake, it might have been her decision not to encourage a proposal of marriage from the young American she met there, a man whose lifetime work would have taken them to England often.

The young American was Jack Heinz, grandson of H. J. Heinz, founder of one of the world's largest producers of processed foods. Helen wrote Daisy Suckley: "My aunt introduced me to one J. Heinz (son of the 'pickle man') and every night I've been in London, he has taken me out." Jack was three years older, a graduate of Yale, visiting England to learn the international side of his family's business. He had classic good looks and a winning smile. Helen was attracted to him, and he to her.

They saw each other for two months, broken only when Helen went to Paris for a week to travel with a friend from Smith.

During this time in London, Helen didn't wear her eyeglasses. She put them on only when she had to. Her mother and some of her teachers at Ethel Walker's had imbued her with the belief that eyeglasses made her ugly.

Here, in the third short story of Helen's that I found, is what happened with Jack Heinz in the spring of 1933. She writes the story in hindsight, placing herself in the Church of the Messiah in Rhinebeck two years later, and learning that Jack Heinz was about to be married to someone else.

She wondered if anyone in the Rhinebeck church would notice her if she took her eyeglasses off. While the choir filed into the chancel soothing the Episcopalian gloom with their monkish purple caps and white surplices, Helen realized that for once in her life she felt a genuine nostalgia. Hitherto, every emotion she had had for the remembrance of things past had been accompanied by a sense of belief in the future. Nothing she had turned down had been worth the promise of an unknown future. To all proposals of marriage, she had been able to laugh gently and sympathetically, and had been able still to smile when her seemingly inconsolable suitors had mailed her announcements of their engagement to somebody else.

But there was one man who had never asked her to marry him, because she had laughed gently, a little ahead of time, and now, she found that because of those unsaid words, her affair with him remained unresolved, endlessly tormenting. That she would have said "no" if he had asked her seemed reasonably certain, but her torment lay in the fact that she was not entirely sure that she could have turned him down. And now, seen two years later, from a point of view sharpened by a constant battle with taxes due, and mortgage interest, and from her knowledge of less desirable acquaintances, she had begun to think of him as the person she could turn back to, if worse came to worst. If no one else asked her, if the rents from a Broadway property came to an end. But not if she lost her looks. She knew that Jack was not the sort of a man to love a woman with her spectacles on.

Her ideal had been a man of intelligence and charm, who would like her mildly bookish appearance and shy, reclusive, satiric wit. There had been men who had told her that her cheek bones were admirably proportioned for wearing spectacles, that they made her look distinguished, but however charming these men were, and however well-read, even into Hardy's *Dynasts*, volubly discussed over a third martini, they were usually more adept in rationalizing themselves into how *au fait* it would be to live on her money, rather than in offering her any advantage from theirs. When she had met Jack she still thought she preferred charm to money in a husband. The charmers were usually charming, and those who had money had an ability to make good husbands and keep their wives moderately contented.

Helen had been to England and returned to Grasmere. She'd returned to the custom of going to church on Sunday. For the first time since her father's death she was finding it peaceful and comforting, rather than a human makeshift stabling with little ironies. She still wanted to smile at the communion of saints, the forgiveness of sins, but the sermon today was unusually good, on the subject of duty. It was better to be in a church than sailing on the *Normandie* with Jack. Or was it, she wondered: was it preferable to clutch the hymnal and sing "Jesus, lover of my soul," than be in the bridal suite, dancing with Jack, having him make love to her, carefully and tenderly? Joan, his new bride, was a lucky girl—Jack would make her a good husband, the men in his family always made good husbands. Helen wondered if she really loved him.

Helen hadn't been thinking of Jack since her return. She let their relationship drop from her heart into the perspective of the past. But the Rhinebeck minister's wife had been brought up in Pittsburgh and had known Jack's family for many years, and had heard that Helen had been "going around" with him when she'd been in England after her father's death. The minister's wife, Mrs. Travers, was a kindly, vital, talkative woman. A few weeks earlier, she'd received an invitation to Jack's wedding to Joan and asked whether Helen, who hadn't, wished she could be there. At that moment Helen realized it was a queer sort of music she'd been called to face. "No," she said, "and I wouldn't want to see Joan wearing white gardenias." Jack had given her gardenias in London.

"Oh," said Mrs. Travers, "it won't be gardenias."

"That's right," said Helen, "it will be white orchids. But I don't think I'd want to go."

No, she couldn't face St. Bartholomew's, carpets rolled to the curb, the reception at the River Club, and the charming young men she wouldn't be able to see unless she wore her spectacles. With spectacles on, she'd look more than ever like a "good old" friend. She wasn't afraid to meet Joan for the first time, in a reception line. It was the remembrance of Jack saying, "Darling, you can have everything you can possibly want, if you'll only love me." She had said she didn't want him. At the time she was more interested in love, excitement, and intellect, than peace, paid mortgages and placidity. Jack did light up when he saw a collection of green sherry glasses and port, but that wasn't enough. His eyes were too close together, he was nervous, and a little flat in his social manner, as of the third generation of meat packers. But he was generous, questioning, solicitous, and didn't drink too much. What man would ever be more? There was Bill with his resonant voice and professional knowledge, but inclined to be boring. There was the earnestness of Bob and his romantic yearnings for her, but he began all his sentences in an adolescent muddle and confined them to baseball performances.

Perhaps the whole trouble had been that given London in April and May for an affair, if you were two young Americans your personalities hardly entered into it. Helen, instead of finishing Smith, had been sent abroad by her trustee. Her English aunt had introduced her to Jack at a luncheon and he'd asked her out to dinner and the theater. She was living in a dingy little room off St. James's and spent her time looking for odds and ends and antiquities. Jack's invitation was manna in the usual wilderness. She put on her evening dress that left no questions to be asked—a brilliant fuchsia crepe—and paid for her dinner by being amusing. Jack found her quaint. She found him simply a man in a dinner coat, with a spectacular little car, and an adequate supply of conversation. It was all that one had ever wanted, and although a comparatively simple state of affairs to most of her relatives, it was little short of a miracle to her. She had been practically born in spectacles, and boarding schools and camp and college had been her straight and wholesome fare. Suddenly, here she was, at seventy miles an hour, heading for the dawn, in an English April, with a desirable young man. It was too perfect to have anything to do with life. It was good Red Book fiction, admirable Metro-Goldwyn.

She discussed it with him. She explained about schools and spectacles. He said she had a lovely profile. She said yes, but without them she hadn't seen any of the play that evening. They parked facing a pond, soft with a low mist. The pond was silent except for a quacking duck. He put his arm around her. "I'm alone with God, the pond, and the duck," she said, "and please don't."

He drove her back to London and came up to her room. She let him soothe and caress her, and was agreeably surprised to find that all men are not avid as the tabloids led one to believe. It was, in fact, a pleasure, and sufficiently platonic. He left at seven a.m. and gave the doorman a pound. He called for her the next evening, with gardenias, and they went to a Hungarian restaurant, mad with music and domestic with families. They treated each day of that week as an epoch of that spring. Neither families, nor friends, nor past, nor future was a consideration. He was to be Prince Charming, she was to be the ugly duckling, with her glasses off, doing all the things she'd read about in novels, with the right person to pay for it, and always with gardenias. He took her to his apartment and introduced her, over five o'clock sherry, to other estimable young men, who accepted her as mistress of the arts of society and seduction, since young Jack was sponsoring her. She had leapt from a vacuum to a spot-light. She learned to put her glasses on as a joke for them to see what she really looked like—and so that she could see, for a moment, which of them was most worthy of her considera-tion. She left it when she went to join a school friend in Paris. She went on a last drive in the little car filled with luggage, the top down, Jack driving fast, and honking, edging mirac-ulously between buses, while London strollers grinned at their ridiculous display. It was a *fait accompli*. It was goodbye.

But Jack wrote her in Paris. He wrote about the women in Manchester, the charms of Birmingham, and wrote pain-fully vulgar jokes. When she found herself back in London, she telephoned him. He was out. She went to the theater and found a note when she came in at eleven. She rang and he came bouncing and shouting through the door, "Darling, whatever are you doing! My God, I'm glad you're here." And he came to kiss. But inadvertently the fool, she said "No, no more, I don't know why I phoned, because neither of us is in love. It's just a convenience to both of us, but I do like to see you."

"Oh my God," Jack said, "You would say something like that. I thought I didn't care about you either, but I missed you like hell when you were gone. I was coming to Paris to see you. I was much more interested than I knew. I've been nearly crazy since I got your message, waiting. And then you say, 'it's just a convenience.' Darling, you could have anything in the world you wanted, if you only loved me, but I see you don't. I'll drop it. It does something queer to me."

And they had dropped it. They had gone as before, seeing each other every evening for two months, but he never mentioned love again. He seemed to have something a little chilled about him if they approached it, as if her moment for their usual honesty had been too perfectly timed, too psychologically explicit, for the romantic hour of a meeting. She was conscious more than ever of keeping the quintessence of their association on an impersonal plane. She knew his friends thought she was his mistress, but she was never, quite. She was too schoolgirl, too consciously saving herself for a more realistically woven future. Their hometowns were too separate, their interests (his business, hers literature) too varied for ultimate contact. All the time she was serving cocktails to his friends, she faced the photograph of the girl he had really loved, Joan, the girl he had wanted for his wife. But Joan had refused him. Helen was rebound. That was another reason for not taking advantage of him.

Now she thought—Helen, rebounds be damned. Here she was kneeling in Sunday church, wearing a dress she paid for by taking in paying guests at Grasmere. Wearing her only pair of white gloves. Actually wearing them, as against carrying them, because her hands were a mess from picking wild strawberries and hulling them for jam, from thinning beets, and from cutting dead roses. While Joan had a new trousseau and was in the bridal suite of the *Normandie*. Helen didn't think Joan loved him anymore than she did. But he was easy to be fond of. But she realized that even if she'd married him, he might still have wanted Joan.

He'd come to Grasmere, a year after she'd left England. He said he'd thought her description of it had been impossible. He was impressed. The halls were as big, the portraits as portentous, and the gardens as lovely as London's. It was a Hudson River estate, and even if one had no more money, it gave one more than it took away. Jack saw she really had come home to live in a house she had to scrub and scrape over, to keep. He knew she had something deep in her background which had made it impossible for her to see him as anything except a Metro-Goldwyn hero. She had more to lose than he had to give. And he stood on the stairway and said, "If I had asked you to marry me, would you have?" And she said, slowly, "No."

She didn't know if that kept him from asking, or if their situation did. She didn't know whether she'd marry him now or not. But she thought she could use a Metro-Goldwyn hero and knew she'd make him a good wife.

Rebounds be damned. Her heart ached for something just the same. Jesus, lover of her soul! "Faith is the guiding principle. An automobile without an engine runs downhill." So did Grasmere without money. And what profiteth her to thin beets, when once upon a time she had a lovely profile, and white gardenias.

While the choir marched sonorously from the nave, and the good women of Rhinebeck rose from their knees, a congregant nudged Helen and said, "Go see Mrs. Travers, before she gets out. She went to the wedding. She's dying to tell you. And Joan wore white orchids."

CHAPTER 12

IT WAS A BLOW TO ELIZABETH when Maunsell died and she realized she'd never have any of his capital. She was still smarting from her older sister Bertha's marriage, at the age of fifty, to a millionaire. Elizabeth's clipping service had failed, and now she tried another kind of business. She knew about developments in the field of transportation, especially motor cars, and approached several prestigious magazines and newspapers about becoming their transportation columnist. She renewed her acquaintance with Maxwell Perkins, now an editor at Scribners, and he encouraged her. She impressed an editor at the *New York Times* with her ability to make car repairs and change tires by herself, and he offered her a byline. Her first published piece was a witty description of wives in the suburbs driving their husbands to commuter trains, still in their nightgowns. She wrote another about the difficulties rich people have finding landing spots for their private airplanes. She was invited to write for the Saturday Evening Post. Buoyed, she wrote Miss Haskell, "They say I could go back to Boston and be received, somehow."

Her income, however, remained marginal, because she didn't live within her means. She was unsure what she could count on from Helen. "Miss Crosby," she wrote Miss Haskell, "is entirely self-contained and to outward appearances needs me not. She hasn't changed since she was three years old. Nor have I. If only someone wanted me." Then she wrote introspectively:

> It's dreadful for you to be inundated with my letters, but I think I'd better. What the matter is, is these things.
>
> I'm lonely. No one comes in and no one telephones, and it can't be helped. They don't know about me. They come when they want to. Then things pile up. It isn't ordered, and it can't be ordered, because I have too many lines out.
>
> Yesterday I signed up the Alexander Hamilton Institute for a little research, and they gave me some good leads, and I may get book reviewing for the *New Yorker*. All that is good.
>
> It's this dreadful mélange, and it's no good my saying I'll do this or that and nothing else. I'm too many kinds of a person to be able to pursue something in single-trackedness. I have to keep fighting down all the sentimental things, and it makes me sick, ill. Miss Mary, I ache with trying.

Through a connection, she was invited to write book reviews for the *Mayflower Log* in Washington, D.C. for fifty dollars a month. This led to an offer to write weekly reviews for *The Outlook*, at twenty-five dollars each. But she was still short of money, and still borrowed from Miss Haskell. It was almost always to cover her Colony Club dues. A typical thank you note was this:

> When June comes, if I pay back $100, will that do for this time? I don't know whether I'd rather have it off my mind, and pay it all, or whether I'd feel better to get a new hat and dress, and have a chair recovered, and get another bust supporter and a new handbag. I shall have to keep a hundred in the bank.
>
> I'm trying to do some stories for Rolls Royce, not much pay, and not, alas, much inspiration on my part. Or maybe I want to do them too well. But I am sort of sodden, not unhappy, but sodden. No point to anything. No lift. That's

why I thought maybe the chair and the dress. I can't even get any satisfaction doing good to others, because they need money, most.

Elizabeth had another growing concern: she wasn't physically well. She'd begun to hemorrhage when she had her period, and her periods were coming more frequently. She had no money for a doctor and prayed each night that God would "please make it dry up by itself, so I won't have to have an operation." She worried that she might be aging too quickly. "I look like Duse wracked by disease when I meet other women." She tried to take to heart Miss Haskell's advice that she consider becoming a private cook, but the advice annoyed her. She didn't think she needed, ever, to descend so low. She wrote Miss Haskell her thoughts:

> I've talked to a new lot of men, and they all say that they'd keep at it, stay here, twiddle with it till I get it right. So that's how I feel today. I may feel entirely different tomorrow. I have got something to sell, my writing talent, and I could never be in the class of the ordinary business venture along stereotyped lines.

She made a final move in New York to 122 East 57th Street. "This place is cheaper and lighter and has a fireplace," she wrote Miss Haskell.

> . . . and is an equally good address and I have the same telephone number. I think the augury is good. But I spent Sunday in Connecticut, and it does seem sort of silly to live in this vile town, with all that lovely country not being lived in.

Six weeks later she asked Miss Haskell for money again. The book reviews didn't pay enough. Miss Haskell begged her to see the light: Elizabeth must find another way to support herself. She couldn't keep living on hope and the help of friends.

True to her nature, which was to make decisions quickly, Elizabeth decided to move to Maine. Her Coolidge family had one last asset, a large house in Alfred that was under lease to a tenant. It was in her mother's name, but her mother, now in her eighties, could no longer maintain it. Mrs. Coolidge signed the house over to Elizabeth, and Elizabeth set out to become a hotelier.

The house, sitting directly on the road from Portland, Maine to Rochester, New Hampshire, had much to offer. Built seventy-five years earlier, it was shaded by elms. It was across the street from the courthouse, three miles from three lakes, and sixteen miles from the ocean. There were thirty-one mostly furnished rooms on three floors.

Elizabeth, as always, had no doubts about her ability to succeed. She asked General Atterbury, who'd sponsored her earlier year on her own, to join her as an investor. He declined. She approached several friends in New York but they declined as well. She went ahead by herself. She would work on rebuilding her newsclipping service and write book reviews from Maine while waiting for the hotel to establish itself.

Helen, wanting to help her mother, arranged for Elizabeth to receive quarterly payments of one hundred dollars, on the condition that Elizabeth not again ask for more. Elizabeth accepted the money. She resigned from the Colony Club. In one of the few letters she wrote Helen from Maine, she said she'd visited the court house in Alfred to look at portraits of two of their ancestors, "Grandpa" Wiggin and Samuel Bradley, "and they looked good."

That the hotel would be profitable was never even a remote possibility. Alfred, in the southern part of Maine, wasn't heavily visited. The court was in session only in January, May, and

September. The country was still in the Depression. Day followed day and there was no sign of life in the house. There are bits and pieces of scribbled-on paper that suggest Elizabeth sat much of the time staring out the window, possibly drinking, certainly smoking. She finally realized that the hotel wasn't going to succeed. One of General Atterbury's friends sent a letter inviting her to a party in Philadelphia. She wrote back, explaining why she couldn't attend:

> It's getting dreadfully complicated. If I had one penny in the world, it would be easier, but then the whole world wouldn't be waiting with bated breath to observe whether or not I succeed. I haven't had any rest recently and I can't be away from my clipping service too long. What I am trying to say is, that I can't sell the Alfred House on a Friday and go to your party on a Monday, and I don't know which is most important. My health, I expect. Both would do it good.
>
> Anyway, my hair still looks like the Mediterranean side of the Rock of Gibralter. I have always felt that a white wig was the solution, but they're so hot.
>
> It does seem a pity to me, that when I can fix the whole United States perfectly comfortably with hot and cold water, in about three minutes, that people should so resolutely oppose me all my life. It's all very well to be regarded as a comic, but look what happened to Jimmy Walker.

Everything came to an end on January 27, 1934. A Justice of the Peace filed a complaint that Elizabeth Oñativia was insane. Two selectmen signed an order empowering a constable to take her into custody. She was committed the following day to the Augusta State Hospital. She was discharged March 23rd. She returned to New York and was briefly admitted to two hospitals there. The first was in Rockland County, the second in Poughkeepsie—the same institution Daisy Suckley had pointed out to Elizabeth in the early 1900s, when she took Elizabeth, as a new bride at Grasmere, on a tour of Poughkeepsie.

Elizabeth was in custody for twenty-two weeks. As soon as she was released, she told Miss Haskell what had happened: "I got so disgusted with the dirt and filth at Alfred House that I just went mad and broke windows—grand! But it's enough to make me sell the house and move. I have my job reviewing books for *The Washingtonian: The Magazine of the National Capital*. I'm going to be fine." She moved to Washington, where she again knew no one. Over the next three years, she lived at 1313 Massachusetts Avenue, N.W., 1256 31st Street, N.W., and 1503 28th Street, N.W. *The Washingtonian* went into bankruptcy and she lost her one meaningful job. She sent a despairing note to Helen:

> I think I shall get a placard saying,
> "I am the daughter of Mrs. A. L. Coolidge.
> "I am the sister of Mrs. Marshall P. Slade.
> "I am boycotted from getting work.
> "I need clothes and a job.
> "PLEASE HELP ME!"

Helen didn't. She wanted nothing more to do with her mother.

* * *

Helen entered Vassar College in the fall of 1934, resuming the studies she'd interrupted when she left Smith. She understood that Vassar would let her graduate in 1935, and she made several good friends in this class. Then Vassar decided that her credits from Smith were insufficient, and that her "life work" in the interim didn't satisfy the academic requirements. Just as had happened at Ethel Walker's, she was told she'd have to study another year. She became a member of the class of 1936. She lived off campus in a rented room and commuted in a roadster to Grasmere on weekends. She never experienced the continuity of undergraduate life and continuing friendships that Edward Sheldon, her father's friend, had said Helen should have.

A few months after Elizabeth lost her job in Washington, Helen received a letter at Vassar. Dated January 16, 1936, it was from an editor at *The Washington Post:*

Dear Miss Crosby,

For weeks and weeks I have delayed in writing to you hoping I might hear something from Mrs. Oñativia. One of her lawyers came out to see me and said my claims were justified. Beyond that, no word.

I am not being very clear though, am I? You see, your mother rented the two back rooms of my apartment, 1503 28th Street, NW, and remained there during part of October and November. One day when I came home from the office I found everything topsy turvy. It really was dreadful. Bottles, a large picture, and a lamp had all been thrown from the window. An old fashioned grandfather rocker was simply smashed to pieces, the phone wire was cut, the electric extension wires also, the wallpaper peeled off in some places and scribbled over in others, books out of the bookcases, the wall mirror under the studio couch, the leg of our old spool bed whittled with a knife, an old Oriental drape torn, the shade in the bathroom window torn, the shade in the living room down and thrown away, my clock and smoking stand precariously balanced on the window sill, and heaven knows what. Glasses—some that made up a set—received for a wedding present—were broken. A three panel screen which had stood in her bedroom also found its way out of the window. Paper had been stuck into the radiator and set fire to. I can assure you the whole episode was nightmarish.

I feel dreadfully sorry about the whole affair and have hated to press matters especially during the Christmas season.

Now, however, editors are pressing me to take action. Some of the items I have not been able to take care of for economic reasons.

Please understand how much I dislike calling this unpleasant matter to your attention but I am simply up in the air about what to do and very badly in need of some assurance Mrs. Oñativia will make good the damages.

Very truly yours,
Frances M. von Lewinski

The trail I've followed in my attempt to get to know my grandmother ends here. No wonder Helen didn't talk about her. I wrote the medical records office at the Hudson River State Hospital, now called the Hudson River Psychiatric Center. Confidentiality laws prevented the hospital from providing more than limited information, but I was grateful for the details they could confirm:

Mrs. Oñativia was originally admitted to the Augusta State Hospital, Maine on January 28, 1934 and discharged March 23, 1934. She was then admitted to Rockland Psychiatric Center on April 6, 1934 and transferred to Hudson River Psychiatric Center on July 11, 1934. She was released various times to live in the community with either her mother or her daughter. Each time she needed to be returned to the hospital because of her paranoid thinking that people were entering her room and going through her belongings. She would begin to destroy furniture and become rehospitalized. The last time she was readmitted to Hudson River was on October 18, 1939 through the petition of Helen Crosby because she was acting irrational and throwing things out of the windows. She remained at Hudson River until her death on September 5, 1960.

CHAPTER 13

ONE WEEKEND AT GRASMERE while Helen was a senior at Vassar, she had a long conversation with Dexter Burroughs, the farm superintendent who succeeded Jacob V. Beach, his father-in-law, as superintendent. She liked him enormously and had hesitated to talk to him about financial matters. She now had no choice. There was no money. He counseled selling. While Grasmere had always managed to 'get by' with infusions of Schieffelin money, the Depression made things different. And, he said, the things Helen was dealing with were normally handled by men.

Helen reflected on his advice, writing in her diary that in the end Grasmere was "translucently beautiful, too good to keep, unless you could work for it, buy it lawn mowers, and have garden parties, and were strong enough to prune and clip for the sake of pruning and clipping, and could solve the problem of unsaleable farming land." She decided to sell the property in two parts, the farm as one, the house as the other. She set aside forty acres and three houses to give to Mr. Burroughs for his retirement. A friend in Rhinebeck recommended Lewis McCabe as someone who could help. "He lives not far away, in Garrison. He works for a real estate firm in New York. He knows the Hudson."

Helen contacted Lewis McCabe. Would he come to Rhinebeck and take a look? Was there a possibility his firm would handle the sale? He came the following weekend. She led him through all the rooms in the house, the attic, and the cellar. They strolled through the gardens, framed by views of the Catskill Mountains beyond. The sounds of the railroad were just audible in the distance, attesting to how convenient Rhinebeck was for people who needed to get to New York.

Lewis told her his family owned wooded land. "We don't have as many acres," he said. "Three hundred, not a thousand. But my point is that our land used to be farmed. It doesn't have to be a bad thing if Grasmere reverts to woods. There's a market for wood in New York. You may not need to look specifically for a buyer who wants a working farm."

Lewis was handsome, just turning thirty, with dark hair and pale blue eyes. He was physically fit. "I enjoy tennis," he said, "and skiing and ice skating. And I like being on a horse."

"I ride too," Helen said. "Or at least I did. My father gave me a pony, and then a horse, and I used to ride along Mill Road in the mornings. What else do you like? Do you read?"

"Yes." Lewis told her he'd studied English and history at Yale. He enjoyed Dickens and Sinclair Lewis. Helen gave him the listing. And when he asked her a few weeks later to have dinner with him, she said yes. And she said yes a second time.

As they got to know each other, they talked about their families. Lewis's forebears were Protestants from Ireland, "before the famine," he said. "The first was Edward McCabe. He emigrated from Dublin in the 1700s."

Lewis's ancestors had settled in New York, some near Utica and Syracuse, others along the Hudson River. His great-grandfather owned a dry goods store on Main Street in Cold Spring, the village next to Garrison. His grandfather was in the wholesale carpet business in New York. There was a family legend they didn't share with everyone that Lewis's grandfather had gotten his start by selling prison-made doormats without labeling where they'd been made. His business grew when he started selling "oriental" rugs. He survived the Crash of '29 and left Lewis's father, a Hobart graduate, a prospering business in Manhattan. The company's customers included Lord & Taylor and W. & J. Sloane.

Lewis's mother, Caroline Partridge, came from Phelps, New York. Her father was a lawyer. Her brother, Bellamy Partridge, was a novelist whose book, *Country Lawyer*, was assigned to first-year law students at Columbia.

"I've never thought of myself as being a lawyer or doctor or writer," Lewis said. "Selling is in my blood. I like the transaction part, matching buyers and sellers."

He told her that his parents' marriage had ended in divorce. "The marriage broke up when my father left in the middle of the night with my mother's niece. My older brother walked out on his marriage too. He left his wife in Cold Spring and went to Florida."

Helen was fascinated. She'd met few people who'd experienced the dissolution of a family through divorce. She felt oddly comfortable that Lewis knew what divorce was like.

The difference in their social standing wouldn't have been apparent to the casual observer. They looked and sounded much like each other. Their Yale and Vassar educations made them equals. But in the small village of Garrison in the 1930s, it would have been noticed that they didn't come from similar backgrounds. Hudson Valley families with inherited money didn't work in "trade." Their names weren't Irish.

* * *

"I don't know if my having an Irish name kept me from being tapped by a senior society at Yale," Lewis said. "I wanted to be asked to join a club. I sat on the fence, on Tap Day, the way we had to if we were hopeful. No tap came."

Gradually, over the next six months, they fell in love. Lewis took her to cocktail parties in New York where she met his friends. "He always seems to have beautiful women around him," she wrote Pig, her friend from Smith. "He told me about his affairs. One a lesbian—should I tell him that I have too? I *almost* think I can discuss with him my own sexual history." Not long afterwards, Helen wrote P, "We went to a cocktail party, and drank six martinis. And he gave me a diamond and I knew everything was all right."

Helen moved back to Grasmere after she had graduated from Vassar. Lewis continued working in New York, and she met him there or in Garrison on weekends. When they met in Garrison, she stopped enroute at the Hudson River State Hospital to see her mother. Elizabeth was sometimes in a violent ward, and Helen couldn't see her; but more often she would be found in a sunroom writing letters. She wrote to every important person she could think of, telling them she'd been imprisoned illegally. The superintendent promised to mail them, then put them in a large envelope and gave them to Helen when she visited.

Helen was happiest when she and Lewis spent their weekends in the country. They took long walks, holding hands, and didn't talk about emotions. Helen wrote later, in her journal, that no one seemed to talk about emotions. She and Lewis acknowledged their unusual families, and said simply that they hoped for the best. Several times they climbed the hill behind his family's farmhouse, looking for a place to build their own. They wanted to live in the country someday.

It was so high and cold and peaceful, so long since I had gone on a long walk, and I felt healthy and hungry, and grateful to him all over again for building up what we do all day into an expression of what we think at night—long excursions here and there, hand in hand—be it movies, real estate, meals, driving, coping with families. I have a lovely splash of joy inside of me at the prospect of an apartment to furnish and keep in order. Please God, don't let me burble too silly.

* * *

But Helen's diary also depicts a woman full of questioning about whether she, or they, should marry. She wanted a stable life and children; but she feared Lewis was enticed more by the status he scented. "I was surprised," she wrote, "to find he's not in the *Social Register*. I thought he would be." When Lewis's sister, Lee, became engaged to Richard de Rham, whose family owned a large estate on the river, Helen wrote in her diary that it would have been "more appropriate if I were engaged to Lee's fiancé."

Some of her concern arose from Lewis's tendency to take control of her business affairs. Helen told Burroughs, Grasmere's superintendent, that she wanted to rent the farm until a sale was completed. When Lewis began to negotiate the terms of the rental, she wondered if she'd regret not assuming her own responsibilities, and how long she could play the "leave it to the male" part. She wondered if his friends in New York would begin to miss him, and what difference she would make to his dinner engagements.

To help make ends meet, Grasmere was briefly rented to a school. Buyers eventually came forward for the land and the house. Most of the contents of the house went at auction. Helen kept the china and silver she cared about, including twelve settings of Tiffany flatware monogrammed with Sarah Minerva Schieffelin's initials, SMS. She kept the Steinway grand piano which had been moved to Grasmere from 665 Fifth Avenue. She found Ernest Crosby's books and Egyptian artifacts where Fanny had hidden them in the attic, and learned about her grandfather for the first time. She stored these items in a barn at Lewis's family's farm in Garrison.

Weeks of intense planning preceded the wedding, which took place on February 5, 1937. Helen worried about her mother, whom she decided not to invite. Oliver Wagstaff and his sister insisted on having the reception at their New York townhouse. A month before the wedding Helen and Lewis signed a lease on an apartment at 47 East 72nd Street. Helen wrote to P:

> I really do love him. We've spent two weekends here and suddenly got peaceful, which the engagement business makes you believe you never can be. I like getting breakfast. He notices things. I buy him soda mints. He finally produced a rose. He probably never will fold bath towels. Anyway, we've been together so much that I know there's much to build well on. I am beginning to stir again.
>
> The paraphernalia of "getting married" helps. It's all comic opera. He's scared now, just the way they all are. But sort of pleased with himself. But he is still a little afraid of the Coolidge women.
>
> Aunt Bertha hates the Wagstaffs. The telephone rings all morning. My pants match my slips. New luggage. <u>Please</u> come to the wedding. The attendants will be in periwinkle blue lace. Me, in what looks like a nightie and miles of train. A darling country-ish church, beams, and a high church young rector. Candles, no palms, freesia, forsythia, daffodils and iris. Reception for drinks at Waggie's—the night at the Waldorf-Astoria. Sail to Nassau for a week the next day at 3. Infinite debts. 4 evening dresses, all full swishy skirts and no backs. Chiffon nightgowns. People, thank God, keep sending cheques and I hope eventually to come out even. Aunt Eleanor is in Australia and is breaking her back to try and find $1,000. Approximate cost, furniture, wedding, reception and clothes is $2,000. Don't think I don't think there's a catch. But everyone says "that's how it's done."
>
> Somehow I've kept him from having complete intercourse. Saved it and saved it. Now I'm doubly glad. Because it will bolster ceremony.

P wrote back that she would come to the wedding and Helen sent a short note in return:

> I am so glad you are coming. Street clothes are O.K. It's a post-business wedding and I wouldn't dress up for it. Them as has clothes may, but the majority are all in the same boat with you and me.
>
> The reception will be embarrassing for everyone anyway. They always are, unless you drink.
>
> No mama. She's written the White House to get her out, but she's in a semi-violent ward, and damned unhappy.

Helen's last task before the wedding was to prepare an announcement for the newspapers. Bertha came to her aid, just as she'd come to Elizabeth's in 1908, and wrote the text. The *New York Times* noted that Lewis had graduated from Yale. Hudson River Valley newspapers included the additional information that he was a graduate of the Scarborough School. This was a little misleading: Lewis did graduate from Scarborough, a private school south of Garrison, but only from the middle school. His high school diploma was from Yonkers High School.

The *New York Times*, as newspapers did in those days, printed every detail of the event:

> Miss Helen Elizabeth Crosby of Rhinebeck, N.Y., daughter of Mrs. Coolidge Oñativia and the late Maunsell Schieffelin Crosby, was married here yesterday afternoon to Mr. Lewis Bates McCabe, son of Mrs. Caroline Partridge McCabe of 830 Park Avenue and Garrison, N.Y., and of Mr. Lewis B. McCabe of New York. The ceremony was performed in the Church of the Resurrection by the rector, the Rev. Dr. Gordon Wadhams. A reception took place at the residence of Miss Mary Wagstaff, 131 East Sixty-first Street.
>
> The bride was given in marriage by Mr. Oliver C. Wagstaff, long a friend of her family. She wore a princess

gown of white crepe with a high neckline, long sleeves puffed at the shoulder and a train. Her tulle veil was fastened to a halo coronet and she carried gardenias and lilies of the valley. Three hundred guests were present for the wedding.

The bride was attended by Miss Lee Selden McCabe, sister of the bridegroom, fiancée of Mr. Richard Dana de-Rham, and by Mrs. Manfred Godfried, both of whom wore gowns of periwinkle blue lace, and carried yellow freesia and daffodils. Mr. Van Buren Taliaferro, of 27 Park Avenue, was best man.

The bride is a niece of the fifth Baron Huntingfield, of Government House, Melbourne, Victoria, Australia. She attended the Ethel Walker School, Simsbury, Conn., and was graduated last year from Vassar College. She is a member of the Junior League and the Colony Club.

Mr. McCabe was graduated from Yale in 1927 and is a member of the Yale Club of New York and the Ex-Members Association of Squadron A. He is with the National Real Estate Clearing House in this city.

When the couple left for their wedding trip, Mrs. McCabe wore a gray suit trimmed with Persian lamb, with accessories of dubonnet.

After the honeymoon, Lewis and Helen settled into the East 72nd Street apartment to begin life as a married couple. Helen hung curtains and cooked and began to enjoy New York as someone who lived there, rather than simply visited. Then, suddenly Helen was pregnant, and I came along in January of 1939. It was a bit of a shock to Helen, but she enjoyed the preparations for my arrival. She used the months before my birth to make the rounds of doctors (an oculist, an osteopath, an allergist) and to brighten up her wardrobe. She'd learned to sew at boarding school and turned up the hems of her dresses. "They look amateurishly done," she said to Aunt Bertha. "I've got to invest in a new dress or two." She bought three large hats.

Friends gave Helen many gifts, including more than thirty baby sweaters. Her godmother, soon to seek a divorce from Vincent Astor, sent a mother-of-pearl teething ring from Tiffany's. The outward symbols were reassuring, but I was Helen's firstborn, she'd never held an infant in her arms before, and she was afraid of taking care of me. She and Lewis made the decision to hire a nurse during my first six weeks.

I was born after a day of labor and Helen, years later, told me that having a child was horrible. "It was the stirrups. They hold your legs apart and the pain is excruciating." The nurse left after six weeks and Helen tried to care for me alone. The nurse said, "Give her five bottles a day, the last at 11 p.m. Don't feed her simply because she cries. If you feed her when she cries, she'll learn she can have things on demand."

"I can't do this," Helen told Lewis after the first week. "It isn't Susan's fault—it's just that in the past week I've had only ten hours sleep." They asked the nurse to return for my last feeding at night and the "hard work" the next morning, preparing my meals for the day, and washing and dressing me. The nurse could come for only two weeks, and Helen confided to Bertha how terrified she was.

Bertha now entered Helen's life in a new way. Because of her wariness of Elizabeth, her sister, she'd stayed away from any close contact with my mother. The only times Helen and her aunt communicated had been when decisions had to be made about Elizabeth's hospitalization. Now, Helen and Bertha had embarked on marriage, both for the first time. Bertha, in her fifties, had no expectation of children. Helen became her surrogate daughter, and I became her surrogate infant. Bertha began to shop, filling in the missing pieces in Helen's wardrobe. She went to Fifth Avenue's most expensive stores. Her first gift to Helen was a housecoat from Tailored Woman.

"The housecoat is divine," Helen wrote in her thank-you note. "It's quite the softest, most luxurious garment in my wardrobe and will be worn constantly at *tête-à-tête* dinners with Lewis. You are an extremely extravagant aunt!" Evening purses and shawls followed. Helen wrote more than a hundred thank-you notes over the next ten years, all of which I have.

Helen still made visits to her mother in Poughkeepsie, though they were increasingly difficult. There was no way to alter the fact that Helen was free and Elizabeth was not, and that their roles were now reversed.

"You should take me home with you," Elizabeth would begin. "You know I don't belong here."

"The doctors think it best," Helen would reply.

"Well, it isn't the best, they don't know anything, they don't have the slightest clue what kind of woman I am."

"What kind of woman are you?"

"I'm your mother and you need me. Why don't you come to see me more often? Why am I so alone?"

Helen usually endured the outbursts and recriminations well, but after a visit on August 8, 1940, when Elizabeth made a scene in a restaurant, becoming shrill about her fury at being "imprisoned," the power balance changed. Elizabeth wrote to Helen afterwards:

> I don't think of myself as here at all, but try to think and live as if I were outside under normal conditions. Whereas you probably think of me as here. Physically I can't help myself. That's why going out occasionally helps. But I wish you could just come up spontaneously and be your own self, and not have one of these ghastly exhibitions. This system certainly turns people nasty. One practically has to be.

Helen replied:

I don't like "ghastly exhibitions" either, and there is nothing I would rather do than just "come up spontaneously and be my own self." But I don't see how I can come any more unless we effect a compromise so that I can take you out for a better lunch and shopping, without having to bear the brunt of being the only person you hold responsible for your present incarceration. The "ghastly exhibition" that occurred at my last visit was due to your feeling that I had completely failed you as a daughter—that I am misguided, misinformed, and either ignorantly or stupidly unaware of all the forces you feel to be at work against you.

I can sympathize from the bottom of my heart with every rage and wave of helplessness you have when seeing me. I would feel the same way if our positions were reversed.

But I cannot come up to see you simply to be a target for those feelings. I can only come to see you when you are able to treat me impersonally and use me for a few hours as a sympathetic ear—and a vehicle for shopping. And I love seeing you and being of assistance in those small ways. I would always rather come than not come.

But I cannot come, and retreat in a cover of lies, indefinitely, and so quite frankly, I had better say that I will not do any of the things you want done in connection with lawyers or public officials or habeas corpus, or trust funds, or banks, or clippings, because I do not feel, no matter how gifted you may be, that you are competent, or that you should be anywhere except where you are. Unless, of course, you should become the clever, but controlled, person that you were when I was younger.

Naturally you can have no comprehension of how queer your letters and remarks seem to other people, who are living what seems to you stupid, but which nevertheless are sane, lives. I know that there is graft and collusion the wide world over, but you have intensified it in your own mind into an insane pattern.

Nothing I say, naturally, will convince you that there is
any truth in what I say. It is useless to talk or argue with you.
I do want to see you, but I cannot, if there is any question of
my doing or promising more than a paid nurse.

Helen became pregnant again. As soon as Lewis heard, he
suggested a change. "Let's leave the city now," he said, "and
move to Garrison. Let's think about that house in the country we talked about." His enthusiasm was fueled by learning that his father was going to spend half the year in Florida
and half in a house in Cold Spring, near Garrison. The farmhouse in Garrison could be theirs. With two young children,
Lewis argued, they should have more space. If they needed to
be in New York, there was the train. The station was only two
miles away.

He proposed that they earn their living selling firewood to
New Yorkers. Many apartments in New York had fireplaces.
"Just like I suggested when we walked through the woods at
Grasmere," he said. "There are acres and acres of woods that
could be cut." He described the comforts of the farmhouse:
four bedrooms upstairs, two bathrooms, and an attic that ran
the length of the house. There was a living room with a view of
stone walls and fields; the east- and west-facing windows provided sunlight all day. The dining room and kitchen overlooked
a three-car carriage house with living space above. There was a
cottage beyond the barn that they could let. Helen agreed with
his idea; she liked Garrison being close to Rhinebeck. "It will
be like coming home," she said. "We can go to parties in both
places. Let's do it."

Maunsell Crosby's estate included two office buildings
in Manhattan. His Schieffelin forebears had invested in commercial buildings in what was now the garment district. Helen
needed to rent the buildings in order to cover their costs.

Her financial transactions still had to be approved by Oliver Wagstaff, despite the fact that she was married. She planned to ask Wagstaff for a higher allowance now that she had a growing family. But Wagstaff worried her; he was anti-Semitic, and most of the tenants in the garment district were Jewish. Thus she was grateful this time when Lewis took over the negotiations with a clothing manufacturer who'd expressed interest in renting one of the buildings.

"We're having to work over O.W.'s recalcitrant body," Helen wrote Bertha. "He insults all Jews over the telephone and refuses to see them if he can possibly help it. They know it, resent it, and accordingly become harder to deal with. We need the rent. Money will trickle in from selling wood and in a year or so it may become a respectable business."

They left Manhattan in the fall of 1940, and Sheila came along on January 4, 1941. To make the family complete, they bought a German Shepherd puppy and named it Waldo. Bertha, worried that the firewood plan was shaky, sent money. Helen was grateful: "The check you sent is enough to keep the Oñativias, Crosbys, and McCabes in pin money for months to come. You really do spoil me dreadfully."

* * *

By the time Sheila was born, Helen had overcome her fear of feeding and dressing babies. But she felt the need for a housekeeper. She hired a white woman named Julia. Julia watched over me constantly, even while Helen was playing with me. She picked me up so often that Helen complained I'd become a "mass of wails to be picked up." Helen wanted me to be left to play quietly by myself. One day she gave instructions to Julia about how I should be cared for while she and Lewis went to Peekskill for shopping.

"Leave Sheila in her crib. Leave Susie in the big porch pen while I go marketing and leave her alone unless she needs dry pants."

"Yes, ma'am," Julia answered.

As she and Lewis were driving back, Helen became anxious. "I want to get home fast," she said. "I think Julia's annoyed at me and may do something to Susie. She may do it unconsciously. I think she wants to prove I'm a tyrant." They arrived to find Julia in the kitchen and my playpen empty.

"Susie cried so long I fixed all her toys for her, and that didn't work, so I put her in the living room," said Julia. And there I was, in the living room, happy as a lark, prancing around with Helen's sharpest scissors and a small cut in my hand.

Julia burst into tears and went into recriminations. "I couldn't let a little baby cry its heart out. You're a lousy mother. I don't understand why you don't want Susie touched."

"I'm sorry," Helen said. "We'll just have to get someone who does. You're fired." They got through dinner that night, with two guests, and Helen resolved to find a woman who'd raised nine children, whether she could cook or not. "At least she'll have experience," she said.

The solution was two black women from Peekskill; a housekeeper and a cook. "The cook, Mary, is 400% quieter than Julia," Helen wrote Bertha, "much more respectful, and her string beans are delicious! Most miraculous of all, they've agreed to eat together and seem quite happy about it. I've gotten nice cheerful uniforms for them and they both seem proud to wear them." Then they both quit, and Helen had to search again. She had better luck with another young white woman, who stayed this time. She was engaged to a young soldier who was about to serve overseas, and having a job in Garrison suited her for several years.

Occasionally, Helen re-entered the upper-class lifestyle she'd enjoyed with her father in Rhinebeck. Bertha and her husband spent weekends and the summer at Woodston, his large estate in nearby Mt. Kisco. There were expansive lawns, boxwood gardens, and a long, reflecting pool with stone statues at each end. They had several servants ("Good colored people," Bertha said, using the language of the day. "They come from freed families and have been educated.") Bertha invited Helen and Lewis to Woodston often, usually including Sheila and me in the invitation.

"Isn't it queer," Helen wrote in a thank-you note after one of these visits, "that only six years ago I didn't really know I had an aunt. Perhaps everyone should have a relative kept intact for their post-formative years."

* * *

The Highlands Country Club in Garrison was another place for relaxing. It offered golf and tennis, and dances on weekends. Lewis saw membership in the club as a way to get to know more people. When the club announced a membership recruitment drive, he volunteered. He was thinking ahead to when he might open a local real estate office; the more people he knew, the better. He organized two successful tennis tournaments with luncheons, teas, and dancing, and brought in a dozen new members.

Helen's pleasure was gardening. She'd tended nasturtiums and sweet peas in Montana and enjoyed digging in the soil. She'd spent many hours in the formal garden at Grasmere. So she was happy when she was invited to join the Philipstown Garden Club, and immediately had ideas for the next annual meeting. "We could have two competitions," she suggested. "'Planting Against a Stone Wall' and 'Planting Against the Garage Fence.'"

She wrote Bertha, "We've just had one of our most successful events ever. We served four gallons of iced tea and the cookies and cakes I got from a very nice bakery in Peekskill were just right. They loved my ideas for the competitions!"

Helen now had a car again, and drove somewhere every day. She was racy behind the wheel, enjoying the feel of the road and the challenge of taking curves well. To reach the village of Cold Spring (there were no shops in Garrison), she took dirt roads past other farmhouses and the occasional gates of large estates. "I'm driving regularly to a volunteer job at the nursery school," she wrote Bertha. "I've been doing my stint from 9–12, plus ferrying two little boys and Susan to and fro. I love doing it, but it takes a big hunk out of the day."

Helen and Lewis watched their money carefully, but always had enough to entertain friends. She was known in Garrison as an heiress, which she did not disown; but since the style of the village was unostentatious, the fact that they didn't have a lot of money wasn't noticed.

What did seem to be a constant was her feeling that she was supposed to "belong." Her Aunt Bertha had traveled with the *Social Register* in her suitcase for all of her adult life. Bertha wouldn't accept invitations from new acquaintances without first ascertaining that they were listed. After she married Marshall Slade, she kept one copy in their New York apartment and another at their Mt. Kisco estate. She was glad that Helen and Lewis were listed, a courtesy extended to husbands who weren't listed when "maidens" in the book married them.

Bertha wanted Helen to join the Colonial Dames of America, an organization she considered far more meaningful than the *Social Register*. To become a member, one had to prove direct descent from colonial times. She helped Helen prepare a genealogical chart. Helen's application was accepted. She wrote a note to Bertha when the acceptance letter came, telling her she was thinking about Lewis's sister, Lee deRham, whose husband's ancestors were Longfellows, Danas, and Appletons. "The Colonial Dames book will sit beside the Crosby and Coolidge chronicles, where it can out-Appleton the deRhams," she wrote. The *Social Register* sat on a bookshelf near our telephone all the years I was growing up.

Differences in their social position were a shadow in Helen and Lewis's marriage, though not talked about. Health issues, spoken about, were another. Lewis constantly complained of minor symptoms. His mother often boasted that she'd successfully toilet-trained him when he was one. She'd forced him to wear high lace-up shoes and short pants to school when his schoolmates were wearing long trousers. She wouldn't let him dress differently even after he told her he was bullied. Throughout his life, he told scatological jokes, but couldn't explain why when asked.

Helen's hay fever was never completely under control, and she had painful menstrual periods. Lewis didn't take the menstrual pain seriously; he said it was psychological, even when a doctor told her she needed surgery. Helen turned to Bertha for sympathy: "It's a cold in the bladder, an awful nuisance. I'm worried about where to get treatment, because a local doctor will gossip."

She decided to be treated in New York, choosing as her doctor William Hitzig, later famous for arranging reconstructive surgery for Japanese women disfigured by the bomb at Hiroshima. "He can probably fix it in a week or two," she told Bertha, "and he charges very little because of our decorative value as Anglo-Saxons." She wrote Bertha:

> My medico has exactly the equipment necessary for this kind of thing—and has definitely got the edge on it. I think I

would have been cured by today if the heat treatments hadn't brought on the curse last night. He tried a 'conservative' treatment first—nitrate of silver and argyrols in the bladder, and twenty minutes of short-wave heat inside the vagina—and drops to relax the contracting muscles on urination. (Pretty, isn't it!) I've never been so mad at getting something more wrong with me.

We've made three flying trips to New York in this heat! But then, the 'conservative' treatment didn't clear out, I regret to say, so for two days I took sulpha thyasol every four hours, which made me fairly nauseated, but reduced the pus to almost nothing. I suppose in the old days one just quietly died—or else, I also suppose, got a fever from the infection, and that cured it. If it comes back, I'll simply have to take sulpha thyasol over again—sans curse.

I am tired. Lewis is exhausted from alternative babies when I can't manage. He at last really understands why I like to go to bed, and a little of what a persistent thing the children's routine is.

Throughout 1941 there was talk of America's entering the war, and after Pearl Harbor the country mobilized. Helen and Lewis thought about the possible hardships they would face. The farmhouse would be difficult to maintain if Lewis was called up. It might also not be safe for Helen and Sheila and me; there were four doors through which an intruder might enter. Villagers were talking about the growing number of poorer people moving to Peekskill from the South. "If they aren't all educated or hardworking, there might be break-ins."

They decided the best thing would be to make the cottage beyond the barn our temporary home. It would be easier to heat than the farmhouse, and the bigger house could be rented. They set to work renovating the cottage. Under layers of wallpaper, they found the original pine boards. "I *love* this cottage," Helen wrote Bertha, "and am primitively happy trotting around fixing it up. When I get the curtains made, we'll have quite a stunning bedroom, and then I shall just lie around and look at it. The clematis and dahlias and roses are lovely, and I feel so proud of my back-handed gardening. And home."

Lewis was classified 3-A, which made him relatively safe from call-up. But the Army was being reorganized and he knew he could be re-classified 2-A. He decided to pursue his one good option. After graduating from Yale, he'd been invited by a Garrison neighbor, an Army officer who owned horses, to join Squadron A in New York. If Lewis could get a commission as an officer in Squadron A, he'd have an easier time.

Squadron A was formed in the 1880s by a group of skilled horseback riders who called themselves the New York Hussars. The group merged with the National Guard in 1889 and became Squadron A. Members served in Puerto Rico during the Spanish-American War and along the Mexican border in 1916. During World War I, 796 saw service and 609 became commissioned officers.

In the peacetime that followed, many members became skilled polo players. They gave sophisticated parties at their headquarters on Madison Avenue. Lewis went to these parties when he was a bachelor in New York.

In 1941, the federal government took over Squadron A and it became the 101st Cavalry. Two troops were mechanized and one remained equestrian, code named "Wingfoot." It was "Wingfoot" Lewis had in mind. He told many friends in Garrison about his plan to join.

His application to become an officer was turned down, and the rejection was soon known to everyone.

Lewis never talked about it. Helen told me she believed the rejection triggered memories of his similar rejection by senior societies at Yale. It was a public humiliation in Garrison just as it had been at Yale to sit on the fence and wait for a "tap" that never came. She didn't at first recognize the enormity of what had happened. She noticed only that Lewis became unnaturally silent. She thought this a character fault rather than something serious. "Cheer up," she said. "It's not all that bad."

Her cheerfulness and support didn't help. Lewis went into a depression, which in hindsight one could understand as coming from a lifelong vulnerability. He stopped logging. Helen confronted him in the living room one sunny winter afternoon when, thinking he was in the woods, she found him reading a book.

"Why are you here? Shouldn't you be cutting wood with the men?" she asked.

"No. I want to read this book." It was Boswell's *Life of Johnson.*

While the scene was peaceful on the surface and they avoided an argument, Helen was angry and thought it odd that her husband, who should have been working, was taking the afternoon off.

This paralysis continued for six months. Lewis read books every day. He finished Boswell and started Gibbon's *The Decline and Fall of the Roman Empire.* When he finished Gibbon, he read Plutarch's *Lives.* Each day, Helen brought him his lunch on a tray.

She did her best to keep Lewis's withdrawal a secret. She didn't want their friends to know, and, most of all, she didn't want Bertha to know. It was hard enough that she had a mother who was hospitalized. She persuaded Lewis to make an appointment with William Hitzig, their doctor in New York. He suggested that Lewis see a psychiatrist. Lewis demurred.

But after six months of only reading books, Lewis started to have terrifying dreams. He was now frightened and asked his sister, Lee deRham, and Helen for help. Again they went to Dr. Hitzig. He had Lewis admitted to Mt. Sinai Hospital

for observation and then recommended that Lewis enter
Chestnut Lodge, a private hospital in Rockville, Maryland, near
Washington. It was known for its innovative psychotherapy and
was attracting some of the best psychiatrists in the country. Dr.
Hitzig arranged for Lewis's admission, and Lee drove him there.
Helen stayed in Garrison with Sheila and me.

CHAPTER 14

CHESTNUT LODGE was a private psychiatric hospital founded in 1910 as a center for the humane treatment of mental illness. It was a far cry from the locked-up institutions of the past. Formerly the site of a summer hotel, the hospital had extensive wooded grounds with no locked gates or high fences. Only a discreet sign at the entrance gave the slightest clue that it was there. Surrounding the hospital were well-tended houses, many with wide front porches overlooking the street. The owners of these houses accepted the presence of the hospital. Patients had permission to walk freely about the town. Many, whose treatment took several years, bought houses of their own. That is what happened to us.

It wasn't immediately clear how long Lewis would be hospitalized, or what his diagnosis would be. He telephoned Helen after his admission and said it might take a long time to find out the reason for his breakdown. "The pattern isn't clear," he said. "They say I'll need to have many sessions before I know." He was concerned about the cost. The director, learning of his forestry skills, offered Lewis a reduction of one hundred dollars a month if he would take care of the chestnut trees. "That's why it's called Chestnut Lodge. There are one hundred and fifty chestnut trees on the grounds," he told Helen. She told him not to worry, that somehow things would work out.

A month later Lewis's psychiatrist telephoned Helen to talk with her directly. He said Lewis had told him when they first talked that it was his father he hated, but now he was beginning to realize that his mother used his father, in fact despised his father, and despised Lewis as well, and played the father against the son, and that Lewis's real problem was that he "never had a mother."

He stayed at Chestnut Lodge through the summer of 1942. Helen wrote him often, pondering what she should do. Her first letters were confident. She described managing the firewood business and coping with mechanical problems like a broken furnace. But she was devastated when Waldo, our German Shepherd, bit a neighbor and the police were called. She had to take him to the S.P.C.A. where it would be decided whether he should go into the Army or be chloroformed. "I left him, oh, so sadly. I miss him as if he had died. He must be so baffled in his pen, wondering where we are."

In September, Lewis wrote that while his treatment was going to take a long time, he no longer needed to be an inpatient. He needed psychoanalysis Monday through Friday and his weekends would be free. Would Helen come? He'd find a house; Chestnut Lodge would help. She'd have to find renters for the farmhouse and the cottage, but he was sure she could do it. He assured her that Rockville was pleasant. "The town opened up in the 1880s with the coming of the railroad. Lots of Victorian houses were built. There are pine groves and oaks and many streams. The countryside in every direction is rural and beautiful. The people are welcoming."

Helen said she'd come. The start of war had made her nervous. She made lists of what to take to Rockville and what to leave behind, uncertain what war shortages there would be. She found, after cleaning every closet, that she had thirty-five pairs of shoes. She wondered which clothes I would outgrow and which would fit Sheila the following spring. "Every day I pack things away so they can be sent on later if necessary."

Garrison friends now openly asked what was wrong with Lewis. Someone started a rumor that he was hopelessly insane. Helen wasn't perturbed by the rumor (she'd heard enough about her mother to be inured to rumors now) and thought it more the rumormonger's problem than her own. But she felt under pressure. One Sunday night she sat down to write Lewis with a drink by her side. She began in a clear hand, "Dear Poops," but by the time she'd finished, she was writing sloppily and her emotions came through:

> I feel so completely exhausted I could cry. It gets me down because I can't think anymore, and when you're rushing, you've got to be able to think what comes next. So then I say, don't rush. But if I don't, we'll have that much more inconvenience later. So if I let anything slip now it will be just too bad, mainly because of all the variety of war restrictions looming in sight.
>
> So when do I come to Rockville? I dunno. Next June if I'm lucky. Now I gotta measure the cottage for the renters and get their god damn oil rations. Trip one. Trip two. Bum up tires getting the god damn rations.
>
> I'm oh so sorry you're oh so alone but how in hell can I get there? It's not my period, it's just the most beautiful fatigue I ever had and I've been feeling so comfortable and now I feel so confused. I just can't think.
>
> I think I can't do it. There's just too much god damn stuff. "Come soon, you say, it's only early autumn here." Oh, you wolf. I am frozen stiff and my hands are wide open from dishwashing and cold and the rats are gnawing in the kitchen. I honestly don't see how I can either get to Rockville or stay here. I am going quite, quite, quite mad, all by myself. So you can toss it around in your precious analysis, and

think what a smart guy you are, because you know what I'm all about, and isn't it too, too interesting.

I know it doesn't seem worth whining about to you, but when you get so that it nearly kills you to get out of bed and you HAVE to, or your kids will get pneumonia, you got something worth dying for. If I could just get one night off and sleep 24 hours I might feel better.

Much love, Peter

Lewis found us a house on the edge of Rockville, a block from the Baltimore & Ohio Railroad Co. station. It was a pleasant two-mile walk to Chestnut Lodge, passing the grocery store and Woolworth's, the post office, the court house, and the Farmers Banking and Trust Company. There was a church on almost every block. Beyond Chestnut Lodge, farmland stretched for miles.

With the finding of a house, and the move now imminent, Helen had to tell Bertha about our plans. Bertha, living closest to the Hudson River State Hospital, would now be the person best placed to look after Elizabeth. Bertha accepted the responsibility, promising to help in whatever ways she could, including financial. But she was saddened that Helen would be living so far away. She confessed a secret. She told Helen that men were difficult, and that she was terrified of her own husband. "Don't have another child," she cautioned Helen. "It's war time, and you'll be alone in Rockville, and it may not be the best thing to conceive another child while Lewis is ill."

Helen packed the car with some of her china and silver from Grasmere, and with Sheila and me. She wrote Bertha after we arrived:

I wrote down the name of every town I should go through and routed us away from all traffic until Baltimore. The back of the car was fixed like a bed, and at 9am we pulled out. Sue napped during the morning. We lunched a full hour below Far Hills. Then Sheila slept two hours. Then Sue threw up briefly, on a rolling road, but we only stopped fifteen minutes for that and then she stayed down on 'the bed' until we got to Rockville. We hit Baltimore at 6pm, just at dark, and that was hard driving in traffic and trolleys and no route signs, but by dint of much questioning we made only one wrong turn, and using my flashlight for signs, we got to Rockville without going to Washington, on the dot of 8pm. 300 miles to the decimal point in eleven hours! The kids were really wonderful and I quite enjoyed the driving as it was a perfect day for it.

Sue and Sheila recognized Lewis at once. Sheila went straight to him without any hesitation and Sue was so delighted to be with him that she began at once to show off for him.

The house on Baltimore Road had two stories with nicely laid out rooms and good light, and a small garden at the rear, but the noise of the trains was ceaseless and the soot inescapable. Helen thought the house the dirtiest she'd ever seen. My earliest childhood memory is of Helen in this house. I'm standing in a doorway watching her on her hands and knees scrubbing the linoleum floor.

"It's a fundamentally good house," Helen wrote Bertha:

The bedrooms are big and sunny and the beds are excellent. But we're inventing ways and means. A sink, but no place to drain the dishes. No tea kettle, no double boiler, no sink stopper, dirty oilcloth, but a good icebox and stove. The living room has presentable and comfortable furniture. The dining room is beyond words hideous. The upstairs walls are so bad, robin's egg blue and pink stippled on yellow, that Sheila cried 'dirty' for a solid hour and a half the night we got here and refused to stay in her room.

She ended with a comment about her summer without Lewis. "I actually enjoyed the time alone," she wrote. "We all know this about me. I've always liked being on my own."

Helen wondered if the cause of Lewis's breakdown was that he'd been doing the wrong kind of work. She had no idea what their future might be. She knew only that they would wait for the final results of his analysis, decide what he was best suited for after such an upheaval, and plan for the future then. Lewis's doctor surprised her by suggesting she might benefit from psychoanalysis as well. He recommended Dr. Marjorie Jarvis, who had an office just six blocks from our house.

Within a month we had a weekday routine. We got up at seven, Helen dressing Sheila and me while Lewis stoked the furnace and started breakfast (he was good with a skillet, both in the kitchen and over a campfire). At five minutes of eight, Helen flew out the door for her daily hour with Dr. Jarvis. At 9:05 she was home again to do the dishes while Lewis got ready for his analysis at ten. Sometimes she took him to Chestnut Lodge in the car, with us, and went marketing afterwards. Other mornings he took the car, while she started cooking lunch and cleaned the house as Sheila and I played outside. She knew I needed a playmate, but there was no nursery school. The population of the town was only 2,500.

Lewis came home for lunch at 12:30. Sheila took a nap afterwards and I, curious about everything, took the house apart. Helen wasn't concerned about the messes we made; she encouraged us to explore. She knew from her own experience that children needed to play.

"Are you sure you want Susie making such a mess?" Lewis would ask, and Helen would reply, "Yes, it's good for her. I remember the few times I could play without my mother telling me to go to my room."

Lewis went back to the hospital after lunch to work on the trees. He came home at five. After being given orange juice on his return, Sheila and I went outside for an hour, while Helen and Lewis talked. At six they fed us and, if they were lucky, got us into bed by seven. Lewis read to us for a few minutes, choosing books that had been in Helen's library at Grasmere.

Once we were in bed, they relaxed over cocktails and their own supper. Their drinks of choice were old fashioneds: a teaspoon of sugar and three drops of angostura bitters stirred with a heavy crystal muddler, then ice and bourbon added to fill the short glass. "Lewis," Helen wrote Bertha, "now sees my summer letters in a different light, and wonders how anything got done at Garrison excepting the needs of the two girls."

Helen began to believe Lewis's breakdown had been good for all of us. "Lewis is fundamentally better in mind and spirit than when we got married, and if we can only finish it up and get started right on whatever new work seems suitable, we may in the long run be better off than we would have been without it." They resumed their sexual relationship and Helen, contrary to Bertha's advice, became pregnant a third time.

* * *

A month after Helen knew she was pregnant again, the owner of 300 Baltimore Road decided to sell the house to a dairy farmer. Dairies in the area were failing. The farmer was a friend and he wanted to move into town. The owner apologized, but he really had to sell.

Few houses were available as rentals and Helen became frustrated after losing several within hours of hearing about them. She had, however, a canner, a kitchen utensil much in demand for preserving food, and this became her good luck charm. A woman owned a bungalow at 704 West Montgomery Avenue, a ten-minute walk from Chestnut Lodge, that she wanted to rent.

Helen quickly went to see it and they fell into talking about preserving food.

"I preserve food every summer," Helen said.

"You do? How?" the owner asked.

"With my canner," Helen said, and quickly they had an agreement. The owner would let us have the house if Helen would let her use the canner once a week. Helen was ecstatic. The house was just what she wanted: small but brand new, in a pleasant neighborhood, and far from the railroad. The garage had a sliding overhead door, a novelty. There was a small yard in back and neighbors' children close enough so that we could have friends and play together safely.

Inside, there was a living room with a fireplace and custom-built bookshelves. The kitchen had built-in cupboards. "After this horror we've been in, it looks like heaven, and heaven comes for $52.50 a month," she wrote Bertha. "The only drawback is that it's unfurnished."

Helen used her analytical abilities to solve the problem of the furniture. She subtracted $52.50 from the $100 rent she and Lewis paid for the house on Baltimore Road and asked Lewis to let her buy what was needed. Aware of the streak in Helen's family that instinctively picked the most expensive chintz, Lewis worried that Helen would go overboard. But he finally agreed, and Helen went off by herself to do the 'great American matrimonial trick,' the furnishing of a house for $500. She drove to Sears, Roebuck on Wisconsin Avenue in Washington, and sat quietly there all one morning, filling in her floor plans with their furniture and prices. She included a double-decker bed for Sheila and me and a crib for the new baby, who would be born September 5, 1943.

Helen kept her pregnancy secret from Bertha for as long as she could. In June she felt she had to confess, and wrote explaining her decision:

The baby was my choice. I could have had a therapeutic abortion, since I was in "analysis" and two psychiatrists had agreed to give the necessary legal permission. Then, when I could have, I simply could not give it up. There were certainly more reasons against having it, than for it, and yet, I knew that if and when it was born, I would never regret it. Any number of times since, in this heat especially, I have thought myself an awful fool—on the other hand, I am stuck to home with children to care for, and it might as well be with the three we wanted, while we can live so simply and cheaply.

There is, of course, the so-called social stigma of bearing a child while Lewis is presumably chez sanatorium. Well, that, while it matters to others, simply does not matter to me, knowing what I now know about the origins of neuroses and mental illness.

Helen didn't know whether she'd been breast-fed herself and asked Bertha if she knew. "Science, heigh-ho, says it makes a difference!" And, several weeks after Judith's birth, she wrote again. This time she said, "A third child is just plain fun!"

* * *

The new house on West Montgomery Avenue had a yard, but no trees. Helen and Lewis both missed them. Several miles away, towards the Potomac River, was a forested area threaded by a brook. Rockville, just fifteen miles from Washington, was becoming suburban and house prices were rising. The owner of the forest decided to sell. He divided the land into two-acre plots and announced an auction. Lewis and Helen decided to buy. "We've no fear of losing a penny on it," Helen wrote Bertha. "It has astoundingly beautiful trees, from poplars to oaks. We've no intention of building. Another family we know is buying as well. We're going to keep the land just the way it is, wooded. We're going to use it for picnics."

The land they bought became the "dam place" because of the large stones in the brook that altered the course of the water. We had many wonderful picnics. We walked on the watery stones, trying to balance ourselves. We chased dragonflies. We cleared paths and played hide and seek. When we were tired of playing, we sat on the grassy bank eating peanut butter and jelly sandwiches while one of our parents read to us. Today this sweet brook lies under a six-lane road, and in every direction buildings with five street numbers in their address blanket what was once open land.

Aunt Bertha continued to spoil us with packages for birthdays, Easter, Thanksgiving, and Christmas. She sent beautifully made cotton dresses, warm snowsuits, velvet party dresses, and winter coats with embroidered collars. Sometimes she sent three matching outfits. I was the luckiest. There were no larger sizes for me to grow into. As Sheila grew, she wore mine. As Judy grew, she wore Sheila's, and then mine. Judy has a stunning, unique sense of dress now, and I like to think she earned it, breaking away from having to wear three times what someone else chose for her.

* * *

Helen knew she'd been damaged by her mother, and also by Alice Nelson, the older cousin who'd seduced her. She was troubled by her lesbian experiences at Smith, and ambivalent about Miss Underhill, the English teacher from Ethel Walker's who'd come to Grasmere. She maintained an on-again, off-again correspondence with her for ten years. She brought these gender concerns to Dr. Jarvis, who encouraged her to try to put Miss Underhill into a broader context. Was there something else, something not sexual, that Miss Underhill represented?

Helen attempted to write a definitive letter in 1945. Careful not to begin with a salutation that would identify Miss

Underhill as the recipient (in case it should fall into the wrong hands), she wrote to her about her marriage.

> I remember once you wrote, rather violently, that I had had no idea what a beating you had taken in our earlier letters. Well, I agree. You certainly did. But you chose me, I didn't choose you. What I am trying to do now is to learn to shake off forever, or at least recognize, that awful pattern I had all those years, learned from my mother.
>
> My marriage and my life will never be healthy until I recover from her. Things went from bad to worse until the war, which looked as if it could solve our personal problems by dividing us. In the midst of applying for a commission in the army, Lewis had a complete nervous breakdown. He came here in July 1942, to the Chestnut Lodge Sanatorium, and was started on psychoanalysis. We rented a house and have been living in Rockville ever since. I started analysis as soon as I got here, and have been analyzing for two years. We had no friends or money the first year, and as usual, I got pregnant three weeks after I got here. Our third daughter was born an hour and a half before my birthday last year. So we have Susan, almost six, and off to kindergarten today, very excited, and Sheila, almost four, who goes to a cooperative nursery school, and Judith, exactly one. They are all beautiful in various ways, and back-breaking otherwise.
>
> We do have friends now, the fringes of Washington are full of Yankees, and a little money again. Maybe we'll be here three years, maybe for life. It all depends on what we find out we really are when and if we ever get through analysis. At the best, it may save our children from repeating our patterns of charming and hurting, and wooing and stabbing if we can control them (the patterns).
>
> At least there is no doubt in my mind that "analysis" has removed fully 40% of the old aches and pains and palpitations and anxiety, and I can address nursery school "study groups" without batting an eye. But it is a horribly prolonged

operation, and during it, it is almost impossible to speak one's mind, because it is in so many contrary pieces. So, my apologies for all my toughness. It's quite possible that if I ever saw you again I might know what you were really like, which of course, I couldn't see for the mote in my own eye before.

Peter

Miss Underhill answered by return mail, sending back Helen's letter.

Dear Peter, Elizabeth, Mrs. McCabe,

What a surprising epistle. I almost let it depress me, but I have troubles enough without resuming feeling desperate about you. I regret your maladjustment. I know you do not want my pity, and I'm no angel to do any pitying. Despair is what I feel for you, the prospect seems so gloomy for you if you really think I chose you and not you me. You'd perhaps better tell your psychoanalyst that he hasn't untied that knot yet. Perhaps it doesn't matter; yet it is a glaring example of your subconscious turning things upside down because you can not face truth, and often cannot tell it. Haven't you seen yet that that is your worst inheritance from your mother, your inability to tell plain simple truth, and your imaginative tendency to yarn.

I just happen to have a lot of written evidence of your seeking me out, at Walker's. I was frightened when you sensed that I had a vibrant wave length, as it were. I was frightened, and furious. I alternated between "praying" and swearing at your not-to-be-denied persistence. You haunted me, hung around, insisted on my paying attention to you. Granted that I should have done a good vicious job of hitting you on the head, hard, but you (unconsciously—artfully) used the old gambit of appealing to my pity.

CHAPTER 14

You held forth on your mother—showed me her letters, told me what a forlorn thing you were, and even gave me a melodramatic version of—apparently—a seduction of you by a woman. You fastened your eyes, literally, on me, and figuratively, clung to me. It used to drive me crazy. You _demanded_ attention. And you _worked_ and _worked_ and on me. Old tricks (that I grant you you went through by instinct) like splashing in the tub water, at Rhinebeck, to emphasize your body. You took pains to do it when there was only a door between us!

Of course you "got" me—I don't deny it. But you did the getting, with a vengeance. Every time I thought you had gone out of the picture—up you popped. (And here you are again.)

I remember how baffled I was when I first knew specifically that you were—inaccurate—about facts—your dramatic imagination so ran away with you.

Your letter as a whole was so encouraging—and so courteous and kind. Alas and alack. I had so hoped that your release from unreality had come. It's not pleasant to know that things are so hard for you. I don't feel fierce—just honest.

Perhaps this letter will help.
Mary Underhill
(who would like to see your three daughters, but thinks she has to continue to try to save her own life and sanity).

Helen wasn't sure "an imaginative tendency to yarn" was the most troubling trait she'd inherited from her mother. She thought it was her desire for independence, so contrary to what was expected of women in marriage. This had been her mother's desire at the same age. Helen wanted time to be alone and time to write. She was becoming conflicted about the demands that children and running a household made on her time. She had enough money to hire servants, which made her life easier than her mother's life had been. But she never felt our house was orderly enough, or that she could enjoy chunks of solitary time. She was afraid of speaking up for what she wanted, worried about using her privilege to berate those who worked for her. She sought help from Dr. Jarvis.

"If you could face why you're frightened to be specific in your demands with your servants, you might find that you would end up with a competent housekeeper, and an outside man, and be free to write," said Dr. Jarvis. "Are you afraid of organizing what you want?"

"Yes."

"Are you afraid you would sit doing nothing?"

"Yes."

"Well, supposing you sat for an hour a day, then another day, and the next. You could call it 'ruminating.' So what? The fourth day you might think of something you would like to write down."

"It's the clutter."

"Why are you so afraid of the clutter that you can't overlook it?"

"Because visitors wouldn't feel they were welcome unless the room was ready for them. I mean it. Maybe it's a hangover from childhood luxuries, the sofa plumped up, the sherry brought in on a tray, the fire going. Just like the ads. I want it to be like the Colony Club. I enjoy it myself. Everything has been tidied and I'm ready for a drink."

"I'm wondering if keeping your house in order and plumping up all your pillows makes you feel whole?" said Dr. Jarvis.

"Of course it does," said Helen. "That's the point. Only that feeling doesn't last very long. If the house is perfect, then I'm perfect. If the house isn't straight to begin with, I feel exposed and as if visitors were finding out things about me that I don't want them to know. There is so much to hide."

"Then why don't you tell me?"

"I do, but it doesn't seem to be the answer. I don't seem to have any real clues."

Further therapy dealt with Helen's concerns about being a good mother. She wondered if her mother's behavior had in some way imprinted itself on her as a model for her own. She loved it when Sheila and I behaved. She didn't feel competent when it came to disciplining us. (Judy was still too young to be punished.) She brought an instance to Dr. Jarvis. Sheila and I had been told not to use paints when we were wearing our good clothes, but we did anyway, and Helen caught us when she went down to the cellar for gin (she and Lewis bought their liquor by the case). She dumped our paint bowls into the sink, at which point I screamed at her in rage, "Wash them up and give them back to us!"

"I won't," Helen said, feeling that if she did, Sheila and I would be getting no punishment for painting. We'd be condoned, and we would paint again. And Helen wanted a cocktail.

"But," said Helen to Dr. Jarvis, "I felt helpless, bullied by Sue, knowing also that nothing could be more confusing to Sue than the feeling in her that I could perhaps be bullied. She was speaking to me as if I were a servant. I went upstairs, forgetting to get the gin."

"Do you remember anyone's speaking to servants like that?" asked Dr. Jarvis.

"Of course, my mother spoke to me like that, but I don't think anyone spoke that way to servants."

"But when your mother spoke to you that way, you must have felt terrified."

"I did. And with Sue, I was terrified. She was the mother and I was the child. And I don't know how to appease her."

The following morning, Helen felt she'd done better, but that disciplining us was still troubling. By mistake, she cut one of my ribbons in half and used it for Sheila's pigtails. I said, "You will have to get me another."

Helen said, "I will, of course."

I said, "And you will get it in yellow velvet this time, too."

Helen said, "No, I won't. If you had asked me pleasantly, 'Mother, will you get me yellow velvet?' I might have. But I will not do anything for you when you are so rude."

Instead of tears, I was quiet. And for the rest of the interim before breakfast, polite and agreeable.

Dr. Jarvis asked why this was troubling.

"I know it's a relief to a child to be limited, to have walls set up for them as limits to their anger. But how awful for her to be the victim of my pattern-in-reverse. To have me, unable to cope with my mother's authority, unable to give her any, so that she becomes in turn a bully, and the old family pattern starts again into the fourth generation."

"Ah," said Dr. Jarvis. "But there's a difference. Unlike your mother, you did not beat her."

* * *

In 1945, Maunsell's common law wife died. Oliver Wagstaff was happy to be quit of his responsibility for Helen's funds. He wrote himself a large check, as his fee, and released the remainder of her capital. It was several hundred thousand dollars.

Lewis was still in analysis, but no longer depressed. He and Helen had a wide circle of friends, both Rockvillians and New Yorkers transplanted to the nation's capital. Several of Helen's Vassar friends lived nearby. The infusion of money caused Helen to think about what she really wanted to do next. She wrote to Daisy Suckley in October of 1946: "I wonder what it would be like to live in Rhinebeck, in a nice, old, big, mansard-y house, not too far from the grocers. . . I sometimes wonder if we couldn't come back to a different way of life there, someday— because Goodness Knows, I'm *not* a southerner, and my roots are *not* Maryland. It may be like, but it certainly isn't, as beautiful as Dutchess County."

In a decision that bound her more to Maryland, Helen decided it would be best not to uproot Lewis when the end of his analysis wasn't known. It did, however, with money now, make sense to buy a house rather than rent. Returning to the Hudson River Valley would have to wait. A former summer house came on the market. Built several decades earlier, its address was 117 South Van Buren Street. It sat on a hill with five acres of fields and trees. It offered remarkable privacy just four blocks from the courthouse and was only a minute's walk through a neighbor's hedge to the new nursery school and kindergarten Sheila and I attended.

There were other attractions to the house. In a little dell near a thicket of rhododendrons, there was a full-size carousel horse in its own pavilion, with stirrups, leather reins, and a horsehair tail. Its platform rocked. None of us had ever seen anything like it on private property. Near the horse were tall oak trees waiting for swings.

The house had nine rooms on two floors, plus a many-roomed basement with interior stone walls. The basement was dark and mysterious with single light bulbs hanging from the ceiling. It offered the potential not only for a large playroom, but also storage. There was room for coal, several cords of wood, a laundry, and a sink and toilet for household help. Lewis and Helen went to the Farmers Banking and Trust Company and co-signed the bank note using Helen's inheritance as collateral. Women were still not generally free to purchase a mortgage on their own. The monthly payment was the same as the previous rent.

They wanted friends to come to the house, and decided to build a tennis court. They knew of only one other family in Rockville that had one. Helen decided on a hard surface that could be painted green ("so that it will look like grass, the way courts in England do," she said). They installed a chain metal fence on all four sides and a backboard at one end.

Helen planted pink climbing roses along the fence. "The tennis court will be a draw for parties," she said, "and the girls will make new friends." That was true. Kids came cascading from neighboring houses, all sorts and sizes. When summer turned to winter, the same children returned for sledding down our hill on snowy days. When it was too cold to play outside, we played in the basement where Helen had packed a steamer trunk with dress-up clothes she no longer wore. In her diary, over and over, she noted how happy she was doing these things.

As individual daughters, we had quiet moments with Helen. For me, a special joy was being allowed in her walk-in closet while she worked at the desk in her bedroom. She had dozens of blouses neatly hung along one side. They were tailored and practical, many of them silk. On the opposite side were her party clothes, understated and elegant. She liked dresses that showed off her trim figure, fitted above the waist and slightly flared below. At the far end of the closet were her shelves of shoes, some high-heeled sandals, others bought for practicality.

It was exciting to try on Helen's jewelry, which she kept in a two-tiered leather box. She wore a single strand of pearls and matching earrings every day. In the leather box, she kept earrings, bracelets, and rings that had diamonds. When I graduated from college in 1960, she gave me a sapphire and diamond ring that had belonged to her grandmother. I was lucky. Not many years later, her jewelry was stolen.

Helen now wore boldly colored harlequin eyeglasses, making an asset of her eyes rather than trying to hide the fact that she was nearsighted. Her eyeglasses matched her clothes. If she was wearing sapphire blue, her glasses were sapphire blue. If she wore dark green, they were dark green. She also wore red frames.

CHAPTER 15

ROCKVILLE WAS ONCE A PROSPEROUS tobacco and dairy town. After the railroad came, connecting Rockville with Washington, D.C., it became a summer haven offering woods and streams to sweltering Washingtonians who could afford a second house or a stay at a country hotel. When we arrived in 1942, there was one traffic light in the center of town, and a blinking yellow light on the eastern outskirts. There were all the basic stores we needed. It wasn't until after World War II, and the G.I. Bill of Rights, that houses began to spring up everywhere. Everywhere, that is, except where blacks lived.

Outside of town, beyond the incorporated limits, there was another Rockville. I got to know it well, because most evenings Lewis drove our cook, Sadie Bell, home after she'd prepared and served our dinner, and washed the dishes. Sadie lived in Haiti, pronounced Hay-tie. Haiti was settled by freed blacks who were joined later by blacks migrating from the injustices of the South. But Rockville was below the Mason-Dixon Line, and Jim Crow, overt and covert, was present. Haiti had no paved roads or sidewalks, and no town sewerage. The houses had outside privies. The only streetlight at night came from the windows of people's houses.

Rockville's white population graded black people stereotypically. The "best" blacks didn't live in Haiti; they lived in the

West End, near Chestnut Lodge, descended from slaves who'd been freed the longest, and able to buy land and build houses before their numbers caused any white person to notice. Whites felt fortunate if they found household help from the West End; Lillian Hart, who lived there, came to our house six days a week to make our breakfast and beds, and take care of Judy. Her sister-in-law, Mrs. Baker, washed our sheets. Sometimes I would go with Lewis when he picked them up. I always longed to be invited into her house. It never happened; the exchange always took place on the porch.

Helen found Southern segregation confusing and painful. She'd encountered very little overt racism. Now, in Rockville, she had to teach us new rules. We could sit in the front of the bus, but blacks couldn't. We sat in the main part of the Milo movie theater, while blacks had to go upstairs and sit on rickety seats in the balcony. Blacks couldn't shop in many of the stores. If they wanted to buy clothes, they could; but they couldn't try them on first.

Helen partly understood that blacks were discriminated against because for the most part they were less educated, but she had trouble understanding why they weren't allowed to go to good schools. She found the lack of education frustrating when it came to teaching our help how to do certain things. Our first laundress came to the house to wash the sheets. Helen had to teach her how to use soap, because the laundress had learned to wash sheets by heaping them into a tub of boiling water and stirring them. Our first cleaner worked in reverse order: she swept the floors, making them sparkle, then dusted the furniture, propelling the dust to the freshly swept floor. "I'm spending more time teaching help how to clean than if I did it myself," Helen complained in her diary. On the other hand, wages were twenty-five cents an hour, so low that any help was better than none. In a letter to Bertha, Helen asked, "Why aren't they killing all of us, for all we've done to them?"

Helen's gentleness with our help may have contributed to the kind of help we had. "An intelligent colored girl walked in yesterday and said she *wanted* to work for us," Helen wrote Bertha, "because her sister, our laundress, had said we were 'such nice people.'"

Helen didn't understand that Jim Crow prohibitions applied to churches as well. She bought three tickets for *Iolanthe*, which was going to be performed in the rectory of the Episcopal Church. It was to be my introduction to Gilbert and Sullivan. At the last minute she and Lewis were unable to go, and she asked Deedee and Kermit Weaver, our babysitter and her fiancé, to take me. The three of us walked to the church several blocks away. I walked between them, holding their hands. Deedee and Kermit were turned away at the door.

"Why?" Helen asked, when we returned half an hour later.

"The reverend was at the door," Kermit said. "He said we couldn't enter. He said he'd find another family for Miss Sue to sit with."

"But didn't you show him the tickets? Didn't he know you'd paid?"

"Yes, ma'am. He said we couldn't go in. We didn't think we should leave Miss Sue without asking you first."

Kermit and Deedee didn't allow this insult to affect their relationship with me. They were married several months later and I was invited to sit in the front pew. It was my first church wedding.

It was difficult for Helen to know when, or how, to explain to us why white people were treated one way and black people another. Bertha wrote Helen that she'd recently enjoyed reading a "darkies" newspaper. Helen wrote back:

We've just been through the race problem with Sue and Sheila—it burst on us with the urgency of a time-bomb as it always does, through the medium of "eeny-meeny-minnie-mo-catch-a-nigger-by-the-toe." Asking them to say mousy meant nothing. They said "nigger" meant a small mouse. So we got out the globe and went into the Japs, the Chinese and the Negroes. Negroes were black. Lillian was a Negro. "But Lillian is brown!" "But Lillian is sunburned." (No, she's brown all over.) "How do you know?" etc., etc. It took three days to straighten out and our hearts were in our mouths every time Sheila yipped it, as yip she did.

Observing black people from a distance never ended. Helen took us by train to Florida a year after the "*eeny meeny*" incident. Segregation began at the Mason-Dixon Line, requiring black people from the north to move to the rear of the train. Helen, Sheila, Judy, and I went to the dining car for dinner. The train had just pulled out of Washington and entered Virginia. Helen and I sat facing the sliding door separating cars. A well-dressed black couple entered and asked for a table. The black head waiter told them to go to the rear of the train to a dining car reserved for coloreds. They weren't allowed to be served. I stared, fascinated, as they turned to leave.

"But Mother, they're hungry," I said. "Why can't they sit at a table here?"

"Because that's the way it is. Don't stare." In a public place, where she might be overheard, Helen didn't explain things.

CHAPTER 16

HAVING MONEY NOW, Helen entered us in private day schools. She arranged piano and ballet lessons and took us to concerts and plays. She bought books, because she believed every home should have a library. It was what she remembered about all the houses she'd known in the Hudson River Valley. She believed in investing in real estate, despite her ordeal selling Grasmere. When the chance came to buy a cottage by the ocean in Delaware, she happily put $8,000 into it. Bethany Beach was founded by alcohol-abstaining Methodists who'd departed after World War II, and Washingtonians were now buying there. Her plan was that she would take the three of us to the cottage in early June and stay until Labor Day. Lewis would join us on weekends. Most of the families who summered there had the same arrangement.

The cottage sat on a sandy street two blocks from the ocean. It was bordered by Pennsylvania Avenue, a two-lane road that went south to Ocean City, Maryland, and north to Rehoboth Beach, Delaware. We often sat on the screen porch watching the occasional cars go by. The living room had a Franklin stove that we lit on rainy days. The tiny bathroom had a claw-foot tub. We got hot water from a gas heater that we lit with a match and let warm up for half an hour. There were two small bedrooms on the first floor, one for Lewis and one for Helen, and a single open room upstairs with dormer windows. Each of us had a bed of our own, plus a bed for a friend.

I didn't understand for many years that Lewis was ill all this time. I had no idea that Helen might be seeking time on her own. They never argued in front of us. I knew they and their friends drank on a daily basis, but I knew nothing about the ill effects of alcohol. Having drinks at the end of the day, or even in the middle of the day, was the norm. My memory of these days is of our being a happy family.

During the week, the mothers at Bethany lived a simple life, doing minimal household chores and spending hours on the beach under colorful umbrellas. Local farmers drove by our houses in pickup trucks, calling out their wares. "Corn today, freshly picked," they would call, and "tomatoes, lettuce, peas, and beans." The milkman came every other day with eggs and bread. The fish man came twice a week with flounder, crab, and mussels, which he kept in a locker with a huge block of ice. We sat on the porch listening for their approach and ran into the street when we heard their calls. We'd put the food away, then don our bathing suits and carry sandwiches to the beach.

Lewis was still in analysis, but now had a job. He'd opened a real estate office in Washington and was working full-time. We loved when he came for the weekend. When he was there, he taught us to float with our toes above the water, and to swim under a wave before it crashed over our heads. Helen kept her eyes on us while we swam, and made sure we covered ourselves with suntan lotion. But she also took a thermos of martinis with her every morning, to sip with her sandwich in the middle of the day.

After the day at the beach, we'd walk home and shower in an outside stall. We'd play kick the can until it was time to eat. After dinner, we played Parcheesi or card games. Helen taught us canasta. She could shuffle a deck of cards so it made a bridge before it collapsed. "Watch," she told us, "the cards are moving so fast they look like a hummingbird's wings."

Long after we were supposed to have gone to sleep, we'd get out of bed and move to the open upstairs windows to listen to the pounding waves of the ocean. When the moon was full, we'd imagine creatures on the sandy street, moving in and out of the shadows, friendly animals that played at night. We had none of Helen's fears while falling asleep, as she had in Montana.

A wooden fence ran along the Pennsylvania Avenue side of our property. Helen planted it with hollyhocks and morning glories. The fence continued along the rear property line, then turned and ran along the east side of the cottage back to the street. On this side of the cottage, there was no room to play. You could touch the fence from a bedroom window. We had to walk in single file, and as we did, we'd pass by Helen's and Lewis's small bedrooms.

I asked Helen about their bedrooms once. "Why do you sleep in two rooms?"

"Because Daddy's sick," Helen said.

"How sick?" I asked, because I didn't think my father looked or acted sick.

"It's nothing to worry about," Helen said. "He's getting better."

* * *

Helen liked using shortcuts when she cooked. One night she gave me a lesson.

"Let's have garden peas with hash tonight," she said.

"How do we make that?" I asked.

"I'll show you," she said. "You take this can of Le Sueur baby peas and open it with a can opener. Put them in this saucepan and turn on the stove. They'll be warm in a minute. The hash comes from this second can and I spread it over the bottom of the frying pan. It'll be hot in a minute too."

Ocean City, Maryland was ten miles to the south. The three of us loved going there because it was honky-tonk and noisy and some of the restaurants had slot machines that whirled and spun out coins. Helen never minded these excursions. It was legal to drink and gamble in Maryland. Weeknights when she didn't want to cook, but felt like driving, she took us to dinner at the Lagoon Restaurant. She gave each of us a handful of coins. She'd nurse one or two drinks while we played the one-armed bandits.

There were two restaurants in Bethany Beach that could have fed us just as well, but they didn't serve alcohol. Helen took us to dinner at one or the other when she didn't feel like cooking or driving. She'd drink two bourbon old fashioneds on the porch and then say it was time to go.

While it was fun to have Helen to ourselves, there seemed to be more to do when Lewis came on the weekend. After dinner he'd take us for a walk on the boardwalk to buy ice cream cones at the bowling alley. We loved bowling, often joining other families. Afterwards, we'd walk home on the quiet boardwalk listening to the waves. Lewis would read to us for a little while after we got into bed. He'd sit at the top of the stairs facing the open room we shared, and read to us from there.

Lewis delighted in taking us crabbing. We'd walk two blocks along Pennsylvania Avenue to Collins Tea Room and cross a little bridge over an estuary. We'd find the rowboat Lewis kept moored there. We'd jump in and take up different positions. Lewis would slowly move one oar at a time, teaching us how to drag a net at the end of a pole. One of us would catch a crab. Another would hold the tin pail that held enough water to keep the crabs alive. It was fun until we got home, when the crabs met their death in a pot of boiling water; but we never said no to the invitation to go out again. On other occasions, he'd take us north to Indian River Inlet where we combed the beach for gold coins rumored to have come ashore when a Spanish galleon sank.

Most weekends, we went as families with all the fathers to the beach for a communal supper in the dunes. We drove to the southernmost end of Bethany, undeveloped and beautiful, and parked our cars. We climbed the slippery dunes carrying food baskets and arm loads of wood. The fathers dug deep holes for fires and started them. The mothers wrapped potatoes and corn in wet newspapers and buried them in the embers. The adults pressed bottles of beer deep into the sand, down to where it was cool enough to keep them chilled. As the night became colder, we put on jackets and sat around the fire. We'd be alone with the sound of the waves and the comfort of being with our families.

CHAPTER 17

CHESTNUT LODGE DIDN'T ENFORCE boundaries between patients and doctors, so patients and doctors often showed up at our house. The town of Rockville had a real love of parties. One couple liked to entertain on Sunday mornings. "Here's an invitation to cocktails at 11:00 a.m.," Helen said to Lewis when the invitation arrived. "It's the same time as church. Do you suppose it *is* church?" They went, drank too much, regretted drinking too much, and accepted when they were invited again. Helen's analyst, Dr. Jarvis, often asked Helen to come back to her house for a drink at the end of the day. She invited herself once to Bethany Beach, renting a cottage directly opposite ours, and then announcing that she couldn't cook. She came to our house for three meals a day for a week.

Here are excerpts from Helen's diary:

Lewis home from a mental hygiene meeting 1:30am by which time I had taken to drink.

A very long day. Tried desperately to diet, which has to include 2 highballs.

Wish I could stop eating 2 cheese sandwiches and 2 martinis.

Went on the wagon for Lent. Spend most of time chewing crackers.

Struggle to stay on wagon acute, accentuating need
of household to relax 5–8 and for mother to sit down.
Otherwise we congregate and quarrel in kitchen.

Felt perfectly awful after a dinner party. All plates too
full. Too many drinks and all unpalatable whisky on ice.

Children's hour. Martinis.
At Bethany. Got very drunk at Nobles.
On beach, with cramps, thermos martinis fixed it nicely.
I am tense. The drinking helps.
Shrimps and rice & martinis on top of old fashioneds at
Newmans.
Took Sheila for eye checkup, then drank too much rum at
Purdons.
Hadleys arrived. Made the men drink beer. Old fash-
ioneds later.

Lewis drank very little. Years later, after he'd had three long
relationships with alcoholic women, I detected his pattern. He
had an advantage with tipsy women. If Helen went to bed early,
he could spend the evening reading. Helen spoke in her later
years of the distance between them. "He slept with me five
times. Two produced miscarriages, three brought my daughters." During the summer of 1946, Lewis began to spend weekends in Rockville instead of coming to the beach. Helen challenged him, asking what he did when they weren't together.

During this time, and afterwards, Helen stayed outwardly
cheerful. Lewis *was* having an affair, it became clear later, and
would have liaisons with other women. Helen threw herself into
volunteer activities, helping to found the Green Acres School
and editing its newsletter. She bought us new clothes and sewed
on endless nametapes. She organized play groups and often
joined us in them. A special project was painting the wooden
carousal horse. "It took us four hours, and to me, was all part

of being able to enjoy being with the children," she wrote in her diary.

But something was in the air. Without knowing why, we began to feel scared. Sheila, Judy, and I began to fight. It wasn't over anything serious, siblings quarreling over who would play the piano, or use the tennis court when. But then we started not to tell the truth. If Helen thought I'd drawn on the living room wall, when Sheila was the one who'd done it, Sheila would point her finger at me. Sheila and I stopped trusting each other, and Judy and Sheila became closer.

In 1951, Helen ended her analysis with Dr. Jarvis. She had tired of Rockville's close-knit society where everyone seemed to know everything about everyone else. She wondered whether she should be "living for Lewis and the children" or "living for herself." She wondered whether she should return to Rhinebeck. She'd accepted Freud's theory that the psyche is organized into ego, id, and super ego, each vying for dominance, but it didn't satisfy her. She wanted to know what kind of happier future she might have. She chose a new analyst, Dr. Hanna Colm, an existential psychotherapist whose interest lay in looking ahead, rather than at what had happened in the past.

Dr. Colm's office was in Washington, near the White House, removed from the peeking eyes of Rockville. Driving back and forth took time, and was complicated when there were other appointments in Washington as well; she could enjoy window-shopping only so much. Helen made a bold decision for herself: she rented a one-bedroom apartment at the LaSalle on Connecticut Avenue, near "L" Street, and made it her retreat. She bought a first edition of Virginia Woolf's *A Room of One's Own,* a radio, a long-playing record player, and a Remington portable typewriter.

I was eleven and in the seventh grade at Sidwell Friends School. When Dr. Colm learned there was squabbling in the family, she suggested I come for therapy. "It won't be such a burden, she's in Washington every day already," she said. Helen picked me up at school once a week and waited in the waiting room while I had my hour. Then we drove back to Rockville. I have no memory of anything I talked to Dr. Colm about; but I did like having this time with Helen.

One afternoon Helen confided in me. She told me about the apartment and took me there. I saw a double bed with a red- and white-striped bedspread and a desk with the typewriter and typing paper beside it. Helen told me she spent time in the apartment between appointments. "My eye doctor is around the corner," she said. "My hairdresser is on 'M' Street. I buy clothes at Joan Roberts." Then she said, "Don't tell your father. I don't want him to know."

Dr. Colm understood the fear Helen had experienced as a child. She knew about the beatings in Montana and Elizabeth's emotional abuse. She listened as Helen described facial tics she was developing in the company of other people. "I don't know what life I'm meant to live," Helen said. "I want a reason to feel alive. I feel I've done the things I was supposed to do."

"What things?" Dr. Colm asked.

"I learned to be polite and kind to people. That's why my grandmother in Rhinebeck let me stay at Grasmere during vacations. I was polite to her even though I was scared of her. I learned to dress well. I worked like hell and got into college. I graduated. Lewis fell for me. He married me."

"And?"

"Well, these were all things I learned to do and did. They were supposed to reward me with something. Now it's starting all over again. I'm trying to make my marriage work. It's not working. But it's supposed to work. That's the agreement, isn't it? That I get married and live happily ever after?"

"Is it?" asked Dr. Colm.

"Well," said Helen, "it just turned into more and more. The kids. Volunteering. All these jobs that have a beginning and then an end. And then what? It's not what men do."

"What do men do?"

"They get up in the morning and go out the door and do something they choose to do and that makes them somebody. I'm propping that up. It isn't enough. I don't feel happy ever after. I feel empty. I don't want to keep doing things for everybody else."

Dr. Colm encouraged Helen to write. "This is the time to try," she said.

Helen told Dr. Colm that her Vassar degree hadn't prepared her for anything practical. She wanted to be more than someone who simply transmitted culture. "I want a real job," she said. "Or maybe I should move out west and ride horses again." Pig Parrish, her boarding school and college lover, was earning her living as an artist in New Mexico.

"I want to control my drinking. I have gin in the apartment. I carry it in my purse sometimes, in small bottles," Helen said. "But I don't really want to stop. When I drink, I feel whole. I feel the parts of me coming together. I don't feel as if I'm two people, one always looking at the other and being critical. Or feeling alone. I think there's something in me that really wants to be a different person, but I can't get at it. I have dreams. In them I'm trying to read the answers, but there's no book."

It was while Helen was exploring these issues with Dr. Colm that she learned that Lewis had started another affair. It was with the wife of a prominent Rockville psychiatrist. She was determined to break it up, quickly; and knew exactly what to do. With her awareness of bi-sexuality, she had no fear. She embarrassed both Lewis and the psychiatrist by initiating a sexual relationship with the wife, who turned out to like it. Helen told me about it over lunch at the Willard Hotel when I was twenty-seven. "I was sick with worry about what was happening to us as a family," she said. "And I was drinking too, and asked for help, but no one believed I was drinking too much."

Bertha Coolidge's husband died in 1953, leaving an estate of seven million dollars. Alone in New York, and in poor health, Bertha was frightened. She asked if she could come to Maryland and live with us. Helen believed that Bertha had inherited her husband's money outright, and that she in turn would inherit from Bertha when Bertha died. She said yes. Bertha moved into the first-floor bedroom normally occupied by Lewis. Lewis moved back upstairs, to a single bed in the master bedroom. Bertha stayed with us for several months, until her presence became burdensome for us all, and Helen made arrangements for her to move to Florida.

During these months, we sat at the dining room table every night with a straight-backed, stern, white-haired New England widow wearing a black full-length dinner dress and a diamond brooch. Bertha studied our manners. She disliked the way we made noise eating soup. "Tilt the bowl away from you when the soup gets low. Make a puddle and slip your spoon in quietly. Hold your breath when you put the spoon in your mouth. An intake of air will make noise." We sat up as erectly as we could, and kept our elbows off the table. Bertha ate slowly. We fidgeted when we finished before she did, because we weren't allowed to leave the table early.

I ended up not liking Bertha. She was complicit with Helen early on when Helen brought her my diary. They thought I was in Sunday school and wouldn't know. I'd developed a crush on a boy who lived down the street and written about it. I came home from Sunday school early and overheard them reading excerpts and laughing at the kitchen table. I fled, mortified, to my bedroom upstairs. I began to wonder how safe I was.

Helen brought up the cost of our private schools with Bertha. "She teased me," Helen wrote in her diary. "She won't say whether she'll help or not." But Helen wasn't being greedy. She'd become concerned about whether sibling rivalry was damaging us. I wasn't doing well at school. A new girl in the seventh grade was a bully. One of her tactics was aiming hockey balls above my shin guard. I began to buy candy bars after school, sometimes eating as many as four, while waiting for the Rockville bus. By the end of the year, I'd gained thirty pounds. I wrote to boarding schools whose ads I saw in the back pages of magazines, and an avalanche of catalogs began to arrive. Helen and Lewis were on the mark. They asked if I wanted to go away to school. They found Solebury, a small coeducational boarding school in New Hope, Pennsylvania, where I found my niche and was happy. I lost all the weight I'd gained, and then some.

When I was in ninth grade, in 1952, Helen received a telephone call from the medical director of Chestnut Lodge asking her to meet him in his office. The director didn't normally see her; Lewis's treatment was Lewis's concern. She knew his analysis was going slowly but trusted it was working. The director was in the front hall and greeted her himself. He ushered her into his office overlooking orchards and farmland beyond.

"Lewis isn't going to get well completely without your help," he said. "To be direct, it's marriage. It's your marriage that's terrifying to him. He sees his mother in everything you do. He can't separate images of his mother from his image of you. When he touches you, he feels he's touching his mother."

"And," he added, "he knows that you're no longer happy in the marriage either."

Helen went cold. She recognized that it wasn't possible any longer to keep the difficulties in her marriage secret. Soon we would know, and so would everyone else in Rockville, New

York, and the Hudson River Valley. Flashes of the times they'd made love raced through her mind. She saw the times they'd held hands and danced before they were married. She saw the times they'd been quiet so as not to wake us. She saw the transition in their bedroom from a double bed to a double and a twin, and how they'd tried not to let us know that their intimacy had ended. But was the marriage itself really ending? How could that be? What were the electric shocks meant to do, the endless hours of analysis, even the fact that they now had money from Maunsell's inheritance, and might, when Bertha died, have even more? Everything should be working, she thought. How can it not be?

"There should be some kind of arrangement that lets him begin a new life," she heard the director say. "Something that allows him to live by himself, but close to the children. It's the only way."

Helen searched for a sentence to speak. "This isn't what was supposed to happen."

"What's supposed to happen isn't always what does," he replied. "Sometimes we choose something that's exactly the opposite of what we want. We do it to keep people from knowing. I don't believe Lewis really ever wanted to marry. He wanted to want to, if you follow me, and he did his best, but now it's stifling him."

"I only wanted to be a good wife and mother. I've done everything I knew how. The children need a father. I'm sure he loves them."

"He does love them," the director said. "And he will be there for them."

Helen understood in that moment that the family history she'd tried to avoid was repeating itself. She and Lewis were going to do the same thing to their children that her parents and his parents had done to them. Despite how hard she'd tried, she was losing a husband just as her mother had. And Lewis was leaving a marriage just as his father had. And her daughters would have separated parents just as she had. And it would be hard for us, because families weren't meant to divorce, and friends would take sides, and we would be talked about.

I was the first to be told. I came home from Solebury for Thanksgiving and Helen took me aside in the kitchen to explain what she called "Life Without Father." She and Lewis had decided to divorce, she said, and she was telling me now because I was home from school and she wanted to tell me in person. Sheila and Judy didn't know yet. The separation would begin at Christmas; she needed to have a hysterectomy first. Lewis would live in another house in Rockville. Sheila, Judy, and I would live with her, but we could see Daddy as often as we wanted.

I was sipping a glass of ginger ale while she spoke. I was concentrating on taking small sips. I said to myself, "Don't cry. You're a grown up now." I bit the edge of the glass to keep tears from coming. The rim of the glass broke but it split cleanly. I wasn't cut. Helen didn't reach out to touch me. We didn't mention the broken glass. We stood there in the kitchen like two utterly rational human beings talking while the world was crashing down around us.

I never enjoyed a normal family Christmas again. From then on, my Christmases involved driving from one parent's house to the other's. In time there would be step-parents and step-siblings and, whether one liked to admit it or not, feelings of jealousy and competition. Lewis would tell me years later that his second wife insisted he spend more money on her children than on his. Her children would live with them, and Helen's children would be visitors. When Lewis walked out on this marriage as well, he left more devastated children.

For this first Christmas "without Father," Helen booked us a Grace Line cruise to Venezuela and Colombia. Lewis stayed in Rockville feeling profound sadness. Bertha Slade died a few weeks later. In her will, she left one hundred thousand dollars of her own money to Helen. The seven million Helen thought she might inherit turned out to have been in a trust and went to Harvard; Bertha had had only the income. Helen was bitterly disappointed. But the money she did inherit gave her more than enough to begin a new life on her own.

CHAPTER 18

SOCIALLY, HELEN KNEW FEW JEWS. But individually, as doctors or actors or writers, she'd encountered many Jews whose sense of humor and kindness impressed her. She concluded that those who helped her the most were in fact Jews. Her trusted doctor in New York was William Hitzig. Her Washington physician was Dr. Steiglitz. She named Judy "Judith" in part because, by giving Judy a Jewish name, "I could make her aware of how helpful Jewish people were before her awareness of them occurred." She had heard Al Capp, the cartoonist, once say, "Jews are just like everybody else, only more so." She'd seen Jeff Chandler, the actor, who'd been born Ira Grossel, on CBS. She wrote the television network afterwards: "It was a long-needed program. Very helpful to an Anglo-Saxon who has always said to her children, our lives have been saved over and over again by Jewish physicians. No Anglo-Saxon ever gave me the laughs, the lovely, necessary, healing laughs, the Jews have given me. I hope you will repeat the program until it penetrates to the heart of everyone who hates."

So it was not surprising that Helen chose Abe Fortas, a former Yale Law School professor, to represent her in her divorce from Lewis. Born in Memphis, Tennessee, Fortas was the son of a Jewish immigrant cabinetmaker from Great Britain. A brilliant student, he was named editor-in-chief of the *Yale*

Law Review. Childless, he lived with his wife, a tax lawyer, in an imposing brick house in Georgetown. A gifted violinist, on Sunday evenings he played in a quartet called "The N Street Strictly-No-Refunds String Quartet." He was a senior partner in the law firm Arnold & Fortas, with an office not far from the LaSalle.

Helen had her first appointment with him three weeks after Bertha died. She started a new five-year diary that year and, after five years, when it was full, wrote on the front page, "This book is the property of Helen Crosby and every other word is double-talk or double-think because, with three daughters reading my diary, I could not record The Truth." In the diary she confirms that she and Abe Fortas had an affair in the spring of 1953. An entry in mid-April reads: "This day I shall Rue." The affair lasted two months, until the day she left for Nevada to establish the legal residence required for a divorce.

During these two months, Helen saw her analyst, Dr. Colm, several times a week. She spent many hours in her apartment, writing many of the pages that appear in this book. She listened to classical music on the radio. She wrote down the names of recordings she liked and walked to the Disc Shop on Dupont Circle to buy them. A favorite was Beethoven's *Sonata in A minor*, "The Kreutzer." She and Abe listened to it together.

Helen hoped to see or hear from Abe the night before she left for Reno, but there was silence. She spent the night alone at the LaSalle. She wrote in her diary, "Cried most of the evening." The radio reported tornados in Ohio and Massachusetts and she was concerned about flying. She sat at her typewriter and wrote him a letter before she went to bed, asking that he return it after he read it.

> Ah yes this is the hour we were waiting for. . . to stay or go. No playing of "Pal Joey" will dull this disaster. How softly the night is coming across the heights of Georgetown where

your wife waits for you to come home and where my husband, miles beyond, is still wondering if I will change my mind. All Judy said was "See you the first of August" and my heart broke. At least she had that much faith in me that going, I would return. Will you telephone and Oh God, I hope you don't, so that at least I can go out of here alone and on the merits of loneliness and not of longing for something I can never have.

I am dissolved and how much worse to have it come so late. You said there will be rough going. . . this is worse than that. . . this is breaking up all the old household patterns of their childhood and ten years of what for this age had been marvelously faithful "help."

And now I know that you can never really love. . . unless, and for one so absorbed in each day's activity, it is a very big unless. . . There are many men who can take love welling up towards them and not feel that they, to be safe, to be their version of free, must annihilate it. I caught a glimpse of this feeling of destruction in you the first time, but thought I could get you to trust me and perhaps learn to accept from another human being, be we male or female, wherever, however, the freedom to love.

"Because it is the man in me," you said. . . "Men are like that." And asked, "Do you think that men can ever give as much love as women do?" Yes Yes Yes. But not if they are endlessly striving for power.

Where were you in that tornado? What a headline to greet us at breakfast. And now one in Worcester. . . and where tomorrow?

Tomorrow. Well my eyes are dry now. I shall go out of here to divorce my sadness with my husband. . . not my sadness over you. Were you in panic that I was going away and that you did not feel sure of me. . . When you did not really want to be sure of me?

Tonight this apartment is worth its yearly rent. I was wiser than I knew when I said I want to come here to think.

And God bless the Good Music Station for roaring onwards and upwards with its symphonies.

Now I can confess to my real meanness of spirit. . . that of never writing you while I am away. . . let it die or let it live according to your lights. Not mine.

Everything you do I love. That you should empty the ashtray into the other before bringing it to the table. . . that you were not hungry. . . that you wanted a little gin. That you found just such a lipstick. That your voice is so deep over the telephone. That your "ah darling" is so light of loveliness before you touch me. That you noticed the delphiniums (blue, geraniums red). That you should leave so quickly. Standing a moment all in blue, framed unforgettably in the doorway. That a vacation should be building a house. That you think I am an alcoholic. . . which I am not. . . Only a terribly distressed person until I could make a decision.

Well, I have loved often enough to let go of you before I am trapped in an impossible situation. I have had my health of you and I thank you. I must go on and find either my life alone or perhaps someone to cherish me and I, him. I am not framed to be a mistress. I care too much where I put my love. I care where you put yours too. You should regard yourself more highly. You are in the prime of life and you could even be a father if you so desired. Only adults so desire. I always want to have children whenever I really love. Since I no longer can. . . I even thought of adopting one in your likeness. Fatuous. Unfair. Below the belt. But I thought it. There and there alone lies the difference, perhaps, between the loving that men and women do, that there is such a profound desire to conceive in the image of one's beloved. Perhaps that is where the tear came from.

Now the lightning flashes around the horizon and the breezes rush softly through the window. Those wretched people next door have let themselves back in from their dinner and there are coughs and conversation. But it is not such a bad apartment after all. It has been an hour glass with the sands running from an emptiness.

It waits now to see if you will call. Either way I can leave
it. I know where you are. Do you know where I am?

The following morning she mailed the letter. She flew to
Salt Lake City and drove to Reno, "a long day over America."
Abe read the letter and sent it back to her with this note:

Helen, my dear,

I have read this many times. I did not know whether I could
send it back, as you asked. But I had better. I suppose, in the
queer way that irrelevancies affect things, it was the notation
on the back: Sonata in A minor, that concluded the issue.

God bless,
Abe

Helen had typed the letter on white typing paper. On the
back side of one sheet, she'd jotted in pencil the name of a new
recording of the "Kreutzer Sonata." Did she choose that piece of
paper on purpose? We'll never know.

I do know, however, what happened next. Abe put Helen's
letter and his note into an envelope and, mistakenly or purpose-
fully (it is said there are no accidents), addressed it to Helen
at Lewis's new Rockville address. Lewis thought it was a legal
communication and opened it. He waited five years before for-
warding it to Helen in 1959. His postmarked envelope survives.
Lewis said:

Dear Peter,

I am glad to be rid of this which came to me in error,
although perhaps it somehow made things a little easier for
me too.

Lewis

Helen spent six weeks at a ranch on Lake Tahoe. Judy, Sheila and I went to summer camp. A dozen other women were at the ranch, also awaiting divorces. They were in various stages of sadness, loneliness, excitement about new freedom, and fear of the same. They spent time together over drinks at cookouts. The cook was Mike Taylor, whose other responsibilities were to saddle the horses, lead trail rides, and take the guests on tours around Lake Tahoe.

Helen's diary tells us she tried to watch her drinking. She fell in love with the scenery and fresh air, and rediscovered her love of riding. Most mornings she went trail riding for several hours. If she felt sleepy, she napped in the afternoon. She re-read Rosamond Lehmann's novel, *Dusty Answer*. "I'm reading it as if it were a textbook," she wrote. "I'm an outsider, and the heroine is an outsider, but I didn't know that the first time I read it."

Three weeks after her arrival, Helen and Mike Taylor went riding by themselves. They continued to ride together for the remainder of her stay. Just before her six weeks were up, she began to bleed from complications related to the hysterectomy she'd had. Instead of arranging for a curettage in Washington, as soon as she got home, she decided to have one in San Francisco. When her divorce was granted, Mike drove her there. ("Mike came for breakfast and Dubonnet," she wrote in her diary the day before they left.) He stayed with her while she convalesced, then drove her across the country back to Rockville. She agonized over whether to marry him. She liked that he was an outdoorsman; but he hadn't graduated from college like the other men she knew. He had a history of changing jobs. He was Jewish. "Loving Jews is one thing," she wrote in her diary, "but marrying?"

Lewis's new house in Rockville was three blocks from 117 South Van Buren Street, and he was at our house when Helen and Mike arrived. The two men actually liked each other, when they met, and Lewis invited Mike to move in with him. I keep wondering, was this more of Lewis's sense of irony? Mike didn't stay long; he was offered a job in Japan and took it. A few years later, he married a Japanese woman.

There were now many decisions Helen had to make about where we would live and go to school, and how often Lewis would see us. When Mike left, Helen saw clearly that Rockville wasn't where she wanted to live. She took us to England in the summer of 1954 to give herself time to think.

* * *

History repeats itself. Sarah and Henry Schieffelin took their daughters, Fanny and Minnie, to Europe in 1876 so that they would become "cultured" and able to hold their own in conversation in New York. General Atterbury helped my grandmother, Elizabeth Coolidge, go to England after the First World War so that she could "think." Oliver Wagstaff wrote a check in 1933 that allowed Helen to go to England as a break from the strain of running Grasmere. Now Helen was taking us to England. Lady Huntingfield, her aunt, had died in 1943, but her widower, Lord Huntingfield, had continued to stay in touch with Helen. He found a flat for us at 69 Chesterfield Gardens, off Curzon Street in the heart of Mayfair. It had three small bedrooms, two bathrooms, a sitting room, and dining room overlooking Chesterfield Gardens.

On June 14th, with twenty-seven suitcases, we took the train from Union Station to New York and sailed to Southampton on the *Britannic* the following day. We spent the mornings in deck chairs with blankets wrapped around our feet. At night, we watched movies in the ship's cinema: Charles Laughton in *Hobson's Choice*, *Return to Paradise* with Gary Cooper, and *Hell Below Zero* with Alan Ladd. The sea was calm throughout the ten-day crossing.

Lord Huntingfield met us at the boat train in London. His daughter, Sara Peel, Helen's first cousin, was with him. They accompanied us to the flat and introduced us to the daily, who would cook breakfast and clean five mornings a week. That night, they took us to the Cavalry Club. Helen was happy to see them. "Uncle Charles and Sara are my family," she said. "When I'm with them, I feel like I'm back in the Hudson River Valley."

Helen made elaborate plans for us to see as much of Europe and her cousins as possible. We went to East Anglia to see where her aunt had lived. We spent two weeks in Paris, Geneva, Zurich, and Venice, returned to London to do laundry, then went to Oslo, Stockholm, and Copenhagen. After another return to London, we went to North Berwick, a coastal village near Edinburgh. Sara Peel joined us with her children and some of her children's friends. Lifelong friendships with my second cousins began.

There was one incident, however, that none of us talked about. In Paris, Helen thought Sheila and I would have fun if we got haircuts. It wouldn't be every day that we could be styled by someone French. My haircut was fine. Sheila's wasn't; she didn't speak French and didn't know how to ask the stylist to stop. Feeling scalped, and embarrassed, she locked herself in the bathroom connecting our hotel rooms and threatened to jump out the window if any of us came near. Helen countered with the threat that she would jump off the bedroom balcony naked if Sheila didn't unlock the door. Several minutes later, Sheila unlocked the door and saw Helen naked on the balcony. I read Helen's diary closely to see how she described the incident to herself. She wrote: "July 27—Sailboats in Tuileries, the Cézanne exhibit being closed. Sue & Sheila haircuts, mildly disastrous. Saw *Bandwagon* pm."

*　*　*

On our return from Europe, Helen sold the Rockville house and bought a three-story white clapboard house at 3411 Lowell Street, N.W. in Cleveland Park in Washington. It had a welcoming front porch shaded by trees, and a large garden at the rear. It was within walking distance of Sidwell Friends. Lewis stayed in Rockville and commuted into Washington to his office on Windom Place, also close to the school. I was torn about returning to Solebury. "How can I see Daddy if the school allows me only two weekends a semester?" I asked. "How do I choose whether to visit you, or him? If I live with you, I can see Daddy after school." Helen agreed, and nimbly arranged for me to rejoin my class at Sidwell Friends. I returned to the class of 1956.

The bully who'd made my life unbearable in the seventh grade was still in my class, but a new girl became my close friend. Linda Griffin was the daughter of an admiral who'd been transferred from Saigon to Washington. During those two last years at Friends, we'd walk home together. We took routes longer than we needed to, avoiding her house and mine. It was only at our 35th Sidwell Friends School reunion that we fully understood why: her mother and mine were alcoholics. In high school, we hadn't had the knowledge to put a name to it. We simply knew that more times than we liked, our mothers seemed weird when we got home from school, and they embarrassed us. I'd been mortified one afternoon to find Helen dancing by herself in a red flannel nightgown. In the confused way children sometimes see things, Linda and I told each other that we liked each other's mother. We both needed mothers, and we projected onto the mother of our friend the admiration we wanted to feel for our own.

CHAPTER 19

LIVING IN A HOUSE WITHOUT A MAN was unsettling for
Helen. There had always been a man in her life before. She
had liked her stepfathers, and had had a trusting and affectionate relationship with Dexter Burroughs, the superintendent at
Grasmere. Lewis had been a good father to her children. Her
growing lack of ease was exacerbated by the sibling rivalry that
was surfacing again in Washington. She was an only child.
Three adolescent girls were not only a challenge to her as a
mother, but were unknown as a situation.

Sheila, Judy, and I had bedrooms on the third floor with
a shared bathroom. Helen's bedroom was on the second floor,
with a dressing room and bath, and a smaller bedroom at the
rear. The first floor had a front hall, living room with a fireplace, dining room, kitchen, and "piano room" for the gold and
cream Steinway piano. In the basement, Helen built a recreation
room and bomb shelter. She built an annex to the side of the
house for guests. It was a comfortable and spacious house, which
she'd paid for in cash.

I spent most of my time studying for College Boards. Judy
and Sheila were under less pressure. Judy liked to turn up the
volume of her phonograph and I lost my temper over this frequently. Sheila made me mad because she borrowed my clothes
without asking.

Helen began to make arrangements for me to be a débutante. It was never questioned: she'd been a débutante in New York, and her mother had been a débutante in Boston. Washington's social life was different from those cities' because it was fluid. Many of my schoolmates were from military, political, or diplomatic families. My first serious boyfriend, Nicolas Rivero, was from Cuba. His closest friend was from the Philippines. There were two annual cotillions, paid for by the parents of eligible young women, and lists of eligible young men.

One December afternoon, at the start of the party season, I put on a new dress for a tea dance. It was emerald-green satin, with a scoop neckline, cupped sleeves, and a soft pleated skirt. I'd been to the hairdresser earlier in the day.

Sheila and I argued in the hallway outside our bedrooms. Our words became heated. Neither of us remembers today what the argument was about. She had a supper tray in her room on which there was a glass of milk. She took the glass and with perfect aim threw milk over my hair and dress. I turned on her with fury and Judy, standing in her doorway, very scared, was afraid we were going to kill each other. Helen stood in the hallway downstairs, not moving. I'm not certain how the fight was stopped. Sheila and I have talked about it again and again, and neither of us knows. I changed into another dress. I managed to salvage my hair. I went to the tea dance and pretended nothing was wrong.

But of course something was very wrong. As sisters, we were losing our bond. Helen's inability to react was based on fear. She didn't come to my defense or Sheila's. The result was that we all felt unsafe. I demanded that I be allowed to live with Lewis. Helen, in turn, began to think she would have to remarry, if only to keep peace in the house.

I moved out the following week and commuted to Sidwell Friends from Rockville. Lewis was glad to have a companion in the house. He was seeing a nice woman who hoped he'd marry her. Leola Williams, a nearly white black woman, cooked for us five nights a week. Lewis drove her home after dinner, while I did my homework.

It must have seemed like a gift from heaven for Helen when, in April of 1955, Harold Glendening, a lawyer from New York, telephoned. He was in Washington on an assignment with the Justice Department. A graduate of Dartmouth and Columbia and a Rhodes Scholar, he'd been given Helen's name by Oliver Wagstaff, her former trustee. He asked if he could take her to dinner.

They went to the Zebra, a cocktail lounge and restaurant just off Wisconsin Avenue, a few blocks from our house. There was a bar at the front, and a room at the back where you could order steak. Two walls of the back room were lined with banquettes covered in black and white stripes. The tables were black, the ceiling low. There were candles on each table and mirrors that reflected their light, giving the room a cozy glow. Helen and Harold each had two martinis before ordering and a third with their steak. He told her about his previous marriages, the first to a duPont, ending in divorce, the second ending with the death of his wife in 1948. He described a humble background; his father was a postman.

Harold's social credentials impressed Helen. He'd moved beyond his origins. He was a member of the Down Town Association, the University Club of New York, the St. Nicholas Society, and the Society of Colonial Wars. He was in the *Social Register* and a member of Phi Beta Kappa. He liked to dance. He owned a tailcoat. He walked Helen back to 3411 Lowell Street and asked if he could see her again. She said yes.

Harold took Helen out to dinner many more times that spring. They went to the Zebra often, and always had drinks. He told Helen he'd called other women in Washington, and that he was frequently asked to dinner parties as an extra man. Helen liked his being in demand, but was bothered by how easy his life seemed. He was never short of invitations, while she, as a woman, received almost none. More than once, she went to the address of a house where she knew he was dining and hid behind a tree (Washington's sidewalks are thick with trees) to see who else was there.

She recorded her dinners with Harold in her diary, and also their many arguments. Still, they continued to see each other. She might have been feeling vulnerable because she understood that Lewis was thinking of remarrying. He'd rung Helen's doorbell three days after Harold first called, to say he wanted to apologize for the suffering he'd caused. He told her about the woman he was seeing. "Please forgive me," he said. "I was fighting for my sanity." (He didn't marry this woman, after all.)

Helen's self-recriminations about drinking continued, but they were complicated by the fact that Harold drank as well. A pattern developed. Harold would lose his temper, storm off, call to apologize, and then send flowers. After one very argumentative evening, Helen packed a suitcase the next morning and left for Bethany Beach. Harold, who didn't know how to drive, hired a car and driver and followed her there.

"Please marry me," he said.

"No," Helen said.

"Please," he said. "Or if you won't marry me, at least have dinner with me again."

The courtship resumed, and Helen made more entries in her diary. "I'm struggling with drink." "Too many martinis, but delicious." "Accident." "Gambling, drinking." "Managed to stay on the wagon." "Had stinger alone at Ritz Carlton." "Vodka'd." "H and I too much to drink."

That summer, I returned from Lewis's to Lowell Street to take an accelerated course in geometry at Sidwell Friends. I had

no talent for spatial thinking and wanted to satisfy the requirement in eight weeks rather than endure it for a year. I was aware
of Harold's presence, though I failed to see the roller coaster ele-
ments; I went out with Nick Rivero most evenings, and if I was
at home, they didn't raise their voices.

Sheila departed in June for summer camp in New Milford,
Pennsylvania. Judy went to the Tetons. They hardly knew
Harold. After my geometry course ended, I flew to Bermuda
with a Solebury classmate whose parents, Helen had been
assured, would be with us the entire time. Hurricane Diane
struck the East Coast a week later. My friend's parents flew back
to New York just before it struck, leaving us in Bermuda alone.
That decision upset Helen. We made our way back to New York
several days later, and I returned to Washington by train after
the storm had subsided.

The hurricane struck New Milford, Pennsylvania, leaving
Sheila stranded in the worst of a major flooded disaster area.
Lewis, who'd offered to pick her up and bring her back to
Washington, telephoned Helen to say they'd be returning later
than originally planned.

Helen misunderstood and thought Lewis meant that he and
Sheila would be returning several days later. She went out to
dinner with Harold the following night. Confident they would
be alone, she invited him in for a drink afterwards. At 9:30 p.m.
Sheila arrived and burst into the living room with excitement at
being greeted by our dog, Poky, who was circling her with joy.
Poky had been in the family for several years and, in Sheila's
mind, was her dog.

Harold was in the living room and called Poky to his side,
commanding the dog to stay. In less than twenty minutes he
told Sheila it was her bedtime. Sheila went upstairs to her bedroom on the third floor, surprised that this man in the living
room should think her dog was his. She heard the front door

open and Harold's voice calling out "Good night. I'll see you tomorrow." She heard the front door close.

It was a hot August night and we had no air-conditioning. Sheila was alone on the third floor. She tried to open her windows. One stuck, and she pushed it harder to break it free. A pane of glass broke and cut her hand. Terrified of the blood on her hand, Sheila flew down the stairs to Helen's room and opened the door to see Harold fully clothed, sitting in a chair, and Helen in her bra and girdle standing before him.

Sheila was shocked. She'd been reading true romance magazines at camp all summer and knew good girls didn't do that kind of thing. She raced back up the stairs and locked herself in the bathroom. Harold departed and Helen pounded on the bathroom door with first aid. Sheila believes that Helen's sense of shame was so deep that she felt the only thing she could do was marry Harold to show her children that she wasn't the prostitute they probably thought she was.

"I ache for us all," Helen wrote in her diary that night. Sheila suffered migraines for many weeks afterwards, and was hospitalized twice. She lost her sight at one time. It wasn't until early November that she started seeing her friends again.

Helen and Harold were married on January 14, 1956, in a chapel at Washington National Cathedral. They held a reception at Lowell Street for a hundred of mostly Helen's friends, then retired to the Fairfax Hotel for the night. The next morning they flew to Montego Bay in Jamaica and spent a week at Round Hill. Helen's diary for their first morning in Jamaica reads, "Woke up to the sound of tropical birds. Harold brought the breakfast tray to bed. Sipped martinis and read the newspapers." It was, she wrote later, "the worst mistake I ever made. I just didn't have the strength to help my daughters without a man in the house."

* * *

In the fall of 1956, I left for Vassar. Sheila went to Solebury as a junior, at Harold's insistence. Judy was left alone in the house with Helen and Harold. She was thirteen, and endured what Sheila and I managed to escape. "During the two years I lived with him," she told me years later, "Harold and Mother verbally fought every night starting at a sit-down dinner required by him. He hit her on three occasions hard enough to break either her glasses or a bone. She needed a cast. She covered up for him. He tutored me in math and said I 'wasn't worth the effort and would never amount to anything.' He was always dressed in a suit with a pocket handkerchief and when he attempted casual it was stiff. He had very flat thumbs and limp hands. He had a huge collection of pencil stubs with complete erasers attached; he never made a mistake. I am not a big fan of his."

Almost from the day they were married, Harold complained that Helen wasn't treating him well enough. He said she had too many friends. He didn't like her going to the theater with them. He said she read too many books. One night, as they went to bed, he called her an "Evil Woman." She was able to tolerate his criticism because he was working on a case in New Orleans and frequently left Washington. But she began to write down his complaints. They were about things that happen in houses everywhere: "Why does this screen have a hole in it?" "Why isn't this porch step painted well?" "Why is my food cold?" "Why is this lightbulb not working?"

In June of 1957, Harold gave two weeks' notice to our cook without consulting Helen. The cook left the next day. Harold fumed for three nights as Helen cooked dinner, complaining that she wasn't getting it ready on time. They went to the Zebra the fourth night. The following morning, a Sunday, he insisted on lunch at home. Helen had planned to spend the afternoon with three Rockville friends. While he was at church, she put out food for him in the kitchen, then left. When she returned, he pulled her by the arm and pushed her through a door. Helen didn't wait for a second broken bone. She fled to the guest annex and locked the door behind her. She slept in the annex all the following week. On July 6th Harold kicked through the storm door and broke the bedroom windows. That night, Helen slept with a small bone-handled pistol under her pillow. The following morning, after reading in her horoscope that she should "avoid people who disturb you," she called Hy Smoller, the lawyer who represented Lewis when he and Helen divorced, and asked for help. Two days later Harold's possessions were massed in the living room, to be taken away by movers. He decamped to his grown-up son's house. By July 17th they'd signed an agreement to separate. Harold arranged for his correspondence to be forwarded to his new address.

Several weeks later, Harold received the *Social Register's* request for address changes that should be made in the next edition. He'd been listed when he married his first wife, and continued with his second. He responded without consulting Helen, providing the *SR* with their separate addresses. Helen had assumed the time to change their joint listing would be when their divorce was granted, at which time she planned to write a letter explaining the situation. "It does rankle that he did this," she wrote the day she learned it, "because the *SR* so often drops wives." That is exactly what happened. Helen, failing in a second marriage, was dropped and never listed again. Her family, going back to the first edition in 1887, meant nothing. Harold's self-made status wasn't held against him.

Helen readjusted her sights and decided she preferred the *Washington Green Book*, a suede-bound directory of people of note in the Washington area. Most of her friends were in it, and eventually she found it much more useful.

In their separation agreement, Helen and Harold agreed that she would go to Reno the following January. He took $5,500 in the form of a check ("That's how much I put into having a dressing room built") and a Chevrolet convertible Helen had bought him after he'd learned to drive. He paid for the broken windows. Then, just a week before she was to leave, he announced he'd changed his mind. He wanted to try again to make the marriage work. "I love you," he wrote. Helen refused to change her mind. She filed for divorce in the District of Columbia Court of General Sessions. Harold wrote again. He wrote more than a hundred letters, keeping handwritten copies of each one. Harold prevailed: the judge ruled that his unending letters affirming his love for Helen demonstrated his desire to reconcile.

It took seven long years for Helen to win her freedom. The Court of General Sessions ruling was overturned by the District of Columbia Court of Appeals on February 8, 1965, by a judge who pronounced that Harold's meticulously handwritten copies of every letter he sent demonstrated not spontaneous declarations of affection, but a premeditated decision to construct a body of proof. Had the judge taken just a few more months to come to his decision, Helen would have been married to Harold for ten years and qualified for Social Security benefits based on his earnings. By the time she was sixty-five, that money would have made a great difference in the way she was able to live.

CHAPTER 20

HELEN'S LIFE AND MINE began to separate at this time. I was at Vassar from 1956 to 1960 and spent my summers elsewhere. Helen's drinking confused me. She knew it and wrote about it in her diary. She asked a close friend, Luther Terry, recently appointed U.S. Surgeon General, to help her find a way to stop. He told her she didn't have a drinking problem. "I've known you for years," he said, "and seen you at parties. You stop drinking before you've had too much. You read books, you go to plays. You're lively and witty. You don't have a problem."

She tried Alcoholics Anonymous. A Rockville friend took her, and she lasted two meetings. She wasn't comfortable speaking the required opening words: "My name is Helen and I'm an alcoholic." Nor was she able to tell her story to people whose backgrounds weren't hers. The one thing that gave her strength was her unquestioned knowledge that she came from a distinguished family. But who in Washington could understand Rhinebeck, and the different kind of life she'd lived there? She wasn't able to bridge the gap and air dirty linen.

There are plausible explanations for why few people realized how much Helen drank. She ordered her liquor by telephone and had it delivered. She took taxis instead of driving. She often had a small carton of milk with her, and a straw. Only she knew that there was no milk inside; the drink was scotch. If she drank too heavily during the day, she took a nap afterwards, looked after by her daily maid or the cook who came at four to make dinner. Since she always had an open book beside her, they assumed she was simply taking a break. In the evening, few people telephoned. I didn't.

Another reason why her drinking didn't raise an alarm was that women weren't perceived as drinkers. In the 1950s, fewer than six percent of American women had a drink more than once a week. No one was looking for alcoholism.

* * *

Elizabeth Coolidge was involuntarily at the Hudson River State Hospital all these years. She was allowed to leave twice a year to present a writ of *habeas corpus* to the Poughkeepsie Supreme Court, where she insisted her confinement was illegal because she was a resident of Connecticut. After a two-minute hearing, her petition was routinely dismissed. She died September 5, 1960. The entry in Helen's diary reads, "Mother died. I wept."

There was no funeral. Sheila was getting married twelve days later in Washington. Helen asked the hospital to arrange a cremation and put the ashes in a simple container. Amidst the wedding preparations, the container arrived. Helen put it on the mantelpiece in our living room where the ashes sat while guests drank champagne and ate cucumber sandwiches.

The following spring, Helen drove the ashes to Garrison, New York, where Lewis's sister, Lee, still lived. Judy, finally able to get away to boarding school, was in her senior year at Oakwood in Poughkeepsie. I was now working in New York. Sheila was pregnant and couldn't leave Washington. Lee welcomed us to the same house in which Helen and Lewis had begun their marriage, and from which Helen, Sheila, and I had set out for Rockville in 1942.

A local undertaker arrived with an ornate urn. Helen and the man went into the dining room. Helen made a funnel with her hands over the opening of the urn. The man lifted the plain canister and poured.

"My ma's ashes spilled dust over everything," Helen wrote. "They were little bits of bone. One had coral colors in it, others were like raisins, all like shale. I had a distinct shock, looking for ashes and finding bones in little bits, two pounds worth."

The following Monday, Judy and Helen drove to Sarah Lawrence College in Bronxville, New York for a college interview. They were stopped by police on the way. They were looking for drugs and searched the car. They opened the urn. Helen said, "It's my mother. We're going to bury her," and the police let them go. Several days after that, Helen and Judy drove Elizabeth's ashes to Saco, Maine and buried her with her Wiggin ancestors.

Judy graduated from Oakwood that June and went to Switzerland for a post-graduate year. Sheila had her baby in Washington. I'd met Al Gillotti, a Yale graduate serving with the Army Security Agency in Germany, and taken myself off to Europe to marry him. The house on Lowell Street, a haven when we first moved from Rockville, was now empty. "Where are my children?" Helen wrote in her diary. She occasionally played the Steinway piano, but there was no one to listen. Poky, Sheila's dog, had died. Helen decided to move to a small townhouse on Eye Street, N.W. near George Washington University. She doubled its size by buying an identical one next door. She found a clerical job in the university library. "I should have gone to graduate school," she wrote. "I should have done something professional with my life. I made a mistake."

"Not one child is helping me," she wrote. "This is what divorces do." The people who helped were Elma, her maid, and

Elma's husband, Edward; Mr. Rose, who sold television sets and jewelry, and whose shop Helen frequented, and a woman who lived around the corner who was now Helen's closest friend. She drank as well; her husband brought her vodka and orange juice every morning in bed.

Friends from Rhinebeck occasionally came to Washington and Helen was mostly glad to see them. When they stepped into the front hall of her townhouse, they were greeted by framed photographs of Grasmere. One visitor was Mrs. Ludlow Griscom, widow of the Boston ornithologist who'd often accompanied Maunsell on birdwatching expeditions. "Mrs. Griscom said my mother was a nymphomaniac," Helen wrote in her diary. "Maybe she was, but why do these old biddies tear my mother apart?"

For respite from Washington's summer heat, Helen bought a log cabin near Front Royal, Virginia, in the Shenandoah Valley. She built a patio, tied tomatoes, and swam in a pond. She invited a few friends to come for the day. In truth, she was very lonely. "Sue has married. The photos of her husband are absolutely delightful. Sheila looks miserable. Is Judy going to be happy? I am in the witness stand trying to get a divorce. Why am I alone? If my daughters wish to know, I am frightened all night long."

Lewis remarried in 1961 and moved from Rockville to Washington with my new stepmother, Elinor. My husband was discharged from the Army in August of 1963 and we came home from Germany. We stayed with Helen on Eye Street, looking forward to spending time with both my parents before going on to graduate school in North Carolina. We arranged to have dinner with Lewis and Elinor at their house on Fulton Street the second night we were home. We were ending dinner when the telephone rang. It was Helen.

"I've taken sleeping pills," she said.

"How many?" asked Lewis.

"A lot. I'm going to sleep now."

Lewis returned to the dining room and told Al and me that we had to go to Eye Street at once. Helen was in danger. She'd taken pills. We raced to her house, ran up the stairs, and found her sitting cross-legged on her bed, laughing. "Oh, you believed me," she said. "I didn't mean it. I just didn't want to be left out of dinner."

Helen was remorseful the following day. In her diary she wrote: "Susan and Al finally home from Germany. Off to Lewis and Elinor at 6:30. At 10:30 I broke. Al wanted to leave the house. Sue finally realized what the strain has been."

After my husband finished graduate school, we moved to Manhattan. Helen came to see us. She stayed at the Colony Club and broached with me the possibility that I join. She tried to make a joke of my married name, pronouncing it with a "Z" instead of a "G." I began to feel nervous; I couldn't figure out whether she thought I was presentable or not. We went to an Italian restaurant where she had two scotches before ordering. When her entrée arrived, she found it lacking and lifted the lamp beside our table off the floor to get the waiter's attention. "Take it back," she said. "It tastes like catsup." I was embarrassed; it was a restaurant Al and I went to often, when we'd saved enough pennies.

The following morning, I telephoned Helen and said I didn't enjoy being with her. She wrote in her diary:

Icy 9 am telephone call from S. saying she had decided the Club was not for her. Enjoyable train ride home. To 'Owls' art exhibit by Emily Wilson, and bought 'The Forsaken One,' a portrait of a crestfallen owl that looks like how I feel. Will give it to Susan for Christmas. After all, my mother didn't speak to her mother for 15 years. I only clammed up for two, and then, when my mother went insane, had her as a burden the rest of my life. Susan is entitled to as long as she wants.

Mother's Day came and went. Helen wrote in her diary: "Pleasant day at Sheila's—and oh so obviously, silence from Sue."

* * *

Helen made one more move in Washington. After five years of living alone in a house, she no longer felt safe with a front door that opened directly onto the street. She bought a large apartment at 550 "N" Street, S.W., overlooking the Potomac. She created a beautiful, open living space with Oriental rugs from Grasmere. She surrounded the fireplace with mahogany paneling. She built bookcases the length of the living room and filled them with the poetry and fiction she'd collected all her life. She swam every morning in an indoor pool. She lunched at the Woman's National Democratic Club and the Sulgrave Club, and afterwards went to art galleries and matinees. But she was still alone. On December 17, 1968, she wrote Daisy Suckley in Rhinebeck: "I spend days & days by myself. When I can't stand it any longer I take off to Cousin Sara Peel in England—who is on tranquilizers but otherwise far livelier than I. . . I just haven't figured out where I belong yet. It is really traumatic when you have really let your children grow up & go."

CHAPTER 21

SHEILA AND HER FIRST HUSBAND divorced after five years. Not long afterwards she met the right man, Harold Hagan. He was a pilot who wanted to teach others to fly. They went to Florida to find just the right place and settled on Venice, a pleasant city south of Sarasota. Sheila became Harold's business manager. For a blissful short period, she thought she was free from everything her life had been in Washington.

But Helen changed that. Without consulting Sheila, or even giving her notice, she followed Sheila to Venice. She settled into a rental apartment overlooking the Gulf and took her time deciding where to live. Several months later, she bought a large mobile home a mile from Sheila's house. My reaction was incredulity. I couldn't reconcile the huge estate in Rhinebeck and the big house in Washington with a trailer park, even if it was Venice's best.

The trailer park turned out to be too neighborly. Seeking greater privacy, Helen moved to a small house even closer to Sheila. She freely let trades people inside, showing none of the fear about living alone she'd felt in Washington. But she began to give conflicting signals to Sheila about whom she trusted. "The workmen make passes at me," she said. One day she left all her jewelry on her bed while workmen were there. She wondered why it was stolen when she left for a swim. She used some

of the insurance money to replace the diamond engagement ring
Lewis had given her and spent the rest on living expenses.

For a long time Sheila had no idea who Helen was seeing for lunch. Helen joined the local branch of the American
Association of University Women and sometimes went to lec-
tures. More often, she drove north to Nokomis to Pelican Alley,
a restaurant on the inland waterway that had a lively lunchtime
bar. Sheila didn't know about the lunchtime drinking until
years later, when the owner made the connection that Helen was
Sheila's mother, and told her.

* * *

There were two people from Helen's childhood with whom
she remained in touch, both of them her age. One was Betty
Nelson, daughter of Alice Nelson, Maunsell's lesbian cousin.
Helen had eventually told Betty about the seduction and Betty
kept the secret. Betty now spent part of the winter on the west
coast of Florida and visited Helen several times. She'd met
Sheila and Harold and liked them. Helen wrote Betty a letter in
which she asked what Betty thought of us and why we weren't
closer as a family. Betty replied:

> I did like Harold so much. . . He was attractive and percep-
> tive, with a good sense of humor, rather the Indiana type,
> also like some people from Maine. I haven't got your mistrust
> of people who haven't had the best of U.S. traditional edu-
> cation, when they obviously are experienced, skilled adults,
> which is what traditional education tries hard to produce.
> I suppose I just met in my younger days, or usually just saw
> in the distance, for I did not attract them, too many too
> rich, passive young men with no particular skills or sense
> of direction, who never amounted to that much when they
> became men.
>
> I know that living five years in France, then in Virginia,
> and much later in Minnesota, and meeting girls from the

Midwest in boarding school, and being enough of a rebel from my mother's pretty stuffy attitude about people, I always had the reaction that being in a roomful of hereditary what are now called W.A.S.P.s was a pretty stifling experience. I never even considered asking home anyone from the Midwest I made friends with at school, because I thought my mother just would have made fun of them behind their backs.

I think now that my mother just did like the excitement of the chase, so to speak. But for her to try something with you was just close to a criminal offense. The writers I have read on the subject have been unanimous in condemning the homosexual seduction of young persons when they are in the vulnerable stage of their adolescence. . .

I am so extra thankful, now that you have told me what my mother did to you, that I had the chance to make one remark to her, not more than a year or so before she died, which I think really sank in. She said something about you, when you were younger, as taking up with rather strange women—that's not her exact wording—and I just said, very firmly: 'Helen was looking for a mother!' At that statement, she really drew in her breath. You see, all our childhood, she would tell us about having lost her mother right after she was born, and how much she missed not having had one, and even how happy she would be some day when she would see her in Heaven. She also, when we were older, said that she did like having the company of older women friends, because they were in a way mother-substitutes.

I was thinking some more about your Sue, who doesn't come to see you, you say. I have the feeling that she may feel that her first responsibility has to be towards her own life—her husband, and her sanity. It just could be that she senses your feelings about what you think is her inadequacy whenever she sees you, and just can't take the discouraged, depressed, pulled-down feelings that such an attitude gives her. . . these daughters of yours are really great successes at being useful, interesting, capable women of the nineteen-eighties, which is the time that counts.

The other person Helen stayed in touch with was Pig Parrish, her Ethel Walker's and Smith College friend. She wrote to Pig in 1976. Not having a response in a number of weeks, she followed up with a telephone call. With Pig, she raised questions of who she was, who Pig was, and what they should accept as facts about their sexuality. Pig replied from New Mexico, where she was living and working as an artist.

FINALLY, Beloved Petie, I've reached that portion of my pile of unanswered letters where I may take up yours and start the weekly process of adding paragraphs, time permitting, until a real letter is built.

You and I are really fantastic. Your telephone call, which I treasure as a white pebble on a field of broken basalt, simply pointed up the rare and limitless nature of our relationship. Not BACK to where we were, as children, adolescents, thank God, but a graceful transition to battle-scarred adults who have been wandering around the "middle mist" of emotional vagrancy and are—STILL—on a wavelength of complete comprehension, 1926 to 1975. Jesus!

Perhaps, because I was enabled to establish a permanent cease fire in the chemical warfare my unformed id was waging with my mind and body, some years before you were, I've reached a more peaceful plateau about my true place in the world I live in. Painting was sent to me as the necessary catalyst. Two years before Pa made his official exit at the ripe age of 95, his mind and memory took a permanent vacation from his head, and I, who had been handsomely supported by him (since my divorce in 1949) on an allowance of $200 a month, suddenly found he was not sending anything. And what had been a pleasant dawdling hobby became something at which I had to earn a living.

So, sensing a dire emergency, my Higher Power put a Santa Fe gallery owner next to a painting I had exhibited at the State fair; he thought it fine, and that I showed promise, and invited me to join his stable. I had no idea what an agent could do for one, but I soon found out! From painting a back-breaking eight paintings every two years and having a wee one-man show, from which I'd make a sum of $500 to $800, in my first year at the Kachina Gallery I painted 30 paintings and made $8,000 gross (33% commission off of that). And so it has gone on, with slight variations, except for last year when the American Artist article, or the national rejoicing over the downfall of Richard IV [Richard Nixon], or a combination, zoomed sales to about $14,000. This year, down again. But in the meantime, from 1965 to now, there have been undreamed-of dividends from Pa's estate (*omnia divisa in partes tres*) so that I don't actually have to paint to eat and have shelter anymore.

But I do have to paint to have life make any sense. The entrapment of the work is complete, and all my power of desire and love is directed, in a mysterious way I don't quite understand, but do accept, into the translation of the lovely things I see in my head into paintings which, alas, are only a vague approximation. When I can no longer do this, I shall (I hope) have the guts to get off the trolley.

I'm so glad you are an alcoholic, too, or I really would have little understanding of the vagaries of your life story. And the tendency to alternate between two types of sexual relationships really does, as I said in my phone conversation, have a very real basis in the disease of alcoholism, at least, in many cases. It figures. Our compulsion to drink, i.e., to heighten what appears to be low, to stimulate what is drab, to add that all necessary aura of luminescence to one's day-by-day, lures us to the forbidden part of the garden, and we find the fruit sweeter and headier there. I'm not at all convinced, though, that the attraction to other women, for those of us who have enjoyed the hetero relationship, is sexual. I think it is an emotional emptiness so compelling in its call that we have confused need with desire. With only one exception, I've found women far more selfish about their own gratification than in a shared experience. But in a few instances where the attraction has been deepest, I have known an unphysical communion which is, without question, the loveliest and most satisfying experience of my life. First, though, I had to realize that it wasn't a sexual attraction, but an emotional and spiritual one. So this kinda put women where they belong, as far as I'm concerned. And men are friends but no bother anymore, because I don't have time for them, and the only attractive ones are happily married. . . so: PAX.

But I'm very glad that all the various types of sexes which have been "in the closet," as they put it, are now coming out and being talked about and are talking. Bi—homo—trans. Television is really doing quite a good job of slowly introducing the taboo subject so that the shock-value is soon to be diminished.

But, back to us, even if alcoholism were not a contributing factor in our sexual confusion, there is the unhappiness of the bi-sexual individual, who can find completion and happiness with one sex or t'other, but for only a short term period, because only half of the person is fulfilled, so the seesaw starts up, and no permanence in marriage or in liaison is possible, as in true heteros or true homosexuals.

For me, age and an overriding interest in my work has made the problem moot. I think I understand what my problem was, how my alcoholism nurtured it, and how—once I was able to sober up in mind, body, and spirit, and lose the fear of really looking at myself—able to laugh at myself—able to appreciate the fact that, whatever I've been or done I'm not stuck with it for life, that I can change whatever I feel needs changing about me. . . well, how wonderfully God damn FREE of anxiety and apprehension I feel. Without my 15 years in AA I doubt that I could have ever learned to be honest with myself, or find my foibles (earlier cherished as distinguished marks of individuality!) laughably ludicrous. Pattern changing is one of the most fascinating miracles which the AA association has brought to me.

This Ethel Walker School syndrome is interesting. I hope you can work your way out of its importance to you. For both of us, I guess, it was a beginning entering wedge for our emotional vagrancy. For myself, it is sufficient to have identified it in all its causative dimensions. Yet it isn't, by itself, the whole bowl of porrich. We brought to it, all naked and receptive, our own personal chemistries and raw sensitivities. And they talk about nuclear fission. Ha!

Loused up as we became, ain't you awfully glad we had such a fearful life—instead of ending up in Greenwich as a wealthy wife of a respectable commuter, dedicating our lives to raising antiseptic children for Walker's and Groton, and becoming a volunteer social worker-board member-bridge player?!

I've a notion that if you and I met up together again we'd have to take quite a bit of time to air all that we've thought about and coped with in our various stages of disintegration and subsequent efforts at integration. The day will come, and you'll come out here and sniff the nice dry air of New Mexico with me.

There's a hell of a lot more to say, and in the time it's taken to say what's here I know I've not touched all the bases. But since our communication deals more with ideas and the evolution of people (mainly ourselves) we don't have to go into big paragraphs about our grandchildrens' marks in school or the childhood diseases they've gone through in the past year, thank God. These are the staple substances of those ghastly mimeographed Christmas letters some people send out to their hundreds of "friends." What a barbaric custom! Even Attila would have had a seizure of aesthetic revulsion. . .

You'll never know how good it has been to know that you still are, and want to stay, in touch.

With much love and delight,
Piglet

From 1971 to 1981, Sheila raised her family and ran her aviation business with Helen living close by, but not in the same house. Helen, now approaching seventy, found the small house she'd bought difficult to maintain. None of us—not I, not Sheila, not Judy—was yet aware of how much Helen's drinking factored into this.

Helen made a proposal to Sheila: she would build and pay for an extension to Sheila's house. Sheila would own it, but Helen would live there. She promised Sheila she wouldn't interfere in her life. Sheila and Harold agreed, glad to have an addition to their house and hopeful that a live-in grandmother would make life easier with two active boys. Helen moved in, bringing her one thousand books with her.

It worked for a while. But Helen was alone most of the day, while Sheila and Harold worked at the airport, and Don and Tim, Sheila's children, were in school. For company, she had only her Irish setter, Nellie, and Sheila's two dachshunds. One day, after being with the dogs outside, she wrote her thoughts on 5 x 8 in. index cards:

> There is nothing easy about living in Florida. One goes from month to month, from the tornado situation to the hurricane situation to the tourist season, when Route 41 to Sarasota becomes a daily death trap for everyone. The garbage still has to go out at dawn, the empty five-gallon bottle for special drinking water likewise every Friday. The dogs have to have a daily heart-worm pill, and now that the man next door is raising chickens illegally, we have to guard against mosquitoes and encephalitis.

I tried to get someone to weed my six roses. He was picked up for 19 burglaries and "borrowed" $50 from me for bail. His brother has just been immobilized by a hit and run driver when he was walking home—two broken legs and double vision. The foster child in this same home cleans for me once a week and is a Hungarian gem. And they've made her into a Seventh Day Adventist. She is college material, but how to free her from the Creationists?

And so it goes, daily, with the ups and downs.

Sheila's hot water heater gave out from doing Don and Tim's laundry, and the new hot water heater came this A.M., and I paid the Flood Insurance, and I must water the plants and the gardenia, and always, forever, be the bag woman for the two dogs. I cook three meals a day for myself. And talk to myself. And watch TV endlessly. And never can keep up with all the publications.

Obviously, I have shed all the trappings of my entire life—all of which were laid upon me by circumstances. I blame it all on the planet Uranus.

Now, they call me the "Ancient Mariner." I walk a mile every day, and sometimes, now that the sun blazes again, my feet burn. Each old man along the mile I walk has his own name for "Nellie." She comes out "Mollie," "Jeannie," and "Susie." I have a great collection of mailbox World War I gentlemen. No one has ever seen a wife in Venice Gardens. Fortunately, they are dying off fast, and the new people are a new breed of "solid citizens," a little better educated and a little wealthier. The AAUW has gone from six members to 284 in six years, and now there are interesting group meetings.

Aside from that, the Hagans have to be constantly on guard against having their planes stolen by cocaine runners. Sheila is on a "hit list" because she refused to rent a plane to a drug trafficker—he is now out of jail and his wife is on trial for shooting the D.A.

But every now and then something makes it worthwhile hanging on. Don woke me up as usual—everybody does—

from a nap, and asked if I had a copy of *Dante's Inferno*. I couldn't believe my ears. Seems he had read a modern version, and wants to write his own!!! So, I produced my *Gustave Doré Illustrated*, an enormous volume, and to my astonishment, he welcomed it—a bit gingerly—and said he either read something straight through, or he started and stopped. Something about it intrigued him. I was delighted.

All of this in our not-very-like Grasmere backyard.

On December 12, 1983, Helen wrote to Daisy Suckley:

Dearest Daisy,

Your letter was my best, or is, my best Xmas present. I have read & re-read the clipping you enclosed—& thought a lot about Us Survivors. You stayed at Wilderstein—& so you keep intact for me all my childhood & adolescent memories of the Hudson. If Allan Ryan had only told me that he was going to sell the "Mansion" to Mrs. Harriman Havemeyer, with 50 acres—for $50,000—two days after he bought all of Grasmere for $35,000 from me, I could either have sold him the house & Lewis & I could have moved to the farmhouse & farm, or I could have stayed in the house with all our lovely furniture & enough land to farm, where the orchard used to be. And then I would be the Heiress in the Kitchen at Grasmere.

CHAPTER 22

HELEN WAS DIAGNOSED with alcoholic cirrhosis that year, but hadn't told us. She stopped drinking from time to time, but never for very long. She had tricks for hiding her glass. One was to cut out the bottom of a cube of Kleenex and remove the tissues. She'd tape one tissue to the opening at the top, so that it looked as if the box were full, and use the box like a tea cozy. It was only when she began to have falls, and twice broke a bone, that it became clear to Sheila how ill she was. Hospitalized for the fractures, she'd go through DTs and have to be put in a straightjacket and moved to the psychiatric floor. She made fewer entries in her diary.

In 1987, Sheila's husband died in a flying accident. With full responsibility for the aviation service, she had no time to grieve. She consoled her children, ran the business on her own until she found a buyer, and kept her distance from Helen. Judy flew to Florida from New York, where she was living, and persuaded Sheila to take a vacation, something Sheila hadn't enjoyed for twenty years. They needed someone to look after Helen and consulted a psychiatrist Helen was seeing. The psychiatrist asked Sheila how she felt about having Helen living with her and Sheila gave an honest answer: "I don't mind it when she doesn't drink, but when she does, I don't want her there."

The psychiatrist recommended a Florida detoxification center. Helen docilely agreed; she had a way sometimes of putting down her head and doing what others told her to do. She voluntarily committed herself for thirty days. Sheila and Judy left her at the reception area, where she was stripped and searched. The following day Helen became livid that Sheila had told the psychiatrist she had a drinking problem, and decided to move into a local retirement community as soon as Sheila and Judy returned.

Lewis and my stepmother, Elinor, were married for twenty-one years. During this time, Lewis stayed in touch with a third woman, Martha Johnson, a Rockville friend with whom he'd had an affair in the 1940s. He found ways to see her every spring and fall on his drives from Washington to Martha's Vineyard and back. Elinor's alcoholism kept her from any possibility of intellectual conversation, which Lewis craved. Part of Lewis's attraction to Martha was that she shared his love of American history. In a clandestine correspondence, facilitated by secret post office boxes, they discussed the books they read when they were apart.

Lewis divorced Elinor in 1982 to live with Martha in New Jersey. The relationship lasted eight years. In the end, Lewis's inability to commit himself paradoxically led to a return to our family life. Martha wanted to be married, but Lewis wanted to remain single. He was stingy with his money and unhelpful around the house. He developed cancer after six years and became truly frightened for his future. Martha understandably hoped he would marry her then, at the very least in return for taking care of him. He refused. She wrote him a letter in which she said: "You use your physical problems, many normal old-age conditions, as an excuse for selfish avoidance of responsibility. . . I used to enjoy cooking, just to show my love for you. But after a year of your pickiness and 84 joyless meals a month without a single break, my delight has turned to bitterness."

The cancer worsened. Martha made the decision to move to a retirement community. Lewis refused to join her, even in a separate apartment. His sister, Lee, had recently nursed her own husband through his dying and didn't want to do the same for another man. Lewis had run out of options. Helen, knowing a little about his life since Sheila, Judy, or I were always in touch with him, got wind of his difficulty. "I hear you've burned all your bridges," she said in a telephone call from Florida early in 1991. "I've moved to the Southwest Florida Retirement Community. Why don't you come here? There's a small apartment near me that's available."

And thus the unimaginable came to pass. Like many children, I'd for years wanted my parents to come back to each other. I'd felt all my life that I lived in only half a world. The void had started in Rockville when Helen told me she and Lewis were divorcing. Lewis moved to Venice, Florida and for six months, until he died in October of 1991, joined Helen for dinner in the residents' dining room every night. My husband and I visited them in Florida and for me a profound healing occurred. I was joyful to have the chance to sit with them as if we were a family once again. Like Helen's parents before, who'd been taught to show good manners even if they didn't like each other, Helen and Lewis were never anything but cordial when I was with them.

It wasn't entirely easy for Helen. While she enjoyed having Lewis there ("He is the one person in this world who actually knows who I am"), she lost some of her privacy with his arrival. The retirement center was Lutheran and she'd held back some aspects of her life when she applied for admission. She hadn't revealed her divorces; she'd told the admitting office that her husbands had died. Lewis blew her cover. He was attractive and sociable almost to the end, and revealed to Helen's new friends many of the personal details of her earlier life. She was proud of her books, though, and some of the residents referred to her apartment as "the library." She was also proud of certain aspects of her background. If one asked, she would tell you that the man in the silver picture frame was Abe Fortas, the Supreme Court justice, and that the dark-haired man in the leather frame was her father, a gifted ornithologist, and that the handsome English sixteen-year-old in court dress was her cousin Sara's oldest son, who had carried Queen Elizabeth's train in her coronation. She didn't keep pictures of Grasmere on display. These she placed in a photograph album in one of her boxes, with a note tucked into it that said: "I dunno. For Sue, I guess. She'll know what to do with them."

* * *

Helen survived another four years. She stayed sober much of the time. I traveled to Florida in the spring of 1994 to see her. One afternoon, she and I drove to the beach and she asked me why I'd stayed away. I said, "I was scared."

She said, "So was I."

I said, "Of what?"

She said, "I was scared of not being strong enough to live with you. I was scared when you and Sheila had your fight and she threw milk on your party dress. I'm sorry I didn't have the courage to break it up. I'm sorry I let you down."

I'd hit Helen once in a pique of anger, when I was nineteen, and her green harlequin glasses had fallen to the floor. I now said, "I'm sorry too. I'm sorry I knocked your glasses off."

She said, "I don't remember your hitting me."

Helen and I spent hours that week on the screen porch of her ground floor apartment. We took a short walk one of those days, stepping gingerly over the exposed roots of the palm trees on the lawn. As always, Helen was beautifully dressed, now walking with a black cane with a silver handle. Sheila drove up in her car as we were returning to her porch and I said I had to go. I put my arms around Helen and held her. Her embrace of me was wooden.

"I told you she can't hold us," Sheila said as I got in her car. "She can't touch us as a mother. I saw her hands against your back. There was nothing there."

I could hardly bear to hear this, though I knew it was the truth. "She was afraid of touching us," Sheila said. "She always was."

During much of the remainder of that year, Sheila would come to Helen's apartment at the retirement center and discover that Helen didn't know her. Helen had become a little child who had to be dressed perfectly. She'd say to Sheila, "I have this dress on. It's a perfect dress. I have to wear it." Several times Sheila found her hiding under her bed, cowering, but at the same time explaining that she had to wear this perfect dress.

In December of 1994, Helen fell and broke her shoulder. The retirement center took her to the emergency room at the Venice Hospital. After being treated, she was returned to her apartment. While helping her into bed, the staff discovered she'd also broken her hip. They took her back to the hospital. Her hip was treated and she was returned to the retirement center, this time to the acute nursing building. She was in great pain. It became clear that she was very ill. Hospice was called. Sheila heard Helen repeatedly ask for more painkillers. The nursing staff finally heard the depth of her plea and increased the dose. Helen died of hepatic failure, alone in her room at night, on January 12, 1995. Sheila was notified early the next morning. She called Judy, who was in Africa, and me in London. "She looked so peaceful," she said. "She looked as if she was free from everything that had followed her all her life."

When we unpacked the boxes with her papers after she died, Sheila and I learned she thought lesbianism was contagious. She thought that if she touched us, it might happen to us. But we also learned that she believed that it was being unloved that had made her vulnerable. She didn't live long enough to learn that there are many normal forms of sexuality. The terrible silences in her family about the facts of life hadn't helped.

Sheila and I, with my husband, Al, and the man Sheila was seeing at the time, buried Helen's ashes in Rhinebeck in the Crosby family plot adjacent to Grasmere. She rests next to her father, where she always wanted to be.

A NOTE ON SOURCES

THE PAPERS HELEN LEFT for her children were stored in three cardboard boxes. When my sister and I first began to look at them, we despaired of finishing. We made piles on her living room floor of letters from Maunsell, Elizabeth, Miss Haskell, and others. We tried to put journals and diaries in the right order. We had no idea how to tell what was important.

My sister understandably didn't want these piles of paper on her living room floor for very long. My other sister was living in Cape Town. It fell to me to ship everything to my house on Martha's Vineyard. I would sort them out, and tell my sisters what I learned.

It took three years to read and organize the material. I made manila folders for the years 1906 (when Maunsell and Elizabeth met) to 1995 (when Helen died). Whatever I handled went into the appropriate year. Fascinating things happened. I would find a letter typed on printed stationery from Elizabeth to Maunsell. Months later, I'd find an onion skin copy of the same letter, retained by Elizabeth. Two pieces of paper that had once been joined by carbon paper now found themselves together again on my dining room table. Eventually I had a chronology of my family from literally one day to the next.

I sat down to write, intending my words for family only. When I'd finished, two years later, I printed sixteen copies.

They went to English and American cousins and to several close friends. Virtually all of them said, "Take this further. There's a story here that will appeal to others." I wrote a second draft, then a third, and finally a fourth.

Here are the materials with which I worked:

Letters
Diaries
Journals
Unpublished short stories
News clippings
Wedding announcements and divorce decrees
Pinkertons detectives reports
Inventories of property and wills
Invitations
First editions of books by Ernest Howard Crosby
Memories of Grasmere by people who'd visited or lived there
Announcements from schools
Yearbooks
Scrapbooks
Photographs
Journals and index cards of notes from Helen's analytic
  sessions

ACKNOWLEDGMENTS

I COULD NOT HAVE WRITTEN this book without the invaluable gift of the documents Helen saved. When it came time to write, I had to decide whose narrative voice to use, and whether I was writing a biography, a memoir, or social history. I concluded it was all three, and that I had to give myself permission to imagine what I couldn't prove. Helen and Lewis gave me this permission. In a dream, Helen came to me and said, "I want to write this book. I don't want you to be the author." Lewis appeared and took her by the hand. He said, "Let's stand together on the other side of a fence and let Sue write the book the way she wants to. You have to trust her now." Helen held his hand and consented. Dialogue then sprang freely, but only when, because of diaries, journals, and letters, I was absolutely certain that such a conversation had to have occurred.

I thank Jordan and Anita Miller, founders of Academy Chicago Publishers, for wanting to publish this book. Their close reading of the text and affirmation of its value have been a gift. I thank Joan Sommers, their talented art director, for her sensitive choice of photographs and graphic design. Longtime Hudson Valley resident Franklin Dennis has been a publicity and editorial consultant to Academy Chicago for more than 30 years, and was especially helpful as I worked through how to present a family history that included imagined dialogue.

I thank Alexander Weinstein, editor and teacher, who is director of the Martha's Vineyard Institute of Creative Writing and read my first draft. I thank Joni Cole, co-founder of the Writer's Center in White River Junction, Vermont, for her ongoing encouragement and stimulating workshops in which many of these pages were shared. I'm grateful more than I can express to Mary R. Morgan, my lifelong friend, who understood from the start the uniqueness of my having so many intergenerational papers coming from women in the same family.

I thank members of my family who helped me accept that secrets should sometimes be shared. They are my sister Sheila Hagan, my sister Judith Conway, and my cousins Jonathan Peel, Charlotte Stevenson, and Emily deRham.

Friends who read the manuscript and offered helpful suggestions include Beverly Barbour, Anne Boswell, Virgil Early, Georgina Forbes, Julie Fortunati, Susan Haedrich, Coleen Lawlor, Tom Miller, Carol Newman, Lisa Whitman Ricketson, and Abigail Sturges. I'm grateful to Mary Otto for her suggestion that I move one word in the title, making all the difference.

Ellen and Harry Pskowski opened their house in Rockville to me, allowing me to revisit the place where I'd grown up, and so much happened. I watched the fields behind Chestnut Lodge surrender to a bulldozer that week, jolting me with the realization that no house can stay forever as it was.

When the manuscript was accepted for publication, I went to Rhinebeck to learn what has happened to Grasmere since. As I write, the house and land are under review for planning permission to become a country house hotel on six hundred acres. I'm grateful to Winthrop Aldrich, who knew my family and over dinner one night shared his memories. He read the galley of the book and made corrections that only someone so close to Rhinebeck could have made.

I'm grateful also to Beverly Kane, granddaughter of Dexter Burroughs, the Superintendent of Grasmere, who filled in many details of her grandfather's relationship with Helen; and to Duane and Linda Watson, curators at Wilderstein Preservation, where I was able to read more than one hundred letters written by my mother to Daisy Suckley between 1925 and 1988.

Colton Johnson, Professor Emeritus of English at Vassar College and Yeats scholar, kindly provided my mother with copies of the letters written by John Butler Yeats to his daughters.

Matthew Hanson, archivist at the Franklin Delano Roosevelt Presidential Library in Hyde Park, New York, was helpful in establishing where (and probably when, 1926 or 1927) the photograph of FDR and my grandfather, Maunsell Crosby, was taken. My sisters and I have made a gift of the photograph to the Library.

I thank, most of all, my husband, Al Gillotti. He had no idea when I received Helen's papers that they would lead to such an exploration.

I am personally responsible for any errors of fact.